ANNEX

ACPL IT

DISCARDED

YO-ACG-014

3-21-60

UNITED STATES
SHIPPING POLICY

SOME PUBLICATIONS OF THE

COUNCIL ON FOREIGN RELATIONS

FOREIGN AFFAIRS (quarterly), edited by Hamilton Fish Armstrong.

THE UNITED STATES IN WORLD AFFAIRS (annual). Volumes for 1931, 1932 and 1933, by Walter Lippmann and William O. Scroggs; for 1934-1935, 1936, 1937, 1938, 1939 and 1940, by Whitney H. Shepardson and William O. Scroggs; for 1945-1947, 1947-1948 and 1948-1949, by John C. Campbell; for 1949, 1950, 1951, 1952, 1953 and 1954 by Richard P. Stebbins.

DOCUMENTS ON AMERICAN FOREIGN RELATIONS (annual). Volume for 1952 edited by Clarence W. Baier and Richard P. Stebbins; for 1953 and 1954, edited by Peter V. Curl; for 1955 edited by Paul E. Zinner.

POLITICAL HANDBOOK OF THE WORLD (annual), edited by Walter H. Mallory.

WHAT THE TARIFF MEANS TO AMERICAN INDUSTRIES, by Percy W. Bidwell.

STERLING: ITS MEANING IN WORLD FINANCE, by Judd Polk.

RUSSIA AND AMERICA: Dangers and Prospects, by Henry L. Roberts.

KOREA: A Study of U. S. Policy in the United Nations, by Leland M. Goodrich.

FOREIGN AFFAIRS BIBLIOGRAPHY, 1942-1952, by Henry L. Roberts.

AMERICAN AGENCIES INTERESTED IN INTERNATIONAL AFFAIRS, compiled by Ruth Savord and Donald Wasson.

JAPANESE AND AMERICANS: A Century of Cultural Relations, by Robert S. Schwantes.

THE FUTURE OF UNDERDEVELOPED COUNTRIES: Political Implications of Economic Development, by Eugene Staley.

THE UNDECLARED WAR, 1940-1941, by William L. Langer and S. Everett Gleason.

THE CHALLENGE TO ISOLATION, 1937-1940, by William L. Langer and S. Everett Gleason.

MIDDLE EAST DILEMMAS: The Background of United States Policy, by J. C. Hurewitz.

BRITAIN AND THE UNITED STATES: Problems in Cooperation, a joint report prepared by Henry L. Roberts and Paul A. Wilson.

TRADE AND PAYMENTS IN WESTERN EUROPE: A Study in Economic Cooperation, 1947-1951, by William Diebold, Jr.

THE ECONOMICS OF FREEDOM: The Progress and Future of Aid to Europe, by Howard S. Ellis.

WAR AND THE MINDS OF MEN, by Frederick S. Dunn.

PUBLIC OPINION AND FOREIGN POLICY, by Lester Markel and Others.

OUR FARM PROGRAM AND FOREIGN TRADE, by C. Addison Hickman.

THE FOREIGN AFFAIRS READER, edited by Hamilton Fish Armstrong.

THE STUDY OF INTERNATIONAL RELATIONS IN AMERICAN COLLEGES AND UNIVERSITIES, by Grayson Kirk.

FOREIGN AFFAIRS BIBLIOGRAPHY, 1932-1942, by Robert Gale Woolbert.

THE UNITED STATES IN A MULTI-NATIONAL ECONOMY, by Jacob Viner and Others.

THE FAR EASTERN CRISIS, by Henry L. Stimson.

LIMITS OF LAND SETTLEMENT, prepared under the direction of Isaiah Bowman.

SURVEY OF AMERICAN FOREIGN RELATIONS (in four volumes, 1928-1931), prepared under the direction of Charles P. Howland.

DOLLARS IN LATIN AMERICA, by Willy Feuerlein and Elizabeth Hannan.

NEW DIRECTIONS IN OUR TRADE POLICY, by William Diebold, Jr.

INTERNATIONAL AIR TRANSPORT AND NATIONAL POLICY, by Oliver J. Lissitzyn.

UNITED STATES SHIPPING POLICY

By

WYTZE GORTER

Published for the

COUNCIL ON FOREIGN RELATIONS

by

HARPER & BROTHERS

New York

1956

The Council on Foreign Relations is a non-profit institution devoted to study of the international aspects of American political, economic and strategic problems. It takes no stand, expressed or implied, on American policy.

The authors of books published under the auspices of the Council are responsible for their statements of fact and expressions of opinion. The Council is responsible only for determining that they should be presented to the public.

UNITED STATES SHIPPING POLICY

Copyright, 1956, by Council on Foreign Relations, Inc.
Printed in the United States of America

All rights reserved, including right to reproduce
this book or any portion thereof in any form.

For information address Council on Foreign Relations,
58 East 68th Street, New York 21

FIRST EDITION

Colonial Press

Library of Congress catalog card number: LS 56-10526

COUNCIL ON FOREIGN RELATIONS

OFFICERS AND DIRECTORS

1115049

JOHN J. McCLOY
Chairman of the Board

HENRY M. WRISTON
President

FRANK ALTSCHUL
Vice-President & Secretary

DAVID ROCKEFELLER
Vice-President

ELLIOTT V. BELL
Treasurer

WALTER H. MALLORY
Executive Director

GEORGE S. FRANKLIN, JR.
Executive Director

FRANK D. CARUTHERS, JR.
Assistant Treasurer

HAMILTON FISH ARMSTRONG
WILLIAM A. M. BURDEN
ARTHUR H. DEAN
ALLEN W. DULLES
THOMAS K. FINLETTER
JOSEPH E. JOHNSON
DEVEREUX C. JOSEPHS

GRAYSON L. KIRK
R. C. LEFFINGWELL
PHILIP D. REED
WHITNEY H. SHEPARDSON
CHARLES M. SPOFFORD
MYRON C. TAYLOR
JOHN H. WILLIAMS

COMMITTEE ON STUDIES

HENRY M. WRISTON
Chairman

HAMILTON FISH ARMSTRONG
GORDON DEAN
BYRON DEXTER
GRAYSON L. KIRK

WILLIAM L. LANGER
THOMAS H. McKITTRICK
STACY MAY
WHITNEY H. SHEPARDSON

JOHN H. WILLIAMS

STUDIES PROGRAM

PHILIP E. MOSELY
Director of Studies

WILLIAM DIEBOLD, JR.
Director of Economic Studies

JOHN C. CAMPBELL
Director of Political Studies

FOREWORD

Mention "merchant marine" to some people and you will evoke a sense of romance and adventure, with perhaps a picture of the Flying Cloud in the background. Others will think only of dull greyness and the "dirty British coaster with a salt-caked smoke-stack" that carried Masefield's "cheap tin trays." But whether merchant shipping seems to you glamorous or humdrum, there is no avoiding the fact that the shipping policy of the United States government is imbued with a substantial degree of public interest.

What happens to the American merchant marine, and to the shipbuilding industry from which it draws its vessels, depends to a considerable extent on what the government does. The merchant marine is often called the fourth arm of defense. Public money is paid to American ship operators and shipbuilders to enable them to meet foreign competition. Preferential legislation provides American ship operators with certain cargoes, and American sailors with jobs on vessels registered in this country. The government itself maintains a small active merchant fleet and a large inactive reserve of vessels. These and other measures not only make a difference to the maritime industries of the United States, and so to the whole American economy, but they also affect the economies of other shipping nations and the relations between the United States and foreign countries, among them some of our principal allies. Shipping policy must be seen, too, as a part of the general foreign economic policy of the United States and assessed for the part it can play in building the kind of international economic life that the people of the free world want and that will add to their wealth and strength.

One cannot solve the problems of shipping policy by generalizations or by looking at only one of its many aspects. The details need to be examined and the many aims of policy —some of them conflicting—must be balanced and brought into the same focus so that each can be seen in proper perspective. The Committee on Studies and staff of the Council on Foreign Relations were aware of the need for this kind of examination of United States shipping policy. In Wytze Gorter, Associate Professor of Economics at the University of California at Los Angeles, we found a highly-qualified man who was interested in conducting a thorough investigation of the problem. By training and profession a general economist, Professor Gorter had already established his competence in the special field of shipping by his work on the maritime industry of the Pacific Coast. Under the terms of a Carnegie Research Fellowship, Professor Gorter spent the academic year 1953-54 in full-time work at the Council in New York. After he returned to Los Angeles he continued his research and completed this book.

While he was in New York, Professor Gorter worked closely with a study group, in the usual Council procedure. This group comprised men of varying backgrounds and experience. Several were from the shipping and shipbuilding industries; they brought to the group's work knowledge of ships, shipyards, and the merchant shipping business, and practical experience of the problems under discussion. Though they participated in the group entirely in their individual capacities they were in a position to state, vigorously and authoritatively, the views predominant in their industries on many controversial matters. Others in the group who were not directly engaged in operating or building ships had special knowledge of the industry as a result of their work in banking, insurance, oil, and the government. A third category was made up of men who professed no special knowledge of shipping but who recognized the importance of the problems being discussed and brought to them a fresh point of view, a variety of backgrounds, and experience in the consideration of problems of foreign policy.

The members of the group were:

Thomas H. McKittrick, Chairman

Robert R. Barker	E. S. Gregg
Gerald B. Brophy	Nathan Habib
William Diebold, Jr.	Warren T. Lindquist
Edward P. Farley	Oliver J. Lissitzyn

C. C. Mallory   George W. Morgan
Walter E. Maloney   Walter A. Radius
Stacy May   Morris S. Rosenthal
Carl E. McDowell   J. B. Smull
Francis McIntyre   Daniel O. Strohmeier
              Walter B. Wriston

In a series of six meetings, the group discussed most of the
principal problems with which this book is concerned. Our
procedure was for Professor Gorter to distribute in advance
of each meeting a paper in which he presented factual data
relevant to the subject of the meeting along with some tentative views of his own and some provocative questions. At
each session some especially well-qualified individual was
asked to open the discussion by giving his own analysis of
the evening's topic. Our discussion leaders were:

   Louis S. Rothschild — Federal Maritime Administrator
   Harvey Klemmer — Department of State
   James A. Farrell, Jr. — President, Farrell Lines
   James A. McCullough — Scudder, Stevens & Clark
   Daniel Marx, Jr. — Dartmouth College
   Robert B. Murray, Jr. — Under Secretary of Commerce

As chairman of the group, I am glad of the opportunity to
express the Council's gratitude to these men, members of the
group and discussion leaders alike, for their help and cooperation in enhancing this study and in aiding all of us in understanding the complex problems of shipping policy.

We made no effort to formulate views that would be acceptable to all or most of the members of the group. Quite
the contrary. Our aim was to go as deeply into a problem as
time permitted, to bring out differing points of view, and to
clarify issues. Only in that way could we hope to make a
real impact on the difficult issues before us. The discussions
were entirely private so men spoke freely and we had many
enlightening exchanges.

No member of the group bears any responsibility for the
views expressed in this book or for the analysis on which they
are based. They are Professor Gorter's alone, arrived at as
the result of his studies and reflecting his own best judgment.
The help he has had from the group, from members of it outside the regular meetings, and from many other individuals,

notably in the shipping industry, he acknowledges in his preface. The Council on Foreign Relations does not endorse the views expressed in the books it sponsors. Its responsibility has been only to assure itself that a book is competently and honestly done and that it is worthy of publication because of the contribution it makes to understanding important problems. The Council's Committee on Studies has no doubt that Professor Gorter's book meets these standards.

Because of the many interests involved, domestic and foreign, public and private, shipping policy abounds in controversial issues. There will undoubtedly be many who do not agree with the conclusions Professor Gorter reaches in this book and who would differ with him in judgment on many of the points that lead him to those conclusions. That is inevitable in matters such as these and is certainly no cause for alarm. Like all good scholarly work, this book makes plain what is fact and what is judgment. It shows how the author reached his conclusions. It presents data from which others might reach different conclusions. It makes clear at what points the author's knowledge stops, and where he is working on assumptions.

In short, this is an honest, able volume, clear in its analysis and reasonable in its conclusions. It fills a great gap, since there is no other up-to-date, objective book treating United States shipping policy as a whole. In a good tradition of American economics, Professor Gorter begins by looking at the industry with which he is concerned and then pursues the major elements of policy that have helped to shape it. At every point he asks: What is the aim? What is the result? Is there a better way? Ought we to have a different aim? The result is a book that is both solid and challenging; an enlightening analysis of where we are, a pertinent questioning about the future.

THOMAS H. McKITTRICK

PREFACE

NOT SINCE the days of the famous Yankee clippers have the United States ship-operating and shipbuilding industries enjoyed competitive advantages over their foreign rivals. To the uninformed this must appear incredible. The United States is blessed with long coastlines punctuated by excellent deep-water harbors. Its volume of water-borne commerce is very large and its industrial and engineering capabilities are great. Yet, despite these favorable conditions, shipbuilders and ship operators cannot generally compete effectively in the international markets for their products and services. Still the existence of shipyards in the United States and of an American-flag merchant marine has been deemed essential to national security. As a result, these segments of American business have received many kinds of governmental assistance.

A substantial body of federal legislation attests to the attempts to promote and maintain a domestic shipbuilding industry and to encourage Americans to sail ships under the United States flag. Since World War I Congress has passed three Merchant Marine Acts (1920, 1928, and 1936) and it has amended them many, many times. It has enacted a mass of other maritime legislation as well. Certainly, maritime affairs have received more than casual governmental attention.

The maritime industries' long-standing dependence upon government aid has resulted in many Congressional hearings and reports on their plight. The executive branch of the government has also made studies of maritime policies. The most recent available during preparation of this book was a review of maritime subsidy policy by the Department of Commerce.[1] An additional Department of Commerce study[2] of aid to ship-

[1] U. S. Department of Commerce *Maritime Subsidy Policy* (Washington: Author, April 1954). For a list of other important studies of United States shipping policies see the bibliography.
[2] U. S. Department of Commerce, *A Review of Direct and Indirect Types of Maritime Subsidies with Special Reference to Cargo Preference Aid.* (Washington: Author, April 1956).

ping appeared as this book was going to press. It is referred to at several points, especially in Chapter IV. In addition to government reports, there have been a number of private, nongovernmental, studies. And the industry itself has, on occasion, published reports on shipping policy. Some industry spokesmen contend that the maritime industries are the "most investigated" in the United States. Why, then, should another study be added to an already long list?

Two basic considerations prompted the decision to write this book. First, except for a few articles and Professor Marx's study of steamship conferences,[3] United States shipping policy has received scant attention from independent economists since the outbreak of World War II. This lack of interest is understandable. The war and immediate postwar years were prosperous ones for American shipbuilders and shipping lines. Shipping was not an irritated area of United States economic policy. However, since foreign-flag ship operators and shipbuilders have regained their pre-war competitive strength, American maritime policies are once again subject to close attention both at home and abroad.

A study of current policy by the industries directly affected can hardly escape the charge of bias. A government-directed study is generally accepted as more "objective" than one made by industry. Still, the reports of a technical staff are interpreted by administrative officials and legislators for purposes of policy evaluation and suggestion. Thus the final report will, in some measure, and justifiably, show the effects of the political climate in which it was born and raised. Therefore, government studies, though valuable, should be supplemented by independent investigations.

The second consideration was that shipping policy, especially in these postwar years, should be examined in the light of United States foreign economic policy. World War II and its aftermath have changed the position of the United States vis-a-vis the rest of the world. Shipping policy as an aspect of foreign economic policy deserves re-examination. This does not mean that the effect of maritime policy upon the mer-

[3] Daniel Marx, Jr., *International Shipping Cartels: A Study of Industrial Self-Regulation by Shipping Conferences* (Princeton: Princeton University Press, 1953).

chant marine should be excluded from the investigation. On the contrary, merchant marine requirements themselves have changed since prewar days and certainly the efficacy of current policy must be judged against these requirements.

United States maritime policy finds expression in many laws, regulations, and administrative and court decisions. These cover a variety of activities, from port procedures to foreign lending. An exhaustive account of all these individual policies lies beyond the scope of this study. Instead, we shall concentrate upon the major aspects of shipping policy. The relevant policies can be divided into five groups: (1) assistance to ship construction, (2) subsidies to the operation of vessels, (3) cargo preferences, (4) cabotage restrictions, and (5) control of shipping competition.

The first group includes construction-differential subsidies, ship mortgage arrangements, "Buy American" provisions relating to vessel construction and repair, and other devices to encourage and maintain a shipbuilding industry in the United States. The second category consists primarily of operating-differential subsidies. The third involves the well-known "50-50" provision for the transportation of foreign aid cargoes, the less publicized policies granting cargo preference to United States-flag carriers for the transport of merchandise purchased with the proceeds of Export-Import Bank loans, and the reservation of military freight and passengers to American-flag vessels. The fourth comprises legislation restricting the coastal and noncontiguous trades of the United States to domestically built and registered ships. And the fifth encompasses the regulation of shipping conferences, the control of rates by manipulation of the size of the government reserve fleet, and the government operation of fleets of commercial vessels under the Military Sea Transportation Service and other arrangements.

Each of these areas of shipping policy could well be the subject of a sizeable volume. Fortunately our objective—to examine United States maritime policies in the light of postwar international economic and political developments—does not require an intensive analysis of many of the technical and administrative details of some of the policies. Nor does it require more than occasional passing references to the maritime policies of other countries. For our purposes, a statement of essential features of United States policy is often sufficient. For the same reasons, it is not necessary to construct an historical account of how United States shipping policy developed. The relevant policies for this study are the current ones. And nowhere shall we discuss the domestic political conditions and alignments that contributed to the formulation of shipping policy. I leave that fascinating subject for the political scientist.

Chapter I begins the book with a broad sketch of American policy. Chapter II draws a statistical picture of the recent history of the ship-operating and shipbuilding industries of the United States and the other leading maritime nations. In Chapter III we examine the government's policies affecting shipbuilding and repair. Chapter IV is devoted to an analysis of the direct assistance given to ship operators—primarily operating-differential subsidies. Another form of aid—cargo preferences—is discussed in Chapter V. Restrictions reserving the coastal and noncontiguous trades of the United States to American-flag vessels are considered in Chapter VI. Chapter VII deals with the regulation of shipping conferences which set freight and passenger rates. In Chapter VIII we explore the implications of the federal government's policy of establishing essential trade routes on which vessel operators must maintain service if they are to receive operating-differential subsidies. The operations of the Military Sea Transportation Service are studied in Chapter IX. Chapter X contains a summary of findings, an appraisal of present shipping policy, and the conclusions I have drawn from this study.

When this study was completed, 1953 was generally the most recent year for which relevant statistical information was available. However, during the interval before submission of the manuscript to the printer, I attempted to extend the statistical series as far forward as possible, including figures for 1954 and 1955 when available.

To some extent the later data required me to modify statements based upon earlier information. However, though conditions in the shipping industry will continue to change, the basic policy considerations examined in this book will probably remain important. I hope that the criteria for the evaluation of policy suggested here will prove applicable no matter how the facts about shipping change.

Shipping statistics exist in a variety of forms. Some show one kind of tonnage, some another. Some apply to vessels above 100 tons, others to those above 1,000 or 2,000 tons. Some data apply only to dry-cargo ships, others to tankers as well. There are active and inactive parts of the merchant fleet. Sometimes we shall want to discuss only ships engaged in foreign trade while at other times the coastal trades must also be included and occasionally the ships on the Great Lakes. I have tried to avoid confusion by careful labelling and by compiling each table for a specific purpose. More general tables appear in the Appendix. The index shows where terms are first defined and also guides the reader to the full citations of reports that are usually referred to by abbreviated titles.

Many people contributed to this book. They deserve credit for its virtues and none of the blame for its shortcomings. Heading the list are the members of the Council on Foreign Relations study group, under the chairmanship of Thomas H. McKittrick, who patiently worked their way through a number of working papers. They offered many valuable criticisms, suggestions, and insights.

The shipping men of this group deserve a special word of thanks. They were very cooperative and were willing to consider any aspect of shipping policy. We often disagreed. Our disagreements about policy were, I am sure, the result of our differing appreciations of the national interest. Obviously none of the shipping men—any more than any other member of the group—is in any way associated with the recommendations I have made in this book.

With few exceptions the shipping industry itself was very cooperative. Frank Braynard, of the American Merchant Marine Institute, provided me with much information and was always ready to discuss my problems. James A. Farrell, president of the Farrell Lines, represents to me the finest in American shipping. He gave an unwarranted amount of time and energy to helping me. These men were typical of those who helped me. Space does not permit my mentioning all the others who were so kind.

Government people, as usual, assisted me at all times. Louis

S. Rothschild, then the Maritime Administrator, led the discussion at the first meeting of the study group. Irwin M. Heine, W. B. Harmon, and R. C. King, all of the Maritime Administration, helped me very much. John McCarron and J. J. Floyd of the Military Sea Transportation Service provided me with very useful statistical data about that service. Harvey Klemmer of the Department of State, formerly with the United States Maritime Commission, gave me the benefit of his experience in dealing with maritime problems. Many other government officials deserve mention, but this listing, already too long, would become unbearably tedious.

I owe the greatest debt to the Council on Foreign Relations. Through their award of a Carnegie Research Fellowship I was able to spend a year free of administrative and teaching duties to concentrate on this study of shipping policies. It was a rare and wonderful experience. Everyone at the Council helped to make my stay there both pleasant and productive. However, there are a few who should be mentioned. Annette Leyden, my secretary, did much to make life easier by acting as stenographer, messenger, and research assistant. Alice Yoakum performed the dreary but very important task of checking the galley and page proofs and even managed to remain cheerful and friendly despite many problems. Ruth Savord, the librarian, and her capable staff did more than librarians should. Percy Bidwell discussed my problems with me and read the manuscript in his usual careful manner. William Diebold Jr. did most of the difficult editorial work and was a constant source of ideas. His patience, tact, and editorial skill did much to clarify my thinking and writing.

Anne Cook, of the Institute of Industrial Relations, University of California, Los Angeles, deserves special thanks for compiling the index.

Customarily, a professor who writes a book ends his acknowledgments by thanking his wife. I shall not do so, although perhaps I should. My wife did no more than the usual wifely chores and to this day remains blissfully ignorant of shipping policy and the contents of this book.

University of California   W. G.
Los Angeles
May 1956

CONTENTS

CONTENTS

TABLES

xix

CHARTS

UNITED STATES
SHIPPING POLICY

1
A SKETCH OF AMERICAN POLICY

WHETHER ranked by number of employees, capital invested, volume of sales, or profits, the peacetime maritime industry is far down the list of United States industries. In good measure, its relatively insignificant rating reflects the long-time experience of American shipbuilders and shipping companies. For many years their foreign rivals have enjoyed the important competitive advantage of lower costs, while at home, railroad, trucking, and airplane companies increased their shares of freight and passengers at the expense of coastal shipping traffic.

In a competitive capitalistic business community the inefficient, high-cost firms may suffer the penalty of extinction. Except for expressions of personal sympathy for those whose businesses are doomed, people casually accept these deaths as necessary to the maintenance of a strong economy responsive to demands for an ever-changing output of goods and services. But in some instances, though the death of a firm or industry may be decreed by economics, public interest requires a stay of execution. In the United States, shipbuilding and ship operation have lived on under a series of such stays embodied in federal maritime policies.

The industry's plea for survival has rested largely upon military considerations. Mindful of the decisive role assigned to shipping during World War II, the federal government has continued since V-J Day the policies laid down by the Merchant Marine Act, 1936. It has also enacted additional laws designed to assist and strengthen the merchant marine and the shipbuilding industry.

Shipbuilders are helped by federal subsidy and other less direct means. Under the construction-differential scheme, a shipping company engaged in foreign trade pays for a vessel

1

built in an American shipyard the same price it would have paid if it had purchased the vessel from a comparable but lower-cost shipbuilder abroad. The difference between this hypothetical foreign price and the real domestic price is provided by the United States government as a construction-differential subsidy. This subsidy cannot exceed 50 per cent of the price paid to the domestic builder minus certain deductions for "defense features" entirely paid for by the government. In recent years this subsidy has averaged about 45 per cent.

All shipping companies operating in the "domestic trades" of the United States—coastwise, intercoastal, and with offshore American territories—must use only American-built vessels. The same requirement applies to companies receiving operating-differential subsidies to help them withstand the competition of lower-cost, foreign-flag ship operators. In addition, all Navy vessels are built in United States yards.

Shipbuilders are also assisted by a variety of other policies. For instance, the government will pay trade-in allowances on ships if their owners order replacements in the United States. Other forms of help include government offers to charter (rent) newly constructed tankers for long periods at favorable rates, government guarantees on ship mortgages, and government loans to shipowners to cover the major portion of the price of new vessels built in United States yards.

Ship operators flying the American flag may benefit from a number of policies adopted to enable them to survive in the rough waters of their maritime economic environment. Subsidies may be given to eligible operators to equalize the foreign and domestic costs of vessel operation. United States shipping concerns are permitted to participate in steamship conferences—cartel-like arrangements under which the companies get together to determine freight and passenger rates. A shipowner who confines his operations to the domestic trades need fear no foreign competitors because they are barred from these routes. American vessel operators get substantial revenues for lifting government cargoes. Under federal law, almost all military cargo and at least 50 per cent of foreign aid shipments must be moved aboard United States-flag vessels.

Despite the shield of protection against foreign competition and the pleasant warmth of the stimulants briefly (and by no means comprehensively) sketched above, the maritime industry of the United States threatens to grow weaker rather than stronger. In only one sector of the industry are there signs of sustained, long-term growth: the noncontiguous trade (with Hawaii, Alaska, Puerto Rico and other off-shore United States territories) is reserved exclusively for United States merchantmen and has increased rather steadily since the early thirties but not sufficiently to offset declines in other trades.

American shipping companies in foreign trade now enjoy roughly double the volume of cargo they handled in 1939. Even so, they are disturbed. Both the tonnage of cargo they have moved and their share of the trade declined in the last few years (except for 1955), even though there has been a significant increase in the commercial foreign trade of the United States (i.e., trade not resulting from foreign aid or government transactions).

Though Chapter II contains a detailed analysis of trade developments, a few general comments are pertinent here. And these must be preceded by a very brief digression on trade statistics and their relation to shipping. In any "trade"— a segment of the water-borne commerce of the United States—shipping men customarily distinguish between dry and tanker cargoes. Tanker cargoes consist of only a few products—mainly petroleum—lifted by special-purpose vessels—tankers. Dry cargo includes all other merchandise and transporting it involves the equipment and organization usually associated with shipping. Therefore, if we measure maritime activity by using cargo tonnage statistics, dry-cargo data will give us a more representative picture.

Sometimes dry cargo is divided into tramp and liner shipments. Liners are vessels operating on regular sailing schedules; they may be freighters or predominantly passenger ships.[1] A tramp follows no regular sailing schedule or route

---

[1] A vessel carrying more than 12 passengers is classified as a combination passenger and cargo ship. Thus the vessels usually thought of as "passenger ships" are included in the data on dry-cargo liners in this book. Except when considering the composition of the commercial fleet deemed appropriate for military purposes I shall not segregate passenger ship operation for special attention.

and ordinarily sails only when fully loaded with one or more commodities.

Returning now to our look at United States commercial foreign trade, we find that since the end of World War II, while dry-cargo imports have more than doubled, the share lifted by United States-flag vessels has been cut nearly in half, leaving the total tonnage carried about the same, although there was a sharp increase in 1955. On the export side, in 1953 and 1954, the total dry-cargo volume was about 7 per cent below the 1946 mark. Meanwhile, the United States-flag share fell from 61 per cent to 24 per cent. Again, there was improvement in volume in 1955, though the share fell to 20 per cent. Even so, in 1955 American shipping lines transported less than one-half as many tons as they had in 1946.

To those who would like to see a growing rather than a shrinking merchant marine, the dismaying situation in the foreign trade is not relieved by developments in the coasting trade. Though total traffic (dry cargo plus tanker) has increased sharply since V-J Day, dry-cargo liftings are far below prewar levels.

Obviously, these trade developments are reflected in the composition of the merchant marine. In June 1939, the total United States merchant fleet consisted of 1,398 vessels of 8.1 million gross tons.[2] More than half of the fleet was engaged in the coastal trades. Roughly one-quarter plied foreign trade routes. The rest was laid up. About half the laid-up fleet was made up of 162 government-owned ships, totalling 1.1 million gross tons.

In June 1955 there were 3,235 merchant ships of 24.8 million gross tons under United States registry. Approximately two-thirds were inactive. All but about 5 per cent of these were in the government's reserve fleet. Of the 1,163 active ships (very nearly the same as the number active in 1939, although the gross tonnage was one-third again as large in 1955), roughly two-thirds were in the foreign trade and the rest in the domestic. In fact, the number sailing in foreign trade in 1955 was about the same as for the domestic trades in 1939.

[2] Gross tons measure a vessel's total enclosed space above and within its hull. One ton equals 100 cubic feet. Deadweight tons (2,240 pounds) measure the total weight of cargo, passengers, fuel and provisions that a ship can carry.

The much larger American-flag merchant fleet, the deteriorating position of American merchantmen in foreign trade, and the reduced importance of coastwise and intercoastal trade, combined to hurt the shipbuilders of the United States. Add to these unfavorable conditions the postwar revival of foreign shipbuilding and the newness of most of the vessels now used by the American merchant marine, and the recent plight of the shipbuilders hardly needs further explanation.

Along with shipping, shipbuilding is often called a "feast or famine" industry. Its periods of prosperity and high output occurred during both world wars. During peacetime it has usually limped or barely crept along, weakened by its near-starvation diet of orders for new ships and repairs. Nine years clustered about the two major wars account for nearly 90 per cent of the industry's total output since the outbreak of World War I. Though recently some new orders have improved its position somewhat, output has fallen precipitously since V-J Day. The industry is now operating at a very low level, both absolutely and relative to its capacity.

At the war's end the shipyards demobilized very rapidly. Output in private yards fell from about 7 million gross tons in 1945 to 700 thousand tons in 1946—a drop of 90 per cent in one year! Meanwhile, shipbuilding increased elsewhere. In 1945, United States shipbuilders launched about four-fifths of the world's output of tonnage. A year later they accounted for a quarter of it. In 1955 they contributed only 1.4 per cent (73 thousand tons out of 5.3 million tons).

If the long-run prospects for American shipping were undeniably bright, then the shipyards might look forward to a great surge of orders within a few years as the vessels built during the 1940's reached retirement age—roughly 20 years. About 70 per cent of the United States-flag merchant fleet is between 10 and 15 years old. If this segment of the fleet were to be replaced within a five-year span, shipbuilding would certainly boom. However, this "block obsolescence"—a serious problem for the merchant marine—cannot be looked upon as necessarily beneficial to the American shipbuilders. Shipowners may not anticipate earnings high enough to make the necessary replacements, although during 1955 and early 1956 some subsidized lines made arrangements to replace a substantial portion of their fleets during the next twenty years. Furthermore, a large part of the fleet that will become obsolete lies at anchor in government reserve locations. A replacement program for these vessels would probably encounter much Congressional opposition.

Since 1945 the United States merchant fleet (including both active and inactive or reserve vessels) has become smaller while the world's merchant marine has been increasing. In 1946, 35.4 million gross tons of shipping flew the United States flag. At that time the world total was 71.0 million tons. The world's fleet included some 3.2 million tons of American-built vessels already transferred to foreign registry. In 1955, 25.4 million tons were registered American, while the world fleet totalled 91.0 million tons. Foreign purchases of some 1,100 United States vessels under the Merchant Ship Sales Act of 1946 accounted for part of the change in the position of the United States merchant marine. The revival of foreign shipbuilding and the scrapping of many American vessels also contributed importantly to the change. However, despite the growth of foreign-flag merchant fleets and the decline of the American merchant marine, the United States-flag fleet is still about three times its size in 1939.

The postwar developments outlined above present vexing problems to those engaged in shipbuilding and ship operation as well as to those responsible for developing and administering federal maritime policies. Shipping companies, alarmed and hurt by the increasing severity of foreign competition, have sought increased subsidies. And reports of the Federal Maritime Board show rising federal expenditures as more companies join the ranks of the subsidized lines. Shipbuilders have pressed for more help from the government as they have stood by nearly helpless while orders for new vessels declined.

Were it not for their foreign policy implications—economic, military, and political—federal maritime policies would be considerably easier to formulate. However, since most of the active merchant marine of the United States sails in the foreign trade, policy often affects foreigners. A policy favorable to the American shipbuilder or shipowner may adversely affect his foreign counterpart. This, in turn, may weaken rather than strengthen the western coalition of nations. Thus, debate over the maritime policies of the United States almost invariably attracts two bitter antagonists. On the one side are the proponents of the nationalistic "go-it-alone" view that only an impregnable "fortress United States" can insure our national security and, on the other side, those who advocate complete reliance on collective security and on the international division of labor.

Both of these views are extreme. They represent the opposite edges of the spectrum of shades of opinion about shipping and its importance to national defense. One can recognize the primacy of defense needs without disregarding the interests of other countries; one can emphasize the importance of allies and collective security without concluding that the United States can safely rely entirely on such arrangements for wartime shipping capacity. Policy makers are bound to try to develop policies that reflect adequate consideration of what is valid in both extreme views.

Defense problems are important to this book, but it does not present new estimates of how much merchant shipping or shipbuilding capacity is needed for national defense. Nor does the book essay a full military analysis. No one not acquainted with all the relevant facts of strategy and new weapons can properly evaluate the argument that shipping is and will be essential to national defense. Based upon the experience of World War II, the argument is certainly plausible. The need for ships was great. Merchant fleets in being at the beginning of the war had to be supplemented by a great expansion of building. Not all the existing shipping in foreign hands could be effectively mobilized in the service of the allies. American shipyards proved essential. To the extent that these problems might exist in a new war, a United States shipping industry larger than that which could be justified by economic considerations in peacetime might well be required.

A future war may be completely different. It is conceivable that merchant shipping should be of no great importance in such a war. There may be neither time nor occasion to use ships, much less build them. Even if they are needed, our allies may be better placed to supply both old and new ships than they were last time. But all this is speculation. As a layman, possessing neither the necessary classified data nor the experience to forecast probable military developments, I believe that this book should accept the present view of the government's policy makers that military prudence demands preparedness in the shipping industry. Adequate shipbuilding facilities and sufficient American- and allied-flag shipping are the components of this preparedness. What is "adequate" and "sufficient," and what disposition is prudent as between American-flag and allied-flag tonnage, are matters that will have to be dealt with in more detail in the course of this book. It is more than likely, however, that so long as the military importance of shipping is assumed, more ships, more yards, and more of both under American jurisdiction, will be called for than are economically justified in peacetime. Therein lies an important part of our problem.

Given the military and commercial importance of shipping to the western nations, the inability of much of the United States industry to survive without government aid, and the predominant position of the United States in western-bloc affairs, it is not surprising that the relatively small American shipping industry receives so much governmental attention. Changes in international political and economic conditions require a continuing re-examination of United States maritime policies. The policy questions may remain the same but the answers must sometimes be changed to fit the new circumstances.

With some modification, the basic policy questions apply to many other industries. For example, the question whether the United States should rely upon foreign suppliers—in this case shipowners and shipbuilders—to provide what may be needed during another war has also been asked about watches, organic chemicals, and electric generators. If the United States should not depend on foreign countries how much should this country provide for itself? And how should it obtain and maintain these facilities? Do the policies now pursued produce satisfactory results when measured by defense standards?

Answers to these questions have both domestic and international implications. Obviously, the foreigners, enjoying competitive economic advantages, protest whenever their economic superiority is reduced by the shipping policies of the

United States government. On the domestic side, the industry objects when the government expands its own fleet of merchant vessels or activity in its own shipyards in order to assure itself of an adequate national defense nucleus in these operations. The taxpayers become concerned when the cost of supporting the maritime industries rises. And the shippers (those who buy shipping services from the shipping companies) may fear that the protection of the United States merchant marine means higher rather than lower freight rates.

Subsidiary policy questions involve similar considerations. Consider the implications of the alternative policies suggested by the following queries. Should cargo preferences be eliminated? Should operating-differential subsidies be offered to all operators in the foreign trade and not merely to liner companies operating on designated foreign trade routes? Should American-flag lines be permitted to participate in steamship conferences? Should shipping conferences be permitted to set dual rates—one for regular and one for casual customers? Should shipping companies engaged in purely domestic trade be subsidized? Should foreign shipping lines be permitted to enter the United States coastal trades? Should the government permit American shipowners freely to transfer their vessels to foreign registry? Should the federal government own and operate the United States merchant marine? Should the government order merchant ships from the domestic shipbuilders even if the vessels are not needed for either military or commercial purposes?

No universally satisfactory policy answers can be given to any of these questions. Federal policy supposedly furthers the national interest. But is there *a* national interest? Certainly it is not purely economic or political or military. Any attempt to develop a policy based solely upon one of these interests would surely be unwise. Policy is essentially a compromise— a deliberate choosing of less than the best under any single criterion in an effort to get the best under several criteria combined. And what this latter "best" is, is a matter of judgment, not of scientific proof. As a result, no particular interest group will be completely satisfied and, as conditions change, even the policy makers may become disenchanted with their creation.

Judgments, like men, are not created equal. Those based upon a sober consideration of facts should ordinarily prove better than those springing full-born from emotion. And those made by a party at interest (other than "the" national interest) are probably more suspect than those made by an informed neutral observer. Even a superficial study of written and oral submissions to Congressional committees investigating federal maritime policies quickly reveals that groups directly affected by shipping policy may contribute more of the proverbial heat than light to a consideration of policy issues. Undoubtedly, these groups recognize that heat is sometimes more persuasive than light—particularly in the political arena where the contests over shipping policy so often take place.

Since an impartial analysis of shipping policies requires a hard look at the facts or a look at the hard facts, the next chapter presents the data relevant to an appreciation of the economic position of the shipbuilding and ship operating industries in the United States. Facts peculiarly pertinent to an evaluation of particular policies appear in chapters devoted to those policies.

II

THE STATUS OF THE SHIPBUILDING
AND OPERATING INDUSTRIES
IN THE UNITED STATES

Describing the status of the shipping and shipbuilding industries of the United States involves many vexing problems of
definition and statistical manipulation. No matter how care-
fully the data are compiled or the definitions cast, objections
to both are bound to be made. This results from the diverse
character of the segments arbitrarily lumped together as *the*
ship-operating or *the* shipbuilding industry. Though often
closely related, these separate parts are sometimes strikingly
different. Their problems are different. Their operations differ
substantially in one way or another. Combining them statis-
tically or by definition obscures these differences and may
lead to erroneous inferences. Still, too much segmentation
can obscure "the forest for the trees." To prevent this, admittedly arbitrary classifications are useful, if the proper
caveat is kept in mind.

To determine the status of the American maritime industries, this chapter compares the size of the United States
merchant fleet with that of other maritime nations, examining
the volume and types of cargo transported in American-flag
vessels; it touches briefly on the relative gross earnings of
American and foreign operators from United States trade; and
then it summarizes the record of output and employment in
the shipbuilding industry in the United States and in some
foreign countries.

THE SIZE OF THE UNITED STATES MERCHANT MARINE

As Table 1 shows, the United States merchant fleet, measured absolutely by gross tonnage, underwent great changes

between 1895 and 1954.[1] It fluctuated both in absolute size

Table 1

MERCHANT MARINE OF THE WORLD AND THE UNITED STATES,
SELECTED YEARS, 1895-1954

[In thousands of gross tons]

Year	World	United States	United States as per cent of world merchant marine
1895	25,086	2,165	8.6
1920	57,314	16,049	28.0
1939	69,440	12,003	17.3
1947	84,356	32,891	39.0
1948	81,074	29,602	36.5
1949	83,346	28,224	33.9
1950	85,303	27,898	32.7
1951	87,961	27,702	31.5
1952	90,868	27,600	30.4
1953	93,978	27,535	29.3
1954	98,046	27,630	28.2

Note: Figures include vessels of 100 gross tons and over. Prior to 1919 tonnage figures are gross for steamers and net for sailing vessels, thereafter gross for both. Wooden vessels on the Great Lakes and vessels on Caspian Sea excluded. Japanese sailing vessels and most vessels belonging to Greece, Turkey, and southern Russia excluded. Figures for Philippine Islands included in United States total.

Source: For 1895-1951, Lloyd's Register of Shipping, *Appendix to Lloyd's Register Book* as cited in United States Department of Commerce, Bureau of the Census, *Statistical Abstract of the United States, 1952* (Washington: GPO, 1952), Table 672, p. 554. For 1952, Lloyd's Register of Shipping, *Register Book Appendix* (London, 1953), Section 6, Table 1, p. 5. For 1953, Same (London: 1954). For 1954, Same: *Statistical Tables, 1954* (London: 1955), Table 1, p. 5.

and as a portion of the world's fleet. Note the decline since 1947. Is it possible that once again less than 20 per cent of the world's merchant marine will fly the United States flag? The trend certainly points that way. Whether it will continue to depends upon decisions regarding government policy and many often interrelated economic and political factors too complex to warrant any reasonably safe guess about the future importance of the American merchant marine.

[1] The United States merchant fleet includes active and inactive vessels and consists of commercial vessels owned and/or operated by the government or citizens of the United States and registered under the laws of the United States. See Frank Henius, *Dictionary of Foreign Trade* (2d ed.; New York: Prentice-Hall, 1947), p. 429.

Table 2

IMPORTANCE OF UNITED STATES MERCHANT FLEET, BY TYPE OF VESSEL, 1939, 1946, 1950-55

[Expressed as percentage of world merchant fleet]

Type of vessel	1939 No.	1939 Dwt.	1946 No.	1946 Dwt.	1950 No.	1950 Dwt.	1951 No.	1951 Dwt.	1952 No.	1952 Dwt.	1953 No.	1953 Dwt.	1954 No.	1954 Dwt.	1955 No.	1955 Dwt.
Comb. pass. and cargo	8.5	11.0	8.7	11.8	7.5	10.5	20.5	28.5	20.3	27.4	20.7	28.5	20.2	24.9	20.0	24.9
Comb. pass. and cargo-refr.	17.1	10.5	19.2	10.8	9.5	4.8	9.2	4.4	9.8	4.6	3.2	1.5	3.2	1.3	3.3	1.5
Freighters	9.0	11.8	42.8	53.6	31.4	41.9	29.0	39.6	28.3	38.7	27.6	37.9	27.0	37.2	25.6	35.2
Freighters—refr.	9.5	6.9	23.2	19.9	18.2	16.4	16.1	14.9	15.0	13.7	15.2	13.8	14.8	13.3	14.4	13.0
Bulk carriers	8.3	14.4	15.2	29.0	10.4	24.5	7.6	23.1	8.9	22.1	9.1	21.9	8.2	19.4	7.2	16.6
Tankers (incl. whaling tankers)	23.1	25.2	46.1	55.6	23.2	27.6	18.1	25.3	19.8	23.0	18.7	21.4	17.0	19.3	15.6	17.4
Total, all types	10.8	14.5	39.1	50.8	26.9	35.6	25.8	34.2	25.0	32.8	24.3	31.7	23.4	30.1	22.2	28.1

Note: Includes seagoing vessels of 1,000 gross tons and over. Excludes vessels on the Great Lakes and inland waterways and special types such as channel vessels, icebreakers, cable ships, etc., and merchant vessels owned by any military force. For detailed notes describing the composition of certain of the data, see the sources.

Source: For 1939 and 1946, U.S. Department of Commerce, Maritime Administration, *Merchant Fleets of the World, September 1, 1939-December 31, 1951* (Washington: GPO, 1953), p. 48-59. For 1950-55, U.S. Department of Commerce, *Annual Report of the Federal Maritime Board and Maritime Administration* (Washington: GPO, 1950-1956).

Table 2 indicates the relative importance of the United States merchant fleet in each of the principal categories of merchant vessels. It shows that (1) combination passenger and cargo vessels increased in importance during 1950-53 but decreased slightly in 1954 with no recovery in 1955; (2) all other classifications declined in significance during 1950-55; and (3) except for tankers and combination passenger-cargo refrigerated ships, all types were a markedly larger part of the world fleet in 1954 than they were in 1939.[2]

These figures apply to ships registered in the United States. Americans also own ships registered in foreign countries. As of December 31, 1955, 374 vessels of 5.9 million deadweight tons owned by affiliates of parent companies incorporated in the United States flew foreign flags. There were 49 dry-cargo ships, 302 tankers and 23 bulk and ore carriers in this group of vessels. An additional 87 ships of 2.7 million deadweight tons were under construction for American parent companies who intended to register them under foreign flags.[3] These vessels are not properly part of the United States merchant marine. They are not included in the general statistics in this book. However their existence ought to be borne in mind, especially in connection with the advantages and disadvantages of an "all-American" fleet and in considering the shipping potentially available to the United States in wartime.

The active fleet

Two important characteristics of the merchant marine have not been mentioned. The first one is the size of the *active* fleet

[2] The sharp rise in percentage of world total combination passenger-cargo vessels of United States registry in 1951 over 1950 resulted from a reclassification of certain vessels. In 1950, the Maritime Administration reported only 77 combination passenger-cargo vessels at 612,000 dwt. In 1951 it recorded 260 of this type aggregating 2,041,000 dwt. In a note to its 1951 figure the Maritime Administration stated that in addition to the 77 ships previously reported, the 1951 figure included "183 freighters of 1,494,000 gross tons and 1,426,000 deadweight tons originally constructed as cargo ships but converted to transports, hospital ships, etc., and included in the freighter classification of previous reports." U.S. Department of Commerce, *Annual Report of the Federal Maritime Board and Maritime Administration* (Washington: GPO, 1951, 1952), p. 58, 100-101.
[3] Data from tabulation prepared by the U.S. Department of Commerce, Maritime Administration, April 24, 1956.

and the second is the *age distribution* among vessels flying the American flag.

After World War II, a large part of United States merchant fleet was demobilized and put into the inactive reserve under the jurisdiction of the National Shipping Authority, an agency of the Maritime Administration in the Department of Commerce. From time to time, during the Korean conflict for example, ships have been withdrawn from this fleet. Nevertheless, a large number has remained there throughout the postwar years. Subtracting the number of ships in the inactive reserve from the total number of vessels in the United States merchant marine therefore throws additional light on the status of American-flag ships in the maritime world. This is shown in Table 3.

Table 3

MERCHANT MARINE OF THE WORLD AND ACTIVE MERCHANT
FLEET OF THE UNITED STATES, 1939, 1949-55
[In thousands of deadweight tons]

Year[a]	World (minus U.S. reserve fleet)	U.S. active fleet[c]	U.S. active fleet as per cent of world fleet	U.S. Maritime Administration reserve fleet
1939	57,500[b]	7,365[b]	12.8	770[b]
1949	83,900	18,126	21.6	18,107
1950	83,446	14,673	17.6	21,853
1951	92,330	17,419	18.9	16,395
1952	95,113	18,520	19.5	17,562
1953	98,732	17,859	18.1	18,395
1954	102,496	16,487	16.1	19,373
1955	107,516	15,331	14.3	19,687

Note: Includes seagoing ships of 1,000 gross tons and over, excludes ships on the inland waterways, the Great Lakes, those owned by any military force, and special types, such as cable ships, tugs, etc.

[a] As of June 30 except for 1939 which is September 1.

[b] Gross tonnage.

[c] Includes temporarily inactive vessels included because they are part of the fleet normally in use.

Source: For 1939, U.S. Department of Commerce, Maritime Administration, *Merchant Fleets of the World, September 1, 1939-December 31, 1951* (Washington: 1952), p. 48; Appendix Table 3. For other years, Appendix Table 3a; *Annual Report of the Federal Maritime Board and Maritime Administration*, appropriate years.

Note that though the sharp fall in the size and importance of the active merchant marine of the United States was temporarily arrested in 1951 and 1952, a decline against set in in 1953. The cease-fire agreement in Korea, the reduction in goverment aid cargoes, and the continued revival of foreign merchant fleets, no doubt contributed to this development.

The age of the fleet

Foreign shipping companies have become more competitive partly because they use newer ships. This is borne out by Table 4, which shows that the age distribution of merchant vessels favors the rest of the world over the United States. Table 4 also indicates that "block obsolescence" is a world-wide problem in the shipping industry. However, it is especially troublesome for ship operators in the United States. About 92 per cent of the United States merchant fleet will become overage (20 years) during a ten-year period beginning about 1960. For the rest of the world the figure is 41 per cent. If the United States is to maintain an adequate merchant marine for purposes of national defense alone, the future replacement problem is indeed formidable.

The story is much the same for tankers considered separately, as Table 5 shows. Here again the current age distribution is disadvantageous to the United States. Tanker tonnage under the United States flag increased from 4.3 million deadweight tons in 1939 to 7.0 million deadweight tons in 1954. For the rest of the world deadweight tonnage rose from 12.7 million to 29.1. Most of the United States tankers were built during the war but roughly 44 per cent of the rest of the world's tanker tonnage was constructed during the five years from 1949 to 1954.[4]

Note that although the 1954 age distribution gives a competitive edge to foreigners, block obsolescence will eventually

[4] U. S. Department of Commerce, Maritime Administration, *Merchant Fleets of the World, September 1, 1939-December 31, 1951* (Washington: GPO, 1953), p. 58 and *Annual Report of the Federal Maritime Board and Maritime Administration* (Washington: GPO, 1955) p. 56. In 1939 the title of the publication was *Annual Report of the United States Maritime Commission.* Hereafter it will be referred to by the current title even though earlier reports bear a different one.

Table 4

AGE DISTRIBUTION OF THE MERCHANT FLEETS OF THE
UNITED STATES AND THE WORLD, 1954
[In per cent]

| | United States | | | World | |
Age Group	Sea-going	Lakes	Seagoing + Lakes	Total Including U.S.	Total excluding U.S.
Under 5 years	3.8	7.3	4.2	19.8	25.9
5 and under 10	21.6	1.3	19.8	19.2	19.0
10 and under 15	70.0	8.8	64.5	34.0	22.2
15 and under 20	1.6	1.4	1.6	5.9	7.6
20 and under 25	0.9	1.3	1.0	3.5	4.5
25 and over	2.0	80.0	9.0	17.6	20.9

Note: Includes all vessels 100 gross tons and over. Percentages apply to gross tonnage distribution. Totals not always 100 because of rounding.
Source: Lloyd's Register of Shipping, *Statistical Tables, 1954* (London: 1955), Table 3, p. 8 and 12.

Table 5

AGE DISTRIBUTION OF THE OIL TANKER FLEETS OF THE
UNITED STATES AND THE WORLD, 1954
[In per cent]

Age group	United States	Rest of the world	Total
Under 5 years	10.9	44.1	37.9
5 and under 10	19.8	18.6	18.8
10 and under 15	58.6	15.8	23.8
15 and under 20	6.1	8.1	7.7
20 and under 25	1.6	4.9	4.3
25 and over	3.0	8.6	7.6

Note: Includes all vessels 100 gross tons and over. Percentages apply to gross tonnage distribution. Totals not always 100 because of rounding.
Source: Lloyd's Register of Shipping, *Statistical Tables, 1954* (London: 1955), Table 7, p. 15 and 17.

become a serious problem for them, too, unless they maintain their recent output of tankers.

The age distribution of United States dry-cargo, seagoing vessels is even more unfortunate, given the needs of national defense and the desire of American operators to compete effectively with foreign-flag companies. As Table 6 shows, about 95 per cent of the American dry-cargo fleet is in the 5 to 15 year bracket, as compared with about 44 per cent for the rest of the world. If the Great Lakes fleet is included the picture is not quite as alarming but neither is it comforting.

Table 6

AGE DISTRIBUTION OF THE DRY-CARGO FLEETS OF THE
UNITED STATES AND THE WORLD, 1954

[In per cent]

Age group	United States		World	
	Seagoing	Total	Total	(World)-(United States)
Under 5 years	2.4	2.8	13.6	18.6
5 and under 10	22.0	19.8	19.3	19.1
10 and under 15	72.6	65.7	37.5	24.7
15 and under 20	0.6	0.7	5.3	7.4
20 and under 25	0.8	0.8	3.3	4.4
25 and over	1.7	10.2	21.0	25.8

Note: Includes all vessels 100 gross tons and over. Percentages apply to gross tonnage distributions. Totals not always 100 because of rounding.

Col. 1 and col. 3 represent total seagoing tonnage minus tanker tonnage. Great Lakes tonnage was added to the figures for col. 1 to get the basis for col. 2. Col. 4 is based on figures representing col. 3 minus col. 2.

Source: Lloyd's Register of Shipping, *Statistical Tables, 1954* (London: 1955), Tables 3 and 7, p. 8, and 12 and 15 and 17 respectively.

CARGOES

Though United States-flag vessels form a substantial part of the world's merchant marine, their record of cargoes handled, except during World War II and its aftermath, is not impressive. In all trades except the noncontinguous the stories are similar. The volume of cargoes carried aboard American-flag ships, though greater than before the war, appears to be headed downward from postwar peaks. The share of United States foreign trade carried in American ships has also declined.

Foreign trade

In 1921, the American merchant marine carried about 52 per cent of the cargo moving in the foreign commerce of the United States—42 million long tons out of a total of 82 million. By 1939 when this trade totalled 93 million long tons, American-flag vessels were transporting only 22 per cent of these cargoes, or a total of 21 million long tons.

Right after World War II, American ships enjoyed both a much higher volume and share of foreign trade cargoes. Leaving out of account purely military shipments or aid shipments aboard military-controlled vessels, or "special category" defense items (see Chapter V), American ships carried 68 per cent of United States foreign trade in 1945. This was their record share—62 million tons out of 90 million. In 1947, though the share had declined to 54 per cent, the tonnage had risen to 88 million. Since 1947 both the share and the volume have fallen. In 1955, after some improvement over 1954, 53 million tons of cargo or about 24 per cent of United States foreign commerce went aboard United States-flag ships. (See Appendix Table 1.)

So far as tonnage volume and share of foreign trade cargoes are concerned, United States operators have generally fared better in the import than in the export segment of this trade. But the long-term tendencies in imports and exports, considered separately, are much the same as for total foreign trade. Both declined after World War I, showed weak recovery after the depression of the thirties, rose spectacularly during and immediately following World War II, and then fell off once again. The highlights of the ups and downs of United States foreign trade and the volume of cargoes handled by American shipping companies appear in the following figures extracted from Appendix Table 1:

	Imports			Exports		
Year	Total (long tons)	U.S. flag (long tons)	Per cent U.S. flag	Total (long tons)	U.S. flag (long tons)	Per cent U.S. flag
1921	33.2	23.5	70.8	48.6	18.6	38.3
1939	37.5	11.1	29.6	55.1	9.4	17.1
1944				49.3	30.4	61.7
1945	35.2	28.0	79.5			
1947				111.0	54.5	49.1
1951	90.2	38.2	42.4			
1955	126.0	33.4	26.5	100.0	19.7	19.7

Note that despite the recent decrease in the share and volume of cargoes handled by American-flag operators, their total liftings remained far above prewar levels. In 1955, despite a drop of nearly 35 million long tons from the postwar high of 88 million tons in 1947, United States flag vessels transported 137 per cent more tons of cargo than they did annually during 1935-39.

Before reaching a final verdict on the experience of the American merchant marine in foreign trade, further statistical refinements are in order. Dry cargo, except for certain bulk commodities (e.g. grain, coal, ores) is transported primarily aboard the freighters that make up an important part of the United States merchant marine. In time of national military emergency these all-purpose freighters are often of greater value than the specialized bulk carriers. Of course, tankers, too, are indispensable during wartime, but they are not interchangeable with dry-cargo vessels. So, unless cargo tonnage statistics are properly segregated into those applicable to dry and tanker cargoes, the experience of the merchant marine cannot be evaluated properly.

American-flag vessels carried 12.7 million long tons of dry-cargo imports in 1946 and 17.7 million tons in 1955. (See Appendix Table 2). The annual average for the period was 14.9 million tons. Except in three instances, the year-to-year fluctuations in this tonnage were not large. However, from 1946 to 1954 United States dry-cargo imports moved aboard vessels of all flags rose steadily from 22.6 million long tons to 51.2 million tons, and then increased sharply to 61.1 million tons in 1955. Therefore, the percentage carried by United States merchantmen fell from 56.2 in 1946 to 28.7 in 1954, and rose slightly to 29.0 in 1955. In 1939, total dry-cargo imports amounted to 27.4 million long tons of which American-flag vessels carried 7.3 million tons, or 26.6 per cent. Thus, though the United States merchant marine increased its liftings of dry-cargo imports between 1939 and 1955 by 142 per cent its share of the trade went up only 9 per cent.

On the export side, during the period 1946-54, American-flag vessels far exceeded both their 1939 share and volume of dry cargoes. They averaged 26.3 million long tons per year—37.2 per cent of total dry-cargo exports—as compared with 7.6 million tons and 22.3 per cent in 1939. However, the postwar tendency for both share and volume is downward. In 1954 the share was 23.5 per cent and the volume 14 million tons, while in 1955 the share was 19.6 per cent and the volume 17.6 million tons.

Summarized briefly, in 1955 American-flag operators carried a slightly smaller fraction of the dry-cargo foreign trade of the United States than they did in 1939. The absolute volume of cargo tonnage, though, was nearly two-and-one-half times that lifted in 1939. This is a substantial gain, and it does not include Department of Defense cargoes and certain "special category" items of military and strategic importance. In 1955, the latter alone added 726,000 long tons to the cargoes aboard United States-flag vessels.[5]

The foreign trade tanker traffic of the United States reflects the shifting position of the United States as an importer of petroleum. In 1939 10.1 million long tons of tanker cargoes entered the United States from overseas. American-flag vessels lifted 3.8 million tons—37.6 per cent—of this total. In 1955, the United States imported 64.9 million tons. About 16 million tons—34.2 per cent—came in American-flag tankers. Both share and volume have been declining since 1950 when 24.5 million tons moved in American-flag vessels, representing 54.8 per cent of total United States tanker imports.

Tanker exports amounted to 21 million long tons in 1939 and only 10.6 million tons in 1955. However, United States-flag tankers transported only 1.9 million tons (9 per cent of

[5] U.S. Department of Commerce, Bureau of the Census, "United States Water-Borne Foreign Trade Statistics" *Summary Report FT 985* (Washington: monthly issues). A note to Appendix Table 2 defines the omission of defense cargoes from the figures given above.

the total) in 1939 as contrasted with 2.1 million tons (19.8 per cent of the total) in 1955. Nevertheless, the outlook is not encouraging for American tanker operators. Since 1950 when 3.5 million tons—43.2 per cent of the total—were moved by United States-flag vessels, volume and share have declined.

As in the case of dry-cargo foreign trade, the tanker merchant marine of the United States handled substantially larger cargoes in the postwar years than it did in 1939. In the early fifties, however, its share of tanker cargoes and the absolute volume of tonnage lifted have declined.[6]

To those interested in increasing or maintaining the share of foreign trade cargoes carried aboard American-flag vessels, the future probably looks bleak. Representatives of the ship operators have emphasized the downward trend in this share. Other observers have stressed the great increase in the volume of cargo moving in United States-flag ships. Little has been said about the relationship of the volume of cargoes to the deadweight capacity of the vessels actively employed in foreign trade. Yet this relationship suggests an explanation of the varying fortunes of the American vessel operators in the foreign trade of the United States.

On June 30, 1939, the inventory of the Maritime Commission showed that United States operators of dry-cargo ships in the foreign trades were actively employing 271 vessels of 2.2 million deadweight tons. During that year, it will be recalled, 14.9 million long tons of dry cargo moved in American-flag ships. On June 30, 1955, 531 vessels aggregating 5.7 million deadweight tons were active under the American flag in the dry-cargo foreign trade of the United States. (This fleet excludes 130 vessels of 1.2 million deadweight tons in "other U.S. agency operations.") In 1955 the 531 vessels handled 35.3 million tons of dry cargo, excluding Department of Defense and "special category" merchandise. Thus, a fleet 2 times larger in number and with 2.6 times the deadweight tonnage, was used to haul 2.4 times the 1939 volume of cargoes. A year, earlier, this fleet was 1.9 times larger than in 1939, had 2.6 times the deadweight tonnage, and lifted only 1.9 times the 1939 volume of cargoes. These figures demon-

---

[6] Department of Defense tanker cargoes added only about 200,000 long tons to the total liftings in 1955.

strate how quickly the relationship between carrying capacity and available cargoes can change.

Not all of the increase in deadweight tonnage can be considered an addition to *carrying capacity* of the fleet. Deadweight tonnage includes fuel capacity and in some instances this may mean relatively less cargo carrying capacity. However, the postwar fleet is faster than the prewar one. Because it could complete more round trips per year, a 1955 vessel would have a greater carrying capacity than a 1939 vessel of the same size. On balance then, it would appear safe to assume that the cargo capacity of the 1955 fleet of dry-cargo merchantmen was more than two-and-one-half times that of the 1939 fleet.[7]

The postwar adjustment of carrying capacity to available cargo appears to have been better in the foreign trade tanker business than it was in the dry-cargo trades. The active fleet of United States-flag tankers consisted of 59 ships totalling 1.1 million deadweight tons in 1955 as compared with a 1939 total of 48 vessels of 0.6 million deadweight tons. In 1954, American-flag tankers, using 79 ships of 1.4 million deadweight tons, carried 19.9 million long tons of cargo (excluding Department of Defense shipments) while in 1939 they lifted 5.7 million tons.

The foregoing figures indicate that at least some of the more recent postwar difficulties experienced by American-flag vessel operators in the dry-cargo foreign trade are perhaps in part attributable to what the shipping industry calls "overtonnaging"—too many ships, too much cargo-carrying capacity, and too little freight to move. This sporadic overtonnaging also helps to explain, as we shall show in Chapter V, why ship operators are so enthusiastic about the United States policy of cargo preferences. By this policy the operators are assured certain cargoes and they can avoid some of

[7] Ship statistics for 1939 taken from *Statistical Abstract of the United States, 1947*, p. 544. For 1954, from U.S. Department of Commerce, Maritime Administration, "Employment Report of United States Flag Merchant Fleet, Seagoing Vessels, 1,000 Gross Tons and Over as of June 30, 1954," *Report* #300 (Washington: August 19, 1954). For 1955, Department of Commerce, *Annual Report of the Federal Maritime Board and Maritime Administration* (Washington: GPO, 1956), p. 62-63; *Report* #300 as of December 31, 1955, (Washington, January 27, 1956). These same references apply to the vessel statistics for the other trades.

the reductions in tonnage that would be forced upon them by an open market for shipping services.

Coasting trades

The Maritime Administration recently published data throwing light on the situation in coastwise and intercoastal shipping. It compared 1939 with 1953 and found that in 1939 total coastwise and intercoastal cargo carrying amounted to about 121 million long tons as compared with 138 million tons in 1953. All of the increase was attributable to tanker cargoes, which amounted to 83 million tons in 1939 and 122 million tons in 1953. Dry-cargo liftings thus fell from 38 million tons in 1939 to only 16 million tons in 1953.[8]

In 1939 there were 675 vessels of 5.8 million deadweight tons in the coastwise and intercoastal trades while in 1953 the totals were 371 vessels and 5.3 million tons. The following informal table indicates the relationships between these fleets and the cargoes they lifted.

	1939	1953
Total number of vessels	675	371
Deadweight tons	5.8 million	5.3 million
Cargoes (long tons)	121 million	138 million
Dry-cargo vessels	378	102
Deadweight tons	2.6 million	1.0 million
Cargoes (long-tons)	38 million	16 million
Tankers	297	269
Deadweight tons	3.3 million	4.2 million
Cargoes (long tons)	83 million	122 million

The adjustment to the drastic changes in cargoes was more easily accomplished in the coasting trades than in the foreign trades because of the differences in the basic conditions. In the foreign trade, the end of World War II required a tremendous reduction in vessel tonnage. Reducing the scale of operations often entails solving difficult problems and hence there is a natural reluctance to do so. In the coasting trades

[8] U. S. Department of Commerce, Maritime Administration. *A Review of the Coastwise and Intercoastal Shipping Trades* (Washington: Author, December 1955), p. 17. Later figures come from p. 10. Short tons in original converted to long tons.

the problem was the exact opposite. No reductions in capacity were required since the coasting trades had been almost completely shut down during the war. Immediately after the war, dry-cargo prospects in the coasting trades were relatively unfavorable. Shipping companies hesitated to renew and subsequently expand their operations.

The Maritime Administration reported that in the coasting trades dry-cargo carryings "continually declined" between 1939 and 1953.[9] Intercoastal trade via the Panama Canal has improved markedly since 1946 but the annual volume of cargo tonnage has generally not exceeded two-thirds of what it was during the late thirties. This has provided little ground for optimism regarding the future of this traffic.[10]

The foregoing figures are hardly reassuring to those who had hoped for a revival of coastal dry-cargo trade. Nor are the data encouraging to those who remember that at the outbreak of World War II, the domestically employed merchant marine was the most readily available for wartime use.

Noncontiguous trade

The student of noncontiguous trade (commerce between the United States and its territories and possessions) is hampered by the absence of data on trade with Alaska and Hawaii after April 1948 and the lack of any published statistics for this trade after 1947. Nevertheless, there is enough evidence to warrant the conclusion that this trade, which grew steadily during the thirties, continued to expand after being interrupted by the war.[11]

[9] Same, p. 17.
[10] For intercoastal trade via the Panama Canal, see Appendix Table 4.
[11] The noncontiguous trade amounted to about 5.5 million long tons of cargo annually during the years 1938-40 with exports exceeding imports by almost 10 per cent. In 1946 and 1947, exports totalled 3.4 and 4.0 million tons respectively. (Complete import figures were not published.) Gorter and Hildebrand, *The Pacific Coast Maritime Shipping Industry, 1930-48,* v.1 (Berkeley, The University of California Press, 1952, p. 29-32) concluded that the trade between the West Coast of the United States and Alaska and Hawaii had expanded since the war. Trade statistics for 1946, Bureau of the Census, *Foreign Commerce and Navigation of the United States, Calendar Year 1946* (Washington: GPO, 1950), v.1 part A, p. 678-695; for 1947, same, "U.S. Trade in Merchandise and Gold and Silver with U.S. Territories and Possessions," *Report FT800* (Washington: May 1948.)

A comparison of the United States-flag active fleets in the noncontiguous trade (the only vessels permitted in this trade) also permits this inference. In 1939, sixty-four vessels of 500 thousand deadweight tons sailed in this trade. There were 10 combination cargo-passenger vessels (49 thousand dwt.), 49 dry-cargo ships (393 thousand dwt.), and 5 tankers (57 thousand dwt.). In 1954 there were 67 vessels all told—about 703 thousand deadweight tons. Five of them were combination cargo-passenger ships, 52 were freighters (538 thousand dwt.), and 10 were tankers with a deadweight capacity of 141 thousand tons. As of December 31, 1955, there were 61 vessels in the trade, four fewer combination and 2 fewer tankers. When due allowance is made for its greater speed, the postwar merchant marine probably has a considerably greater capacity than the one operating in 1939. Since cargoes are larger than prewar it is doubtful if any appreciable excess vessel tonnage exists.

EARNINGS OF UNITED STATES VESSELS

Available figures (see Table 7) indicate that since 1951 foreigners have earned more than Americans in the carriage of United States foreign trade cargoes. Note that the earnings do not include receipts from military-controlled export cargoes. Although 1946-54 is too short a span of years to warrant any inferences about trend, the annual figures show that foreign operators rather steadily increased their share of these earnings from 1946 to 1954.

The share of American and foreign shipping companies in the earnings from United States foreign trade is only part of the story. Since the end of the war, United States citizens have received more from foreigners for shipping services than Americans have paid to foreigners for the same purpose. However, during the period 1946-54 the position of the foreigners improved. Table 8 sets out the relevant figures as they appear in the United States balance of payments. The table shows that foreign countries have generally earned more in passenger fares than they paid to Americans. However, this gain has been more than offset by higher payments to the United States for the carriage of freight and for port charges.

Table 7

Estimated Freight Earnings of United States-Controlled
and Foreign-Controlled Vessels in the Carriage of
United States Exports and Imports, 1946-54[a]
[Millions of dollars]

Year	U.S. Controlled			Foreign Controlled		
	Dry Cargo	Tanker	Total[b]	Dry Cargo	Tanker	Total
1946	1,061	96	1,157	494	64	558
1947	1,210	118	1,328	871	78	949
1948	719	136	855	624	76	700
1949	637	87	724	596	38	634
1950	560	100	660	576	53	629
1951	878	169	1,047	1,084	188	1,272
1952	777	160	937	925	202	1,127
1953	594	141	735	764	122	886
1954[c]	597	129	726	839	106	945

[a] Data are for ocean freight.
[b] Does not include freight on military-controlled export cargo.
[c] Preliminary figures.
Source: U.S. Department of Commerce, Office of Business Economics as cited in letter to author from Walther Lederer, Chief, Balance of Payments Division, November 8, 1955.

In 1937 the relative positions of the foreigners and Americans were reversed, Americans paying more to foreigners. This was also the case in each year during the period 1919-39, except for 1919-21, when Europe was recovering from World War I. From an historical standpoint, then, the post-World War II position of United States shipping in the balance of payments is unusual.[12]

Unfortunately, the available statistical information does not permit additional analyses of earnings and related matters. Except for subsidized carriers or those subject to regulation by the Interstate Commerce Commission, the financial data regarding shipping are not amenable to the kind of examina-

[12] This conclusion based upon the close correspondence between "balance—ocean shipping" and "balance—transportation account," since only the latter were available for the period 1919-39. See U.S. Department of Commerce, Bureau of Foreign Domestic Commerce, "The United States in the World Economy," *Economic Series No. 23* (Washington: GPO, 1943), Table 1, Appendix.

Table 8

INTERNATIONAL TRANSPORTATION ACCOUNT OF THE BALANCE OF PAYMENTS OF THE UNITED STATES, 1937, 1946-54

[Millions of dollars]

	1937	1946	1947	1948	1949	1950	1951	1952	1953	1954ᵖ
Receipts:										
Ocean shipping	220.4	1,277	1,597	1,181	1,085	883	1,353	1,286	992	979
Export freight earnings	65.2	893	961	531	455	347	657	524	371	378
Coal	—	184	257	83	52	1	129	73	9	6
Grain	—	82	67	44	38	23	142	57	21	21
Other dry cargo	—	594	608	389	353	311	358	373	323	339
Tanker	—	33	29	15	12	12	28	21	18	12
Military-controlled export freight earnings[a]	—	93	197	223	192	51	44	72	17	4
Freight earnings on shipments between foreign countries	3.7	79	100	112	100	110	201	175	103	98
Passenger fares	9.3	28	39	35	21	26	18	22	21	24
Port expenditures	142.2	162	281	268	291	313	411	462	465	462
Charter hire	—	22	19	12	26	36	22	31	15	13
Other transportation	15.7	106	145	154	164	176	211	228	239	243
Total, receipts	236.1	1,383	1,742	1,335	1,249	1,059	1,564	1,514	1,231	1,222

Table 8 (Continued)

	1937	1946	1947	1948	1949	1950	1951	1952	1953	1954ᴾ
Payments:										
Ocean shipping	328.7	349	456	501	549	643	787	911	843	777
Import freight payments	186.4	115	141	193	214	295	384	428	402	354
Dry cargo	—	109	133	175	191	255	279	318	320	281
Tanker	—	6	8	18	23	40	105	110	82	73
Passenger fares	96.7	17	47	63	90	121	102	133	134	130
Port expenditures	45.6	186	231	198	177	138	183	190	142	130
Charter hire	—	31	37	47	68	89	118	160	165	163
Other transportation	36.8	110	127	145	152	175	186	204	216	224
Total, payments	365.5	459	583	646	701	818	973	1,115	1,059	1,001
Balance—Ocean shipping	−108.3	+928	+1,141	+680	+536	+240	+566	+375	+149	+202
Balance—Transportation account	−129.4	+924	+1,159	+689	+548	+241	+591	+399	+172	+221

ᴾ Preliminary.

ᵃ Military end-items included 1946-52; economic aid only 1953-1954.

Source: For 1937, Department of Commerce, Bureau of Foreign and Domestic Commerce, "The United States in the World Economy," *Economic Series No. 23* (Washington: GPO, 1943), p. 210. For 1946-1954 Department of Commerce, Office of Business Economics, as cited in letter to author from Walther Lederer, Chief, Balance of payments Division, Nov. 8, 1955.

tion that would be useful here. However, this lack of information, though unfortunate for those desiring completeness, is not detrimental. The character of the available evidence suggests that additional information would probably support rather than weaken the general conclusion regarding the fortunes of the United States merchant marine.

THE SHIPPING POSITION IN BRIEF

By the end of 1955[13] the United States-flag merchant marine had apparently adjusted fairly well to the changes that had occurred in the volume of cargoes available to it. We cannot be sure because coastal trade figures are not available. However in 1953, that trade, too, reflected a good adjustment of deadweight tonnage to cargo tonnage.

Since 1937, the geographic disposition of the American merchant fleet has shifted markedly from operating mainly in the domestic trades (coastwise, intercoastal, and noncontiguous) to sailing primarily in the foreign trade of the United States. Of the 1,091 vessels (9.2 million dwt) in the active merchant marine in 1939, 319 ships (2.8 million dwt) carried foreign trade cargoes. As of December 31, 1955, 606 vessels (6.9 million dwt) out of a total of 1,072 vessels (13.6 million dwt) operated in the foreign trade of the United States.

The contrast is even more startling for dry-cargo ships. In 1939, only 271 (2.2 million dwt.) were in foreign trade as compared with 551 (5.9 million dwt.) in 1955. The domestic trades used only 142 dry-cargo vessels (1.5 million dwt.) in 1955 as contrasted with 468 ships (3.0 million dwt.) in 1939.

Tankers continued to be concentrated far more heavily in the domestic trades than in the foreign, with an increase of about 500,000 deadweight tons over-all, with more than four-fifths of the tonnage sailing in the domestic trades as contrasted with a lower ratio (2.6 to 1) in 1939.

[13] December 31 rather than June 30, 1955 is used in this summary in order to give a more recent picture of the status of the merchant marine as compared with its characteristics in 1939. The totals for 1939 given in this summary differ from the totals obtained by summing the figures in the preceding discussion. Earlier I used the Maritime Administration figures as found in its *A Review of the . . . Intercoastal Trades* for the coasting trades. These differ slightly from those cited in the source I used for other 1939 figures. However, the differences are not significant.

If we assume that the ships in the domestic trades are more readily available for emergency use than those plying foreign trade routes, the United States was in a more favorable defense position in 1939 than in 1955. However, as regards the capacity of its active merchant fleet the United States was much stronger in 1955, with 13.6 million deadweight tons available as compared with 9.2 million tons in 1939. Furthermore, the postwar fleet is much faster than the previous one.

Even so, this strong general position contains weaknesses. United States diplomatic and military commitments are expanding. The dry-cargo merchant fleet, an important auxiliary military element, is largely concentrated in the foreign trades. Here it faces stiff competition and there are some signs that it is going to continue to shrink in size and importance. The coasting trades are not taking up this slack and the inevitable result appears to be a further decline in the merchant fleet. Economically this decline is justified. Politically and militarily it may not be. This makes governmental policy decisions difficult. Later chapters will deal with the means by which these issues might be resolved.

SHIPBUILDING

The recent history of shipbuilding in the United States can be related briefly. It is the story of an industry twice rescued from near extinction by the outbreak of large-scale war. As an industry importantly dependent upon merchant shipping, its history is one of instability. For example, after an unprecedented burst of activity during and, to some extent, after World War II, the industry reported as follows on April 1, 1955.[14]

Paradoxically, although shipyard employment dropped over 20% during 1954 and gross tonnage of commercial vessels under construction or on order dropped even more, the gross tonnage of commercial vessels delivered was only slightly less than 1953 which established a record for peacetime construction. The deliveries are the result of orders placed several years ago and, instead of indicating a healthy condition in the industry, they are symptomatic of current decreasing employment trends inherent in a complete lack of new orders, at least until recently, and then to a

Figure 1
STEEL SELF-PROPELLED MERCHANT SHIPS DELIVERED BY PRIVATE SHIPYARDS UNITED STATES, 1914-55

(MILLIONS OF GROSS TONS)

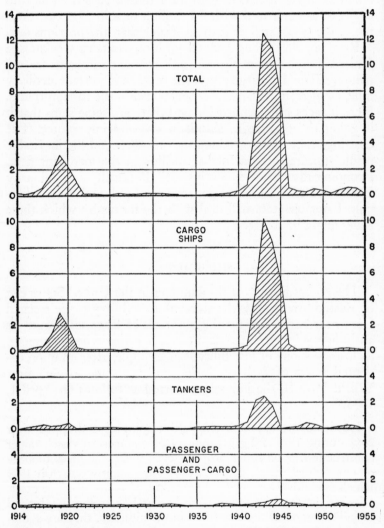

Source: Shipbuilders Council of America, *Annual Report* (New York: April 2, 1956), Appendix.

very limited extent. This condition highlights the spasmodic severity of the business cycles to which the industry has been subject and will continue to be subject until sufficient ship construction is available to provide reasonable continuity of operation, which in essence constitutes a long-range program.

The downturn of the present cycle started in the first quarter of 1953, and has extended through 1954. It has applied to both shipbuilding and ship repair, although during the last quarter of 1954, the downward trend in ship repair has been arrested, at least temporarily. Ship construction employment, however, has continued to decrease. There are sufficient orders in prospect for 1955, if and when they materialize, to likewise arrest that trend in shipbuilding and start it upward again.[14]

Figures 1 and 2, taken from the 1956 *Annual Report of the Shipbuilders Council of America*, vividly depict the experience of the shipbuilding industry since 1914. Little comment is required. It is interesting, though, to note that the annual output of private yards exceeded 100 ships of 2,000 or more gross tons only nine times during the forty-year period shown. These nine years, five of them in World War II, two in World War I, and two immediately following World War I, saw the construction of nearly nine-tenths of all merchant vessels built in private yards between 1914 and 1955. These vessels accounted for 86 per cent of the gross tonnage of this 41-year output of merchant ships. Nearly two-thirds of all the merchantmen built in American private shipyards were delivered during World War II (1942-45).[15] Surely, merchant ship construction in the United States has been primarily an industry called upon to manufacture vessels used principally to sustain large-scale military actions.

As Figure 2 indicates, private shipyards also built many combatant and auxiliary naval vessels. Over the 41-year period under consideration they delivered nearly four-fifths of the vessels constructed by the combined efforts of naval and private shipyards. In only eight of these years did the private yards deliver more than 50 ships to the Navy. However, as

[14] Shipbuilders Council of America, *Annual Report* (New York: April 1, 1955), p. 8. Only eight merchant vessels of 2,000 gross or over were built and delivered by private American shipyards during 1955. (See Appendix Table 6.) Prospects for 1956 are much brighter. (See p. 48, below.)

[15] Statistics showing output by type of vessel appear in Appendix Table 5. All statistics are for vessels of 2,000 gross tons and over.

Figure 2
STEEL NAVAL VESSELS DELIVERED BY NAVAL
AND PRIVATE SHIPYARDS UNITED STATES, 1914-55

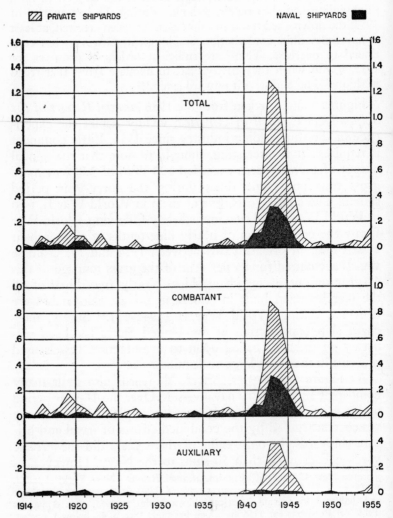

Source: Shipbuilders Council of America, *Annual Report*, (New York: April 2, 1956), Appendix.

might be expected, most of the 41 years' output occurred during these war and postwar years. About 85 per cent of the private-yard production of naval vessels took place during 1918-20 and 1942-46. During World War II these yards built a little over two-thirds of their entire output of combatant naval vessels for the period 1914-55.

The annual average volume of employment in naval and private shipyards is illustrated in Figure 3. The now familiar wartime hump furnishes additional mute proof of the expansion potential of the shipbuilding industry. From a low point of 56,500 employed in 1933, employment rose to 1.7 million in 1943. Though the industry shrank swiftly after World War II, employment remained well above the 100,000 mark. Though it fell sharply after 1952, it was still over 200,000 in 1955. After the first World War, in contrast, employment did not rise above 100,000 until 1937, probably under the impact of the government's building program under the Merchant Marine Act, 1936. From 1923 to 1936, the annual average level of employment was 75,250. From 1947 to 1955 employment averaged 214,000. (See Appendix Table 7).

1115049

Foreign shipbuilding

After V-J Day shipbuilding activity in the United States receded rapidly from its wartime levels. Meanwhile, foreign shipyards were swinging back into action after a necessary interval of repairing and refurbishing their yards and assembling the required work forces. The demand for vessels of all types was high. Though many foreign ship operators had taken advantage of the Merchant Ship Sales Act of 1946 to obtain vessels, some considered these ships as stop-gap until new ones could be built to replace them.

Foreign shipbuilding revived rapidly under these favorable conditions. In 1955, the world's shipyards delivered 594 new merchant vessels of 1,000 gross tons or over (6.9 million dwt.). Of this total American shipyards accounted for 19 ships totalling only 483,000 gross tons. The United Kingdom, with 163 ships of 1.9 million deadweight tons, was the leader followed by Germany, Sweden, Japan and the Netherlands. The United States was tied with Italy in eighth place in number

Figure 3
MONTHLY AVERAGE NUMBER OF EMPLOYEES
IN THE SHIPBUILDING AND REPAIRING
INDUSTRY, UNITED STATES, 1923-55

—— TOTAL

---- PRIVATE YARDS ······NAVY YARDS

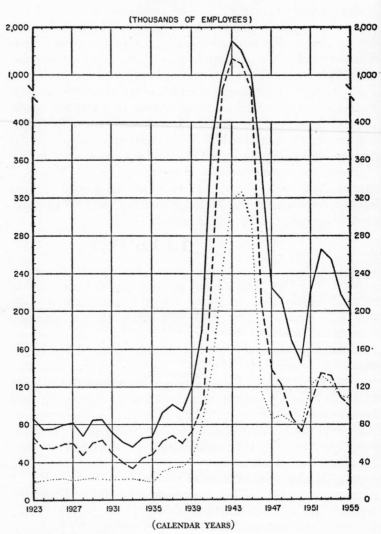

Source: Appendix Table 7.

of merchant vessels produced. For the entire period 1948-55, the shipyards of the world delivered 3,928 vessels of 38.5 million deadweight tons. Shipbuilders in the United States contributed 201 vessels of 4.1 million deadweight tons to this total. Their rivals in the United Kingdom delivered 1,324 ships of 13.2 million deadweight tons. (See Appendix Table 8).

Though the volume of merchant-ship building in the United States dropped spectacularly immediately after World War II, as Figure 1 shows, it recovered somewhat in 1949 and generally remained well above the 1930-38 level. The United States' postwar share of the world output of merchant vessels has fluctuated around the mark for the late thirties. For example, in 1955 American shipyards contributed 1.4 per cent of the deadweight tonnage of the vessels launched by the world's shipbuilders. In 1954, the figure was 8.5 per cent as compared with 10.4 per cent in 1953 and 7.3 per cent in 1937, which marked the beginning of the pre-World War II upsurge in shipbuilding activity in the United States. Even at its lowest point in the postwar years, the American volume in gross tonnage was more than six times its low for the thirties (11,000 gross tons in 1933). Figure 4 illustrates the shifting importance of United States merchant shipbuilding in the world total.

As these figures make clear, shipbuilding in the United States is primarily a war industry. This is borne out by the fact that it produced about nine-tenths of its 1914-54 output of vessels during two periods of national emergency or war covering a span of eight or nine years. After World War II, production remained above prewar levels. There was a tremendous demand for new tonnage especially for tankers. Delivery by order-choked European yards was slow and business spilled over into high-priced United States yards. In addition, the government's program to construct thirty-five Mariner vessels, (13,400 dwt. each) gave American yards a welcome boost. (See Chapter III.) Current prospects, indicated earlier, are somewhat brighter than they were in 1955 but still modest.

Figure 4
PER CENT OF WORLD GROSS TONNAGE
OF OCEAN-GOING MERCHANT SHIPS LAUNCHED
IN THE UNITED STATES, 1937-55

(VESSELS OF 100 GROSS TONS AND OVER)

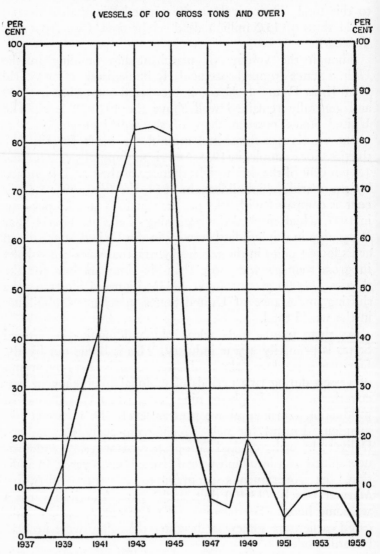

Source: Appendix Table 9.

THE STATE OF UNITED STATES MARITIME INDUSTRIES

At the time of writing the American-flag operators' share of United States foreign trade cargoes is tending downward. So is the absolute volume of these cargoes. However, it is nearly double the prewar volume. In the coastal trades, cargo tonnage is larger than prewar. However, this total combines larger tanker cargoes with smaller shipments of dry cargoes. Only the noncontiguous trade shows steady growth, but it is not enough to offset losses in the coasting trades.

The active merchant fleet is not much larger in number but bigger in carrying capacity than it was before the war. In contrast with 1939, it is much more heavily employed in foreign trade where it is less accessible should war break out. The age distribution of the vessels in the merchant marine, both active and inactive, is uneven. About four-fifths of the ships will become 20 years old within an eight- or nine-year period beginning about 1961 or 1962. Block obsolescence threatens the merchant fleet.

Shipbuilding activity in the United States has come to the end of its second great war-induced era of high profits and large-scale activity. The merchant fleets of the world are being rapidly rebuilt. Not until the early 1960's will most American-flag operators be faced with important replacement problems as their ships reach 20 years of age.

Briefly sketched, these are the principal features of the status of the American maritime industries today. More detail will be supplied later when we discuss the kinds of maritime policies the government should consider in the light of conditions in the ship-operating and shipbuilding industries and the political and military climate of today.

The next chapter is devoted to a close look at the shipbuilding industry in the United States, a description of governmental policies affecting it, and to an evaluation of the efficacy of these policies. In succeeding chapters this same procedure is used to analyze the operations of ship operators and their performance under policies designed to help them.

III

ASSISTANCE TO SHIPBUILDERS

The commission expects to take delivery of the
first C-2 design ship in the spring of 1939, thus
terminating an 18-year hiatus of cargo-ship construction in American yards.

U. S. Maritime Commission, *Report to Congress*, 1938, p. 7.

WITHOUT help from the government, many American builders of seagoing merchant vessels would soon be forced to
employ their yards and use their talents to manufacture primarily nonmarine products. Some might shut down completely. In the strictest sense, most merchant shipbuilding in
the United States is not economic. And this has been true for
many years. Most observers agree that when steam and steel
supplanted sail and wood, foreign shipbuilders fell heir to the
mantle of lower costs.

These harsh judgments must be kept in mind when discussing shipbuilding in the United States. The following
statement made by the National Industrial Conference Board
over twenty-five years ago provides a good springboard for a
leap into the muddy, rough waters of United States maritime
policy. The Board said,

The profitableness of the shipping industries as a whole, which
rests upon the economic soundness of their position, is a basic
consideration in the merchant marine policy of any nation. If a
nation can not engage in the building and operation of ships profitably, it is obvious that that industry can not be considered in
itself an economic asset in the industrial life of the nation. Such
a country may make shipping profitable to those engaged in it by
means of governmental aid, through which part of the cost is paid
by the general public in the form of taxation, but this does not
make that industry an economic asset in itself. In such case the

importance of the industry must be measured in other terms than as a part of the business life of the country, and its preservation and development must be justified by other considerations than those of its value as a business. . . . They [the considerations] relate to the importance of shipping for the development of foreign trade of the nation and for its security.

Obviously, however, the question of the relation of the shipping industry to the foreign trade and defense of a nation would not be likely to become an issue of national policy if its shipping industries were on a profitable and sound economic basis.[1]

Some observers contend that since many of the shipbuilders in the United States cannot meet the tests of the market place, the problem of their survival is not an economic one and hence not susceptible to analysis by the economist. They go on to espouse the view that "policy is politics" and thus beyond the realm of economics. They abhor the existence of an economically unjustified industry. They dismiss the "problem" by saying that "ships should be built where they can be produced cheapest."

Economists with a bent for *political* economy may sympathize with this view but they recognize that shipbuilding industry may be essential for noneconomic reasons. This is especially true in the United States where military considerations play the decisive role as regards government policy toward shipbuilding. The importance of the military aspect of shipbuilding was stressed in a special report prepared toward the end of the last war for the Maritime Commission and the Navy by the Graduate School of Business Administration of Harvard University. It stated,

It must be clearly recognized that the demands of national security so outstrip all other demands for ships and shipyards that national security becomes the controlling factor in determining the characteristics of ships and shipyards in the United States. Since the Federal Government is responsible for the national security, and since with respect to ships and shipyards private enterprise will not and cannot of itself alone relieve the Government of this responsibility by doing the whole job, the Government must assume its full responsibility and see that the job is done. Thus, the country through its Government must set as

[1] National Industrial Conference Board, *The American Merchant Marine Problem* (New York: 1929), p. 3.

its goal the maintenance of the ships and shipyards which are necessary if the United States is to be adequately prepared for national security. This goal must be clearly defined and then, with the goal defined, the Federal Government must develop, adopt, and execute a long-run policy designed to attain that goal. In this fashion the Federal Government will assume its full and true responsibility.[2]

Admittedly those writing the *Harvard Report* in 1944 and 1945 were importantly influenced by the war then being fought. Yet eleven years after V-J Day, the exigencies of the cold war and the fear of hot war underscore the importance of their general observation.

Despite widespread agreement about the vital role of shipyards in the national defense plans of the United States, there is much disagreement as to the appropriate national policy. Many groups are dissatisfied with current policy. Included among them, of course, stands the shipbuilding industry, crying long, loud, and insistently that it will fail in its military mission if it does not obtain more orders for new ships.

In this chapter we shall attempt to present the essential facts about the condition of the shipping industry, critically examine the current policies of the federal government, and suggest some changes in policy.

AMERICAN SHIPBUILDING

Shipyards

In 1939 there were 38 shipbuilding yards containing 119 shipways of 300 feet and over. By 1944 these totals had risen to 84 shipyards and 614 shipways.[3] In 1954, fifteen private shipyards with 81 shipways capable of handling ocean-going vessels 400 feet or more in length were in existence.[4] Of these six were listed as "operating" yards and the rest as "reserve"

[2] Graduate School of Business Administration, Harvard University, *The Use and Disposition of Ships and Shipyards at the End of World War II* (Washington: GPO, 1945), p. 37. Hereafter called the *Harvard Report*.
[3] Same, p. 180.
[4] *Maritime Subsidy Policy* (Washington: 1954), a report prepared by the office of the Under Secretary of Commerce for Transportation (Robert B. Murray, Jr.) and the Maritime Administration, p. 26-27. The quotation that follows is from p. 24. Hereafter called the *Murray Report*.

yards. The *Murray Report* limited its study to these yards because ". . . our shipbuilding problems have been confined to ships of the . . . size [these yards produced]." In February 1955 the Maritime Administration reported that there were 44 ways available for the construction of merchant ships over 400 feet long.[5] These were operated in seven shipyards. An additional 63 ways in private yards could be put into operation after some rehabilitation. In addition, reserve yards contained 31 ways also available after rehabilitation.

The Harvard study showed that at the post-World War I low point in United States shipbuilding in 1928 only 11 yards were open; these were the "larger private" yards of the 25 in existence in 1916. The National Council of Shipbuilders (now the Shipbuilders Council of America) stated that in 1928 only 10 of 60 shipways operated by 5 private shipyards on the East Coast were in use.[6] Thus, rapid, extensive contraction is not a novel experience for this industry.

In addition to the larger private shipyards there are many smaller ones. For example, including shipbuilders on lakes and rivers, the Shipbuilders Council of America lists 79 companies as included in its statistics on employment in shipbuilding and repairing.[7] These concerns are available to manufacture and repair a wide variety of craft essential to amphibious military operations.

Though shipbuilding activity has dropped off precipitously from its wartime peak, experts agree that the facilities in use and on hand in reserve status are adequate as a nucleus from which to expand in time of national emergency. Apparently they are far larger than needed to accommodate the demands of commercial ship operators.[8]

[5] U. S. House of Representatives, *Study of the Operations of the Maritime Administration and the Federal Maritime Board*, Hearings before the Committee on Merchant Marine and Fisheries, 84th Cong., 1st sess. (Washington: GPO, 1955), p. 8. The text refers to "400 long tons" but this is obviously a slip for "400 feet long." Subsequent figures come from p. 24.

[6] *Harvard Report*, p. 170-173.

[7] Shipbuilders Council of America, *Annual Report* (April 2, 1956), Table 6, Appendix.

[8] According to the *Murray Report*, p. 26, on the basis of a 40-hour workweek, each shipway can handle two ships per year. Taking the Maritime Administration figure of 44 ways available, then 88 ships—a number far exceeding current demands—could be built each year.

Workers

Without a trained, well-organized working force shipyards are of little use. Despite a plethora of figures on employment in the shipbuilding industry, some significant statistics are missing. Any attempt to estimate the manpower currently employed in the critical segments of the industry founders on the rock of controversy about which groups of workers should be included. As a result, there are many different estimates of the size of the essential nucleus of workers to serve the needs of national defense.

The great swings in employment in shipyards from 56,500 in 1933 to 1.7 million ten years later and back to 254,000 in 1953, have already been traced (p. 35-36; Appendix Table 7). These total employment figures include employment in Navy, as well as in private, yards of all sizes and locations and also repair yards. They have some barometric value for estimating the expansibility of the industry but they do not tell us the status of the critically important private yards capable of producing merchantmen and war vessels 400 feet long or longer.

Since 1952 employment has been fairly evenly divided between Navy and private shipyards. In 1955, for example, 107,000 workers were employed by Navy yards and 100,000 by private shipbuilders. This was only the fourth year since 1923 during which Navy yards employed more workers than private yards. Other estimates provide a further breakdown of shipyard figures. The *Murray Report* estimates that about 23,000 were employed by "major coastal yards" constructing only merchant ships during 1953 and that 63,500 were employed by private yards building both Navy and merchant ships.[9] The Shipbuilders Council reported that as of December 31, 1955, there were about 33,000 people employed by the "principal" private shipyards engaged in new construction. The roughly comparable figure a year earlier was 37,000, and for two years earlier, 52,000. Including "principal" repair yards, employment totalled about 65,000 on December 31, 1955 as compared with 67,000 a year earlier and 85,000 a

[9] P. 35. These estimates include both direct and indirect labor. A Maritime Administration estimate seems to confirm the former figure for January 1953. *Study of the . . . Maritime Administration . . .* , cited, p. 8.

year before that.[10] However, the Maritime Administration reported that in 1954, in the private yards it considered essential, "less than 6,000 men [were] employed in shipbuilding, which is an all-time low."[11]

The range of the figures cited above is great and their coverage varies. Judgment as to the level of employment necessary to maintain the nucleus of shipbuilding labor needed for war involves an assumption about the "dilution ratio." This ratio shows the extent to which the skilled and experienced shipbuilding workers can be diluted by additional men—some of whom may be skilled and experienced, though not currently employed in the industry—to make up the larger supply of labor needed for increased output when demand rises, as in war. What ratio is proper is subject to some disagreement. The *Murray Report* said, "Experience has shown that a ship construction labor dilution of 12 to 1 during the mobilization build-up is the maximum that is acceptable. Consequently, a mobilization nucleus during peacetime of approximately 36,000 workers is necessary."[12] However in 1953, Earl W. Clark, Deputy Maritime Administrator, testified: "On a rapid expansion of a shipyard load the efficiency rapidly falls off with dilution of the skilled workers with unskilled workers. The exact dilution possible is not fixed and depends on many circumstances. However, a rapid dilution of over 10 to 1 does not appear possible. On this basis, a skilled labor force of about 50,000 production [workers] in shipyards appears necessary to meet a mobilization requirement of 500,000.[13] Subsequently, the Maritime Administration has indicated that the dilution ratio applies only to certain types of workers employed in the essential private yards. *These* yards alone must employ 36,000 men to meet the mobilization requirements as envisaged in 1955.[14]

---

[10] Shipbuilders Council of America, cited, Table 6, Appendix. Thirty-nine yards reported to the Council in December 1955 as compared with 40 in December 1954, and 45 a year before. This probably accounts for a small part of the decrease.

[11] *Study of the . . . Maritime Administration. . . ,* cited, p. 8.

[12] P. 29.

[13] U.S. Senate, *Merchant Marine Studies,* Hearings Before a Subcommittee of the Committee on Interstate and Foreign Commerce, 83rd Cong., 1st sess. (Washington: GPO, 1953) pt. 1, p. 345.

[14] *Study of the . . . Maritime Administration. . . ,* cited, p. 7-8, 23.

If the mobilization requirement is estimated at 500,000 workers and a 10 to 1 dilution rate is assumed, then employment of 65,000 in the principal building and repair yards at the end of 1955 (as reported by the Shipbuilders Council) was sufficient for national defense. Using a 12 to 1 ratio, the *Murray Report* put the essential minimum at 36,000 workers. According to the Maritime Administration's estimates—based on the view that the 36,000 must be employed in essential private yards—the necessary minimum would be employed in the second quarter of 1956. But after that the number would drop rapidly to between roughly 5,000 and 10,000 in 1957.[15]

Shipbuilding requires many skills. One of the principal arguments for government support of the industry is the necessity for maintaining certain critically important unique skills. Loftsmen, shipfitters, and marine engineers and draftsmen are usually included among them. There is no question of the importance of these skills to shipbuilders. However, shipbuilders complain that when their business slackens employees in these key occupations seek and obtain work in other industries. This is *prima facie* evidence that either the skills are *not* unique to shipbuilding or the men having these skills have been able to adapt themselves to other jobs. Conversely, then, we should expect that an increase in the volume of shipbuilding can provide means (higher wages) to draw these workers away from other jobs. Further, in the case of skills especially scarce and important to shipbuilders, workers having these talents will be available unless the industry collapses completely. True, the skills may not be employed as intensively or necessarily directly in shipbuilding, but they will be *in* the industry ready for any emergency.[16]

We should, however, recognize that insofar as the demands for these skills by the shipbuilding industry have declined, the total demand by *all* industries for these skills is not as great as it would have been if the decline in shipbuilding had not occurred. Moreover, the men who find jobs outside shipbuilding may not be employed at their specialties. This, coupled

[15] Same, p. 23.
[16] In a shiprepair yard the author visited in 1954, the guide told him that 90 per cent of the work in its shops was nonmarine. See the *Harvard Report* for examples of how shipyards kept skeleton forces of key personnel together after World War I.

with the less-than-full-time use of these skills in shipbuilding today, could discourage some men from acquiring them. Then, if during war these skills were to be in great demand by a number of industries, a shortage might occur. All this assumes that these skills will be as necessary tomorrow as they were yesterday. Yet we know that great strides have been made in reducing tasks, once the exclusive province of highly-trained, skilled workers, to a series of simple operations performed by workers of little training and average mental and physical endowment. Thus the shortage may never materialize. Nevertheless, without evidence that this will be so, the military prudence that has been adopted as a working basis for this book requires us to regard the maintenance of a core of shipbuilding skills as a central problem of American shipping policy.

Vessels ordered and under construction

On December 31, 1955 private shipyards in the United States were constructing 25 commercial vessels totalling 315,340 gross tons. During the year they had received orders for 18 ships—195,760 gross tons. A year earlier 15 vessels of 210,316 gross tons were under construction and orders had been placed for 7 ships aggregating 122,360 gross tons.[17]

Private shipyards had 43 naval vessels of 253,460 displacement tons[18] under construction at the end of 1955 as compared with 44 ships of 302,840 displacement tons a year earlier. Thirteen vessels totalling 92,670 displacement tons were ordered during 1955. In 1954 the Navy ordered 26 vessels with a total of 138,420 displacement tons.[19]

In mid-1953, L. R. Sanford, president of the Shipbuilders Council of America, testified before a United States Senate subcommittee that only 35 vessels would be completed in 1954, leaving just one vessel under construction in 1955.[20] His prediction was valid for more than a year. Then in August 1954,

[17] Shipbuilders Council of America, cited, Table 5, Appendix. All data are for vessels of 1,000 gross tons and over.
[18] Displacement tons measure the weight of the water displaced by a fully-loaded vessel.
[19] Shipbuilders Council of America, cited, Table 5, Appendix.
[20] *Merchant Marine Studies,* cited, p. 490.

Congress passed and the President approved legislation to help the shipbuilders. The bills provided for the construction of 20 tankers, 4 new passenger liners, the conversion of four Liberty vessels on an experimental basis, the reconditioning of ships in the reserve fleet, and the payment for national defense features included in tankers built under the trade-in and build program.[21] On December 31, 1954, the Federal Maritime Board announced the signing of a long-term agreement with American President Lines for the purchase and construction of $175 million worth of vessels in the next ten years. This, however, meant only some conversion of four Mariner-type ships in 1955. The total order for the ten-year period will be eighteen to twenty ships.[22] The Grace Line later agreed with the Maritime Administration on a replacement program for two passenger liners and twenty-four cargo ships during the next twenty years.[23]

On October 12, 1955 *The New York Times* reported that the Maritime Administrator had told the National Propellor Club that "projected ship construction plans . . . will add up in the next fifteen years to more than $1,200,000,000." If the average price per vessel is assumed to be about $8 million (a reasonable figure in the light of the cost of building the Mariners), this will mean about 150 vessels. Even if 200 ships are constructed this amounts to only 13 each year for the 15-year period.

Helpful as this batch of new orders may be, it affords only temporary relief. Developments in late 1955 and early 1956 indicated that over the longer pull prospects were better than they were a year or so earlier. If all goes well, perhaps twenty ships annually may be ordered for a number of years to come. However, according to the *Murray Report*, sixty ships per year must be built if the essential nucleus of the shipbuilding industry is to be maintained in a state of readiness for a national emergency.[24] Thus the patient has been momentarily revived. Collapse has been postponed. Repeated postpone-

[21] *Public Law 575*, ch. 665, 83rd Cong., 2d sess. (Aug. 10, 1954); *P.L. 663*, ch. 935, same (Aug. 26, 1954); *P.L. 608*, ch. 777, same (August 20, 1954).
[22] *The New York Times*, December 31, 1954.
[23] *The Economist*, January 21, 1956, p. 206; *The New York Times*, January 18, 1956.
[24] P. 29.

ments based on sporadic government action are conceivable. But they do not represent a very good answer to the industry's problems. Unless an even flow of orders can be maintained over the years, the industry's output will fluctuate sharply from time to time. This will be inefficient and costly.

Shipbuilding costs

The cost of building ships in the United States is usually much greater than in foreign yards. Normally this handicap would be insuperable under market conditions. Only when the demand for tonnage is great can American shipbuilders compete effectively. This has happened in some years since the end of World War II. The shortage of tankers placed a premium upon early delivery of new vessels. American shipbuilders obtained contracts in the open market at high, profitable prices because they were able to deliver the ships long before their order-choked foreign rivals were able to do so. In more "normal" times, foreign shipbuilders can underbid their American competitors by substantial margins.

Congressional committees, special commissions, and executive agencies of the federal government, have been deluged with shipbuilding cost information. The costs of building ships in American yards are known with a high degree of accuracy. Over the years the Maritime Administration has been obtaining data from applicants for construction-differential subsidies. Fairly reliable estimates have been obtained of the costs of constructing vessels in foreign shipyards. These foreign estimates have been critized but nonetheless accepted in determining the cost differentials between foreign and American shipbuilders.

Generally speaking, recent comparisons show that the buyer can purchase a ship from a European shipbuilder at from 55 to 70 per cent of the price he would have to pay the American shipbuilder. For example, the Federal Maritime Board approved a construction-differential subsidy of about 46 per cent for the purchase of the *Constitution* and *Independence* by American Export Lines from the Bethlehem Steel Company.[25] In July 1953, a special subcommittee of the

---

[25] U.S. Department of Commerce, *Annual Report of the Federal Maritime Board and Maritime Administration*, 1953 (Washington: GPO, 1954) p. 13.

United States Senate (the "Potter Committee") received evidence indicating that foreign prices generally work out to about 60 per cent of the American price".[26] More recently, the Federal Maritime Board decided that on construction of Mariner-class vessels the construction differential ranged from about 40 to 45 per cent.[27]

In 1950, John E. Slater, president of American Export Lines, offered as an exhibit before a Senate subcommittee, a list of firm bids received by the Argentine State Line for the construction of three sister ships. The bids from twenty foreign and United States shipbuilders were opened in Washington on July 15, 1946. They thus reflect immediate postwar conditions. Nonetheless, the figures are worth noting. They show that, except for two French shipbuilding companies (whose bids were about 20 per cent above the lowest American bid), foreign bids ranged from about 49 per cent to 92 per cent of the lowest American bid. Other United States shipbuilders submitted bids ranging up to 26 per cent above the American low bid. In delivery time the United States yards were well ahead of their foreign competition. Two of the three American shipyards offered delivery in 15 months. Foreign shipbuilders promised deliveries in from 20 to 48 months.[28]

Why are American shipbuilding costs so much higher than foreign? Basically, the answer lies in the technique of shipbuilding. The construction of ocean-going vessels is emphatically not susceptible to the mass production methods of the assembly line. Ordinarily the number of ships to be built is

[26] *Merchant Marine Studies,* cited, p. 660, Exhibit II in the testimony of Adolph Kurz on behalf of Charles Kurz, president, Charles Kurz and Co., Inc. The Kurz estimate was based upon quotations he had received as to the "cost of construction of vessels in the United States yards and in foreign yards." (Same, p. 645.)

[27] *Murray Report,* cited, p. 50. For details see Federal Maritime Board, *Sales Prices of "Mariner" Class Vessels,* Staff Hearing September 9, 1953 (Washington: n.d.), mimeographed. The differentials are exclusive of the rise in costs that occurred between the date of the hearing and February 7, 1951. Thus, the Board concluded that the actual cost of building a Mariner in the United Kingdom might be less than 50 per cent of its cost in the United States.

[28] U.S. Senate, *Merchant Marine Study and Investigation,* Hearings on S. Res. 50, Subcommittee of the Committee on Interstate and Foreign Commerce, 81st Cong., 2d sess. (Washington: GPO, 1950), pt. 7, p. 1584-1585.

small. Each one is a "custom job" tailored to unique specifications as required by the prospective owners' intended use of
the vessel. Even when each ship is not unique, traditional,
assembly-line mass production methods cannot be used. The
unit to be manufactured is large and complicated and cannot
be manufactured in the manner of an automobile or a washing
machine. When high rates of output are necessary, multiple,
not mass, production occurs. The number of yards or sub-
assembly points is increased but the labor-intensive "hand-
craft" methods of manufacture and assembly largely remain.
Some improvements in technique occur but the basic method
of production is retained.

Foreign and American shipbuilding techniques are fundamentally alike although there is evidence indicating that
American shipbuilders use labor somewhat more efficiently.
For example, investigations of foreign costs in connection
with the construction-differential subsidy to be paid for purchase of the *Constitution* and *Independence* indicated that
the productivity of labor in the Dutch shipyards was between
10 and 20 per cent below that in the Bethlehem Steel Company yard. To be exact, the ratio of productivity of Bethlehem to Dutch shipyard labor was estimated to be 118 per
cent. This means that for each manhour expended in the
Bethlehem yard their Dutch counterparts would need 1.18
manhours.[29] More recently, the Maritime Administration confirmed this estimate in calculating the construction-differential
subsidy for the building of a Mariner-type vessel. It compared
British and American (Bethlehem, Quincy) manhour requirements. British hull and machinery item prices, however, were
about 80 and 90 per cent of American prices respectively.[30]

Though American shipbuilders achieve higher labor productivity than the Europeans do, their superiority is not
enough to offset the higher wage rates they must pay. In the
American Export Lines case the Federal Maritime Board declared that in 1948 the average shipyard worker received

[29] U. S. House of Representatives, *Redetermination of Vessel Sales Prices
of S. S. Independence and S. S. Constitution,* Hearings Before a Special Subcommittee to Review Redetermination of Vessel Sales Prices of *S. S. Independence* and *S. S. Constitution* of the Committee on Merchant Marine and
Fisheries, 82d Cong., 2d sess. (Washington: GPO, 1952), p. 126-127.
[30] *Sales Prices of "Mariner" Class Vessels,* cited, p. 15-16.

$1.71 per hour in the United States and 40 cents per hour in the Netherlands. In 1951 the Board found that a United States rate of $1.72 per hour compared with 46 cents per hour in the United Kingdom.[31] Obviously the 10 to 20 per cent advantage in productivity of labor in American shipyards did not compensate for wage rates three-and-a-half-times as high as those paid abroad. The Federal Maritime Board's study just cited suggests that the labor cost of building a Mariner in the United States was almost three times the British labor cost. United States labor cost was roughly one-fifth of the total sales price as compared with about one-tenth of the British sales price.

Apparently some reduction in American shipbuilding costs occurred during World War II. Because the same types of vessels were constructed in large volume, extensive prefabrication was possible and there was a gain in manufacturing skill. The small peacetime market for ships precludes the effective use of many of the wartime techniques and severely reduces the chance for marked increases in productivity resulting from repetitive processes.[32]

At present there are no technical developments in the offing that will enable American shipbuilders to cut costs enough to compete successfully in an open, unsheltered, worldwide market. Shipbuilders in the United States can retain their skilled and other employees only by paying wages sufficiently high to keep them from being employed elsewhere. But paying these wages raises their costs above the internationally competitive level.

Our conclusions regarding the status of the shipbuilding industry in the United States can be briefly summarized as follows:

1. The industry is primarily a war industry. Nine-tenths of its output over 40 years has occurred during wars or immediately afterward. Between World War I and II it barely survived. If left alone it will again run down to very low levels of operation. It is a declining industry in an expanding economy.

[31] *Redetermination of Vessel Sales Prices...*, cited. *Sales Prices of "Mariner" Class Vessels*, cited, p. 16, 20.

[32] For an interesting discussion of this point see the testimony of L. R. Stanford, president of the Shipbuilders Council of America in U.S. Senate, *Merchant Marine Studies*, cited, p. 493-496.

Employment and output have fallen during a period of high prosperity for most of the rest of the economy, since the end of the second World War.

2. The plant and equipment available far exceed the peace-time or cold war requirements of the United States.

3. Undoubtedly there are key employees and teams of workers who would be difficult to replace or re-assemble should they leave the industry. Exactly how difficult or costly cannot be foretold.

4. At this time the industry faces insuperable cost disadvantages in its competition with foreign shipbuilders.

GOVERNMENT POLICY

The declaration of policy appearing in the Merchant Ship Sales Act of 1946 clearly states the official position of the United States government towards domestic shipbuilding: "It is necessary for the national security and development and maintenance of the domestic and the export and import commerce of the United States that the United States have an efficient and adequate American-owned merchant marine . . . composed of the best-equipped, safest, and most suitable types of vessels, constructed in the United States . . . supplemented by efficient American-owned facilities for ship-building and repair. . . ." (Sec. 2 [a].)

This statement is stronger than the declaration of policy appearing in the Merchant Marine Act, 1936. There, the only reference to shipbuilding is that the merchant marine necessary for the development of the foreign and domestic commerce of the United States and for the national defense shall be "constructed in the United States." (Sec. 101.)

The increased emphasis upon shipbuilding and repair in the postwar Act reflects a divergence in the fortunes of the ship-builders and the ship operators rather than a basic change in national policy. After World War II, except for certain types of ships, the American merchant marine was well equipped. Shipbuilders were painfully aware that their own continued prosperity could no longer depend solely upon a build-up of an American merchant fleet. Their impending decline could best be publicized by calling attention to their own plight.

Thus, even though the 1936 Act provides a number of methods to help shipyards, it does so indirectly in the interest of building and maintaining an adequate merchant marine. Under the declaration of policy in the 1946 Act, the provisions of the earlier Act can be "interpreted" to aid shipbuilders foremost and ship operators incidentally, instead of the other way round.

Basic features of governmental assistance to American shipbuilders

Most government aid to the shipbuilding industry consists of inducements to entice prospective American buyers into ordering vessels from American shipyards. To this end, liberal trade-in allowances on old or obsolete vessels, (not less than 12 years old and for some tankers not less than 10 years old), low down payments on new ones, and long-term loans at low interest, ship mortgage insurance, accelerated amortization, limited tax deferment for funds deposited in special construction reserve funds, are added to construction-differential subsidies and allowances for national defense features under which the federal government pays a sizeable portion of the total price received by the shipbuilders.

In the case of the superliner *United States*, for example, the price was approximately $70 million of which the government computed its share at $42 million. Of the $42 million, $18 million represented the construction-differential subsidy and $24 million national defense features.[33] In the controversial American Export Lines case, the Bethlehem Steel Company's successful bid was about $23.4 million per ship for the *Constitution* and the *Independence*, plus escalation (the additional charge for increases in certain costs, during construction). The sales price to the American Export Lines was calculated to be $14 million. About $700 thousand of the difference in the figures represented national defense features to be paid

[33] *Report on Audit of United States Maritime Commission.* H. Doc. No. 465, 81st Cong., 2d sess. (Washington: GPO, 1950), p. 160. "National defense features" are items of construction or equipment not required for commercial operation but desirable if the vessel is to be used as a naval auxiliary; for instance, heavy bulkheads, reinforcement of decks to take gun emplacements, and, in some cases, greater speed than is needed for trade.

for by the federal government. The rest was a construction-differential subsidy.[34]

In addition, the government has assisted shipbuilders by ordering vessels—both military and commercial—for its own account. Since 1949, for instance, the Maritime Administration has ordered 35 Mariner-class freighters. These are large cargo vessels incorporating many features that make for quick conversion to naval auxiliaries. Maritime Administration officials had hoped that American-flag shipping companies would buy the Mariners. To date, only a few have been sold. Most of them have been operated for the Military Sea Transportation Service for a few months (usually six in order to take advantage of the guarantee period during which the builder must correct certain defects that may appear) and then placed in the government-administered reserve fleet. Commercial operators have stated that the Mariners are generally not suited to their needs. In the spring of 1956 shipping companies, particularly those operating in the Pacific area or round-the-world, showed increased interest in purchasing these vessels. Their interest was no doubt whetted, and some of their objections overcome, by the price recently announced by the Maritime Administration—roughly $4.4 million to $4.9 million per ship. The government paid approximately $8.4 million for each one.[35]

The Merchant Marine Act, 1936, as amended

Though the principal features of United States shipbuilding policy can be quickly grasped, a thorough understanding requires a look at some of the details. The main features of a policy are sometimes substantially modified or amended in the administration of its details. Further, the details themselves can be altered in a way that either fosters or negates the broad policy objectives. The Republican administration in Washington since 1953 has emphasized sections of the Merchant Marine Act, 1936 that were not stressed by its Democratic

---

[34] U.S. House of Representatives, *Construction Subsidies on SS INDE-PENDENCE and SS CONSTITUTION*, Hearings, 83rd Cong., 2d sess. (Washington: GPO, 1954), p. 53.
[35] See *The New York Times*, April 6, 8, 1956.

predecessor. As a consequence, maritime policy today, though still rooted in the 1936 Act, is somewhat different from what it was in 1936. We therefore turn next to a consideration of some of the details of the Act.

Under the provisions of section 501 of the Act, any qualified American-flag vessel operator in the foreign commerce of the United States is eligible to receive a construction-differential subsidy. To receive this subsidy the Maritime Board must find ". . . the plans and specifications [of the applicant] call for a new vessel which will meet the requirements of the foreign commerce of the United States, will aid in the promotion and development of such commerce, and be suitable for use by the United States for national defense or military purposes in time of war or national emergency . . . [and] the applicant possesses the ability, experience, financial resources, and other qualifications necessary to enable it to operate and maintain the proposed new vessel and . . . the granting of the aid applied for is reasonably calculated to replace worn-out or obsolete tonnage with new and modern ships, or otherwise to carry out effectively the purposes and policy of this Act."

The subsidy is paid only for ships constructed in "a shipyard within the continental limits of the United States." In the building of a subsidized vessel, the "shipbuilder, sub-contractors, materialmen, or suppliers shall use, so far as practicable, only articles, materials, and supplies of the growth, production, or manufacture of the United States . . ." (Sec. 505 [a].)

Construction-differential subsidies cannot exceed 50 per cent of the price of the vessel paid by the federal government exclusive of national defense features. A subsidy in excess of 33⅓ per cent will be paid only if "convincing evidence" dictates this action. The percentage allowed is determined by a comparison of foreign and domestic costs. Foreign cost in this instance is "the fair and reasonable estimate of cost, as determined by . . . [The Federal Maritime Board], of the construction of the proposed vessel if it were constructed under similar plans and specifications (excluding national defense features. . .) in a foreign shipbuilding center which is deemed by the . . . [Board] to furnish a fair and representative example for the determination of the estimated foreign cost of construction of vessels of the type proposed to be constructed." (See 502 [b].)

A vessel purchaser can use one of a number of schemes to pay for a ship built under the subsidy program. First, he can pay cash. Second, he can pay 25 per cent of the sales price to him (full sales price received by the shipbuilder minus subsidy and national defense features allowances) and borrow the balance from the federal government. This must be repaid in not more than twenty equal annual installments at an interest rate of $3\frac{1}{2}$ per cent per year on the unpaid balance. (Sec. 502 [c].) Third, he may buy a vessel built on government account. He will pay the subsidized price minus depreciation (if the vessel is sold sometime after its delivery to the government). If he has chartered the ship and then decides to buy it, he may apply the excess of the charter hire payments over the accumulated depreciation allowance on the down payment. Again the down payment is 25 per cent of the Board's sales price of the vessel. The balance must be paid in equal annual installments during the remaining part of the twenty-year period beginning at the time the vessel was delivered for charter. Interest is $3\frac{1}{2}$ per cent annually on the unpaid balance. (Sec. 714.) Fourth, he can borrow money in the private capital market (ordinarily at rates not to exceed 5 per cent or in some circumstances 6 per cent). He can then insure his mortgage against default by paying a premium of not more than $\frac{1}{2}$ per cent per annum of the unpaid balance to the federal government. Such mortgages may be insured up to 90 per cent of the unpaid balance, or in the case of special purpose vessels certified by the Secretary of Defense as essential to national defense, 100 per cent. (Title XI.) For the purchaser of a nonsubsidized vessel the loan and guarantee provisions described above apply to $87\frac{1}{2}$ per cent of the price he pays for the ship. He, too, may obtain 100 per cent mortgage insurance on eligible special-purpose vessels.

Vessel purchasers may sell their old or obsolete ships to the government. They must then use the proceeds in partial payment for new vessels to replace those turned in. (Sec. 510 [b].)

As noted earlier, the government is authorized to build ships for its own account. The language of the authority is worth repeating. Avowed national policy as regards the shipbuilding industry is stated in unequivocal terms. The pertinent passages of Section 701 and 702 read,

Wherever the . . . [Board] shall find and determine, and such determination shall be approved by the President of the United States, that the national policy declared in section 101 of this Act and the objectives set forth in section 210 of this Act [long-range program of replacements and additions to the merchant fleet], cannot be fully realized with a reasonable time, in whole or in part, under the provisions of titles V [construction-differential subsidy scheme] and VI [operating-differential subsidies], the . . . [Board] is authorized and directed to complete its long-range program previously adopted. . .

The . . . [Board] is authorized to have constructed in domestic yards, on the Atlantic and Gulf and Pacific coasts, such new vessels as it shall determine may be required to carry out the object of this Act, and to have old vessels reconditioned or remodeled in such yards: *Provided*, that if satisfactory contracts for such new construction or reconstruction, in accordance with the provisions of the Act, cannot be obtained from private shipbuilders, the . . . [Board] is authorized to have such vessels constructed, reconditioned or remodeled in United States Navy yards.

These various provisions for aid have become increasingly important to American shipbuilders. Though the 1936 Act was concerned primarily with building up the United States-flag merchant marine, shipyards have been important beneficiaries. And if the declaration of policy found in the Merchant Ship Sales Act of 1946 represents current thinking, vessels can be built primarily to support shipbuilders even during times when the merchant fleet is deemed large enough for commercial and national defense purposes.

An economist would summarize the shipbuilding provisions of the 1936 Act by pointing out that the subsidy, the payment plans (long-term, low-interest, and insured mortgages), and generous turn-in allowances on old and obsolete vessels, were designed to stimulate the demand for ships. If these measures fail to increase the demand for ships, then the government itself will enter the market to buy vessels. Thus, the 1936 Act provides both mixed private and public and also purely governmental means to help the shipbuilders of the United States.

Experience under the Merchant Marine Act, 1936

Between 1936 and June 30, 1953, 247 vessels were built under the construction-differential subsidy provisions of the 1936 Act. The subsidies amounted to $425 million.[36] An additional $6 million in subsidies were granted for reconstructing and reconditioning vessels,[37] bringing the total for overt construction subsidies up to $431 million. In addition, of course, the government paid out large sums for vessels it bought. Insofar as these vessels could have been bought from foreign shipbuilders, the government paid premium prices for its ships. This, too, then was a subsidy paid to the United States shipbuilders. We can therefore conclude that the total subsidy—overt and covert—was much more than $425 million.

The evidence certainly supports the inference that without the very substantial assistance of the federal government, the shipbuilding industry in the United States would not have reached its present size. And without continuous governmental support, the industry would shrink markedly. The interval between World Wars I and II saw such a development.

Since V-J Day, the industry, though generally prosperous, has been substantially aided by the Mariner-class building program of the Federal Maritime Board. However, with the last of the 35 Mariners scheduled for delivery in 1955 and relatively few commercial orders on the books, private ship-

[36] Data from U.S. Maritime Administration, *Net Construction Differential Subsidies on Vessels Sold Under the Merchant Marine Act, 1936, From Inception of Act Through June 30, 1953* (Washington: n.d.), mimeographed. Their figures are very nearly the same as those used in the *Murray Report.* Apparently, there is (or has been) considerable confusion about the number of ships and the amount of subsidy paid for their construction. For instance, in 1953 Earl W. Clark, Deputy Maritime Administrator, offered some exhibits showing that American shipping companies had acquired 163 ships. (*Merchant Marine Studies,* cited, p. 309-310.) The information used in the text was the latest available from the Maritime Administration as of December 14, 1954.

[37] *Report on Audit of United States Maritime Commission,* H. Doc. No. 465, 81st Cong., 2d sess. (Washington: GPO, 1950), p. 7. This figure is for the period 1946-50. It is estimated that an additional $3.3 million were set aside during 1950-53. (From letter to the author from S. C. Manning, Jr., Public Information Officer, Maritime Administration, December 15, 1954.)

builders again faced a sharp curtailment of operations. And once again the government has come to the rescue. (See p. 48).

EVALUATION OF CURRENT POLICY

The crucial role of ships in World War II convinced even the most skeptical of the importance of the United States shipbuilding industry to national defense. The government, whether controlled by Republicans or Democrats, has frequently indicated its desire to maintain a strong shipbuilding industry and enacted this desire in legislation from 1936 to the present.

Providing support for Navy shipyards is a relatively simple matter. They are recognized as military installations supporting the fleet. Except in unusual circumstances, Navy yards confine their work to the building and repair of Navy craft.[38] The size of the peacetime Navy and the prospects for war largely determine their level of activity.

Private shipyards, however, presumably exist primarily to serve the privately owned and operated *merchant* marine. If this view is accepted, then they should gear their peacetime operations to the needs of the merchant fleet and in time of war they should convert to the production of miltary requirements. The automobile industry is a good example of this type of industry. However, it is supported at a suitable (i.e., profitable) scale of operations by *private* orders for its products. Not so private shipbuilding. *Purely* private orders for vessels would not support the industry at a level considered adequate for national defense purposes.

Current policy is still firmly anchored to the 1936 Act's conception that shipbuilding is supported in order to maintain a merchant fleet. Shipbuilders usually receive aid only if private ship operators are also involved. There is still a strong conviction that commercial-type ships ought not to be built unless they will be used commercially. In 1936 this was appropriate. The merchant fleet was deplorably run down. New

---

[38] Under Title V of the 1936 Act, for example, the Federal Maritime Board may order construction of a vessel destined for private ownership under the construction-differential subsidy if no satisfactory bids are received from private shipbuilders.

vessels were needed. With the aid of construction-differential and operating-differential subsidies it was hoped they could be operated "profitably." Rebuilding this fleet was sensible, if not immediately economically justified. It helped to revive shipbuilding. The impetus to shipbuilding activity provided by the construction program initiated under the 1936 Act contributed importantly to readiness of the industry to expand rapidly during World War II.

Even the generous terms of the 1936 Act failed to attract sufficient orders to keep shipyards "adequately" busy. The Maritime Commission developed the designs for many types of cargo vessels now prominent in the United States merchant marine. It then built prototypes and proceeded to build vessels for its own account. And this occurred during a period when most of the ships in the merchant fleet were around twenty years old. Obviously, receipts were inadequate. As the Commission put it, when it embarked upon its program to order 50 ships per year for ten years to replace the 800 vessels in the "aging and obsolescent cargo fleet. . . ,"

The possibility of private operators being able to absorb even 50 ships seemed beyond the realm of likelihood in the light of the facts disclosed by the Commission's Economic Survey of the Merchant Marine in 1937. Nevertheless, the urgent need for new, fast, and efficient cargo carriers outweighed considerations of a probable deficiency of private capital to acquire them under Title V of the Merchant Marine Act . . . .

When the ships which had been contracted for by the Commission in 1938 became ready for delivery in the following year the Commission's doubts that private purchasers would not be found were not substantiated. Increased revenues derived from improved shipping conditions in our foreign trade and the sums received from the sale of obsolete vessels at rising prices enabled the subsidized lines to purchase, or make commitments to purchase, about 100 new ships.[39]

Today, the American merchant marine is middle-aged. Much of it was bought at bargain prices after World War II. Though it carries far greater cargoes than prewar, its share

[39] United States Maritime Commission, *Report to Congress* for the period ended October 25, 1941 [Washington: GPO, 1941] p. 9, 10. In addition to these orders, the Commission also received orders from nonsubsidized lines.

of total cargoes is declining. Its liftings have shown no tend-ency to increase—varying sharply from year to year. Foreign competition is intense on the international sea lanes. In the sheltered domestic trades, trucks and railroads provide such rugged competition that dry-cargo carriers move substantially less freight than before the war. These developments alone would be sufficient to inhibit orders for new ships.

There is, however, an additional factor of considerable importance. In the Maritime Administration reserve fleet about 2,100 vessels ride at anchor. This fleet includes almost all types of seagoing vessels although the nearly 1,500 Libertys predominate. An increase in the demand for ships can, and has been, readily accommodated by withdrawals from the reserve fleet.

Today there is little commercial justification for replacing the middle-aged vessels of the American merchant marine. Certainly expansion is economically unjustified. Under these circumstances, the private shipbuilding industry in the United States is condemned to extinction unless it can somehow exist between the sporadic increases in demand for seagoing ton-nage. Helping shipbuilders by helping ship operators at the present level is clearly not the best way to sustain a shipbuild-ing industry. Operators must anticipate profitable operations or they will not invest in new ships.

According to those best qualified to judge, a private ship-building industry located in the United States is essential to national defense. Though some may perhaps wish to quarrel with this conclusion, particularly in the light of developments in atomic weapons, let us accept the verdict for purposes of analyzing policy. This means that regardless of the commer-cial needs for ships, a defense nucleus of the private shipbuild-ing industry must be maintained at all times.

The Mariner shipbuilding program clearly demonstrated an understanding of the postwar position of American ship-builders. It was a forthright, though expensive, program. The Mariners were designed for easy conversion to military use. The Maritime Administration hoped that these ships would be useful commercially as well. It has been disappointed. Nonetheless, as a scheme to keep the shipyards busy and to strengthen the military effectiveness of the reserve fleet, the

Mariner program should be judged a success. Thirty-five ships of excellent design for military use were built, thus strengthening the reserve fleet. Shipyard production teams were kept together, thereby preserving the essential nucleus. From a policy standpoint, the outstanding feature of the program was that it was a "clean" national defense operation and not a mixture of commercial and military endeavors.

Recently the mixture has reappeared. The aid to the shipbuilders has become less direct. The twenty-tanker program *permits* the building of fifteen tankers with appropriate government aid. However, the *orders* for these vessels depend upon the successful arrangements of charter parties between the Navy and private operators (i.e., contracts between the owners of the vessels and those renting them). Only five tankers will be built for government account with government funds. The other fifteen will be privately financed. This program reduces government expenditures for ships but increases its outlays for charters. The shipyards get assured assistance only through the construction of the five vessels. Construction of the other fifteen depends upon the attractiveness of the charter parties and the availability of private capital.[40]

It seems odd indeed to make a defense measure—vital assistance to essential shipbuilders—depend largely upon the availability of private capital. This, in effect, makes the private money lenders of the country—the bankers, insurance companies, private investors—the final arbiters as to whether these critically important national defense facilities should be kept in operation. Ultimately, then, under this scheme shipbuilders must compete in the open market for funds. More attractive alternative opportunities for investment will move funds away from shipbuilding. This may not be in the national interest.

Similarly, the new ship mortgage guarantee provisions[41] are

[40] *Public Law 575*, ch. 665, 83rd Cong., 2d sess. (Aug. 10, 1954), authorizing this procedure was implemented in 1956 when the government authorized the construction of 14 tankers under this law. See *The New York Times*, February 2, 1956.

[41] *Public Law 781*, ch. 1265, 83rd Cong., 2d sess. (Sept. 3, 1954). This is called an act "To amend certain provisions of Title XI of the Merchant Marine Act, 1936, as amended, to facilitate *private* financing of new ship construction, and for other purposes." (Italics mine.)

indirect means to aid the shipbuilders. Merely offering to guarantee payment of 90 per cent of the unpaid balance of a ship mortgage (100 per cent in some cases) will not bring orders to the shipyards if the prospects of ship operation are not favorable. Only in the marginal instances in which a guarantee is the necessary catalyst to the conclusion of a loan will the guarantee be helpful. Again the emphasis is upon private capital to sustain activity in an industry whose existence is justified primarily because of its contribution to national defense.

This brings us to the last element of current shipbuilding policy—the experimental conversion of reserve Libertys. Here shipbuilders and shiprepairers benefit immediately and directly. The outlay under the program is to be relatively small—$25 million for "reserve fleet modernization and repair."[42] All of the $25 million will therefore not be spent on conversion and modernization of Libertys.

Some shipbuilders and vessel operators have recommended against any scheme to improve the performance characteristics of reserve Libertys. They prefer to have new ships built incorporating the latest improvements in marine engineering. However, such a program would apparently be far more expensive than the remodeling of the Libertys. If these reserve vessels can be markedly improved at relatively low cost, the national defense of the United States will be strengthened by having an improved reserve fleet and a shipbuilding industry whose skills will have been preserved in the course of revamping some 1,500 Libertys.[43]

The outstanding weakness of government policy toward shipbuilding is the apparent failure to recognize that to

[42] *Public Law* 608, ch. 777, 83rd Cong., 2d sess. (Aug. 20, 1954.)

[43] Douglas C. MacMillan, president of George G. Sharp, Inc., a firm of naval architects and engineers, stated that his firm had concluded that the World War II Liberty ship could be modernized to increase its speed from 11 knots to 18 knots. They found that this could be done by fining (making the forward part of the vessel into a sharper point) the lines by the number 1 and 2 holds and installing a new bow and propulsion equipment. The estimated cost was $2.2 million per ship. This is about half of what a new ship of the same specifications and estimated performance would cost. (U. S. Senate, *Maritime Subsidies*, Hearings before a Special Subcommittee of the Committee on Interstate and Foreign Commerce, 82d Cong., 1st sess. [Washington: Holmes Reporting Co., Oct. 23, 1953], vol. 29, p. 1886-1891. Mimeographed.)

achieve national defense aims shipbuilders must be helped regardless of the needs of the American merchant marine. If it is essential to have shipbuilding facilities in the United States, then there are grave risks in letting peacetime shipbuilding dwindle below a given level. United States government policy assumes that this country will be called upon for the production of ships in the event of war. These ships will be built in time only if the nucleus of the shipbuilding industry has been preserved regardless of whether the peacetime merchant marine has use for them.

If we accept the view that an essential nucleus of the industry must be preserved, then the only problem left is to determine how many ships must be under construction at all times in order to sustain this nucleus. The *Murray Report* recommends that 60 ships per year be built. It states that this level of output meets the mobilization requirements of the Department of Defense but exceeds the number that can economically be absorbed into the privately operated merchant marine for at least the next ten years. It then indicates that this excessive output will be justified because it will reduce the impending impact of block obsolescence. It states further that "considerable additional government assistance and incentive would be necessary for private industry to attain a 60 ship a year construction program in the next ten years."[44]

To absorb these ships in the merchant marine, shipowners will require more than the construction-differential subsidy. While it may seem natural for the *Murray Report* to be concerned with the disposition of these 60 vessels, this consideration is not strictly pertinent to a discussion of aid to shipbuilders intended to preserve the defense nucleus.

We should clearly understand that building ships in the United States is usually uneconomic. This includes building them for the American merchant marine under the provisions of the Merchant Marine Act, 1936. The American merchant marine does not gain by this, either. Only the shipbuilders do. The only sound reason for enabling shipbuilders to make profits by their uneconomic endeavors is their essentiality to national defense. Clearly, then, the only relevant consideration is how many vessels should be constructed each year to keep

[44] P. 29-30.

shipbuilding activity at a "safe" level. Under these conditions, the potential usefulness of the ships is of no importance when deciding how many to build. *After* they are completed sound policy dictates that an inexpensive (or perhaps profitable) way be found to employ them. This is disposal policy and is quite different from *construction* policy.

Accepting this dichotomy of policies leads to the following suggestion. Except during periods of national emergency or when the worldwide demand for tonnage brings foreign orders to the United States shipyards, the shipbuilders of the United States should produce only enough ships to keep the essential nucleus occupied. Without access to classified data no estimate can be made of the number and types of ships to build. Only a principle for choosing the number can be suggested. Under this program the government would merely make up the difference between privately-inspired orders (including those under the construction-differential and other such private aid programs) and the number required to keep the nucleus fully occupied. The government would not subsidize orders that would raise shipyard activity above the level decided on; this would be sound policy both on grounds of economy and in order to stabilize the domestic industry. If private domestic orders exceeded the "national defense" level, American ship operators would be permitted to place their surplus orders in foreign yards without later losing the benefit of operating-differential subsidies.

Our suggestion would not conflict unduly with United States foreign economic policy. It would make clear that the American shipping industry will be maintained at a given level for purposes of national security. The maritime nations in the anti-communist bloc, mindful of the contribution of the United States shipbuilding industry during World War II, can hardly protest against this proposal to keep the industry in a state of readiness in this uncertain world. Furthermore, the international economic repercussions of the proposal are surely not important, given the very small output of the United States shipbuilders compared with that of foreign yards.

IV
VESSEL OPERATING AID

Our American ships in the international trades must compete with the products of foreign labor, both in the acquisition of equipment (the building of ships) and in their operation. Because this competition takes place upon the high seas it cannot be brought under protection of our tariff system as is the case with other American enterprises.

The Congress, in the Merchant Marine Act of 1936 therefore, sought to effect the same result by what I shall call the 'tariff operation in reverse.' When the cost or market value of a foreign product—in this instance shipping services—cannot be brought up to the level of fair competition with its corresponding American product, this is equalized under our subsidy system of lowering the American cost (rather than raising the foreign cost) through Government aid.[1]

> Frazer A. Bailey, President, National Federation of American Shipping, April 26, 1950

Like shipbuilding, operating ships is more expensive in the United States than in most foreign countries. To maintain a merchant fleet of a certain size in such unfavorable circumstances, the United States government has offered assistance to American ship operators in various forms. As we saw in the last chapter, the subsidy to shipbuilding has been conceived largely

[1] U.S. Senate, *Merchant Marine Study and Investigation* (*Government Aid to Shipping*), Hearings on S. Res. 50, Subcommittee of Committee on Interstate and Foreign Commerce, 80th Cong., 2d sess. (Washington: GPO, 1950), pt. 7, p. 1642.

as a means of enabling operators to buy American-built ships at competitive prices. Many American operators also receive direct subsidies based on the difference between their operating costs and those of foreign competitors, the "tariff in reverse" that Mr. Bailey speaks of. Still others, especially in recent years, have been the beneficiaries of legislation requiring that half the goods sent abroad under various government aid programs be shipped in American vessels. This chapter and the next deal with these two major forms of aid to ship operators, examining their rationale, their means of operation, and their result.

THE AIM OF POLICY

The first section of the Merchant Marine Act, 1936 reads as follows:

It is necessary for the national defense and development of its foreign and domestic commerce that the United States shall have a merchant marine (a) sufficient to carry its domestic water-borne commerce and a substantial portion of the water-borne export and import foreign commerce of the United States and to provide shipping service on all routes essential for maintaining the flow of such domestic and foreign water-borne commerce at all times (b) capable of serving as a naval and military auxiliary in time of war or national emergency, (c) owned and operated under the United States flag by citizens of the United States insofar as may be practicable, and (d) composed of the best-equipped, safest and most suitable types of vessels, constructed in the United States and manned with a trained and efficient citizen personnel. It is hereby declared to be the policy of the United States to foster the development and encourage the maintenance of such a merchant marine.

Certainly this declaration shows that the government is committed to support an American-flag merchant marine. But more careful study raises questions about this apparently clear-cut statement, and an examination of actual policy shows, as is so often the case, that execution has not always fulfilled the hopes of those directly concerned with maritime matters.

Perhaps the politics of 1936 were such that the Merchant

Marine Act could not be enacted into law unless military and commercial considerations were intertwined in the statement of policy. Surely the requirements of straight thinking did not call for this mixture. A little thought exposes serious weaknesses in the declaration. It also yields clues indicating why United States maritime policy has been so erratically implemented.

Commercial considerations

The 1936 Act states that the United States needs an American-flag merchant marine to develop its foreign and domestic commerce. This is debatable. Consider the arguments. The *Kennedy Report* of 1937 summarized the commercial reasons for supporting an American-flag merchant marine as follows:

(1) To insure continuity of service.

(2) To protect American shippers against exorbitant rates.

(3) To improve the service given to American shippers.

(4) To prevent discrimination against shipments by Americans on foreign vessels.[2]

The *Kennedy Report* then noted that only reasons (1) and (3) had "sufficient validity to be worthy of inclusion in a fact-finding report." The others were "either undemonstrable or seemingly at variance with the facts." "Nevertheless," said the report, "the survey indicates that we are justified in concluding that an American merchant marine is of national value in the development of our foreign commerce."

There can be little disagreement that American-flag lines, operating on regular schedules, can provide dependable, satisfactory service. Few would quarrel with the contention that the projection of such lines into hitherto unserviced areas may stimulate American commerce. In this respect, the ship operators are in somewhat the same position as the early railroad men who established lines in the virgin west of the United States.

Moreover, there may be commercial disadvantages to reliance on foreign ship operators. Economic, political, or mili-

[2] United States Maritime Commission, *Economic Survey of the American Merchant Marine* (Washington: GPO, 1937) p. 5. Joseph P. Kennedy was chairman of the United States Maritime Commission at the time.

tary interests of foreign governments may outweigh the purely private commercial interests of their ship operators. American shippers might therefore receive relatively slight attention and, as aliens, might have little influence on the foreign governments. In this case, a United States-flag merchant marine may well insure more dependable and satisfactory service for the domestic shipper.

Certain intangibles may also give additional strength to the two reasons under consideration. The American shippers and shipping companies may have mutual interests. Thus, good service is beneficial to both and is likely to be provided. The ship operators and some of their important customers may share a common background that tends to draw them together. This will reinforce the basis for sharing the same interests in foreign commerce. Though obviously the influence of these and other intangibles cannot be measured, it should not be dismissed as negligible.

Despite the Commission's curt dismissal, in 1937, of the other two commercial reasons for having an American merchant marine, they should be examined. These reasons—the prevention of discrimination against American shippers and the forestalling of exorbitant rates—continue to be offered in defense of United States merchant marine policy.

Does the existence of an *American* merchant marine tend to prevent exorbitant shipping rates? High rates occur when the amount of shipping space available is too small to handle the cargoes that need to be shipped. American shippers would find rates high if there were a shortage of ships regardless of national flag or they would encounter high rates if foreign-flag companies were discriminating against American shippers. In the first instance, a general shortage of tonnage would bring high rates to all shippers regardless of nationality. In the second case, it is conceivable that shipping space could be plentiful but Americans would be charged higher rates than foreigners.

Some proponents of the exorbitant rate argument mistakenly draw support from the behavior of rates during both world wars. Rates rose sharply. The American-flag merchant marine was not generally available for private use. If it had been available the rates would have geen lower. But they would also have been lower if some *other* merchant marine similarly engaged in war work had been diverted to haul private cargoes.

Insofar as American steamship lines belong to international shipping conferences, the government may be able to exert pressure upon them to urge moderation upon a conference determined to raise rates. Such pressure and influence may not be important during a "feasting" period for the shipping industry.

Possibly the presence of the American merchant marine may discourage foreign lines from setting discriminatory high rates for shipments by United States exporters and importers. Such discrimination is more likely to occur when tonnage is scarce. Obviously, those favored by the discrimination gain advantage in sales and profits. If ample tonnage exists, competition for cargoes will be keen and discrimination less likely. While the presence of American-flag vessels may protect some American shippers from foreign discrimination, those unable to ship on United States-flag vessels will still be discriminated against. To some extent, then, an American merchant marine is helpful. However, a surplus of foreign tonnage will mitigate against discrimination, too.

Discrimination against American trade might result from the action of the governments of foreign countries having merchant fleets. Then, the existence of an American merchant marine would, of course, be useful in countering the effects of such actions. But the supposed danger of this kind of a situation's arising seems rather unlikely. No foreign merchant marine has a monopoly. Instead there are a number of national fleets, and private firms of different registries, plying the seas and interested in getting as much business as they can. Moreover, the picture of the United States isolated in the world, with all governments—among them very friendly ones—discriminating against American shippers seems rather fanciful. Perhaps in times of a shortage of shipping, nationally-set priorities abroad would have the effect of general discrimination against the United States, but as long as the supply of shipping is generally adequate the need to have ships to counter potential discrimination resulting from the policies of foreign governments would hardly seem to be a major factor in justifying the maintenance of an uneconomic American merchant marine.

From this review of the commercial arguments for the maintenance of an American merchant fleet—including the considerations rejected in the *Kennedy Report*—we conclude that there are a few positive advantages in the existence of such a fleet and some protection against potential discrimination. To a considerable extent these protective elements relate to times of general shipping shortage. Taken all in all, the commercial arguments for the maintenance of a national merchant marine in the United States have some slight validity but are not very weighty.

Even if greater weight is given to these arguments, does it follow (as the 1936 Act and subsequent legislation would have it) that the United States merchant fleet has to be predominantly "all American"? That is, must the vessels be built in the United States, the crews hired at United States ports, and the vessels registered under the United States flag? Clearly American citizens should manage and own the ships under the laws and jurisdiction of the United States government. This will give the government the necessary legal authority to enforce whatever regulations and policies have been deemed necessary to insure the condition and availability of these vessels. In other respects, however, an "internationalized" American merchant marine would appear capable of performing the required services. An "internationalized" American merchant marine would consist of a fleet of ships under United States registry, purchased from shipbuilders all over the world, manned by seamen of any nationality, and managed by companies subject to the jurisdiction of the United States government. The United States government could have undisputed jurisdiction over such a merchant marine. This assures the shipper proper governmental support should shipping companies owned by United States citizens charge unduly discriminatory rates. Armed with suitable laws, the government could then take appropriate action.[3]

---

[3] In a sense there is an "internationalized" United States fleet, in the form of American-owned ships registered abroad (see p. 14). Since the vessels are subject to the laws of the countries in which they are registered, they do not conform to the conditions set out here. However since many are registered in Panama, Liberia, and Honduras—not strong maritime nations—the practical difference in a time of crisis might not be very great.

Considering the weakness of these "commercial" arguments for maintaining an American merchant fleet, we may well wonder why they continue to be advanced. Perhaps one of the reasons is psychological. The subsidy-dependent, aid-conscious people in the shipping industry may feel a compelling need to be considered commercially useful—surely important for the self-respect of many businessmen.

National defense needs

The 1936 Act and present policy are based on the view that an American merchant marine is essential for national defense. As the Maritime Commission's Postwar Planning Committee put it in 1946: "If we were living in a peaceful world, where there was never any warfare—either military or economic—we might well entrust the carriage of our goods to those who could do it at the lowest cost. Since this is not a perfect world, and since it has been characterized by recurring warfare—both military and economic—it behooves us to keep some shipping subject to our own control in international trade." [4]

This view is widely accepted and only occasionally challenged. In its essentials it will be accepted in this book as a conclusion demanded by caution and military prudence. One might have doubts, as was suggested in Chapter I, whether the character of future wars would necessarily call for an American merchant fleet—or allow time for its use. But if, as seems to be the case, our military planning must allow for several kinds and sizes of wars, then the established view about the essentiality of a merchant marine remains valid. Accepting the need for a large merchant fleet in wartime, one might still question whether this would have to be an *American* fleet. Present United States strategy and defense policies rest in part on military alliances. Our allies in NATO include most of the principal shipping countries of the world, whose merchant fleets are not only numerous but capable of operating in peacetime more cheaply than American merchant ships can operate. Why should not the United States depend on these

[4] *The Postwar Outlook for American Shipping*, A report submitted to the United States Maritime Commission by the Postwar Planning Committee (Washington: GPO, 1946), p. 4.

merchant fleets for wartime needs and so avoid the necessity of costly and uneconomic subsidies and preferential policies in peacetime? The question is a serious one and will be touched on at various points in this book. For the present it should suffice to point out two general reasons why this otherwise attractive suggestion cannot be accepted out of hand. First, the experience of war has been that *additional* merchant shipping tonnage was needed, not just the amount that sailed in peacetime. An active American merchant fleet enlarges the mobilization base from which wartime expansion can take place. Moreover the countries that are the most economical shippers may not also be best able to maintain large reserves of shipping. Second, although alliances play a key role in American strategy, military planning cannot rest entirely on them. There must be some independent military capability. It follows that if the United States is to maintain some fighting power independent of alliances, and if a merchant marine is a necessary ancillary to fighting power, then there must be an American merchant marine of some size.

In the pages that follow we shall be dealing with estimates of the amount of merchant shipping the United States needs to maintain in peacetime in order to provide an adequate nucleus for potential wartime expansion. Lacking access to the data of strategical planning, we have to rely on the estimates made by the military. But to avoid giving undue weight to any particular statistics, or assuming that a military calculation is more nearly infallible than other policy or economic calculations, a few cautionary considerations should be borne in mind. For one thing, there is little evidence that wartime planning in this field has taken full account of the possibilities of working out a joint merchant shipping policy with our allies. For another, the arts of war are obviously undergoing great changes and it is likely that whatever rethinking of the military significance of a merchant marine is necessary has not yet taken place, or at least not found expression in policy.

Furthermore, while the policy arguments stress the flag under which a ship sails, the ability to use ships at the outbreak of war is predominantly a physical matter—their location. Enemy ships in the ports controlled by the United States and its allies can be controlled. Western bloc vessels in hostile ports will be lost. Some allied ports may be captured or destroyed quickly, and ships with them. Western bloc ships in neutral ports cannot be wholly counted on. Getting the ships out of these ports may well depend upon the exchange of neutral ships in allied ports for allied ships in neutral ports. Ships engaged in the United States coastal trades or in the laid-up fleet will be available. Thus flag alone—the basis of planning—is not sufficient to assure a specified supply of vessels.

Time is another uncertainty. It takes time to bring laid-up vessels into service. The pattern of demand for vessels is largely unpredictable. Will they be needed in great quantities at the outset? Can one make do with the diversion of vessels already in service for six months? A year? This depends on the character and geographical scope of a war. Since we cannot forecast what kind of war there will be or what conditions will prevail on the day war breaks out or what the geographic disposition of the world's tonnage will be on that day, we cannot realistically estimate the size of the available American-flag merchant fleet we should keep in operation at all times.

Another fact worth bearing in mind is the experience of the two world wars. Both times merchant shipping was of crucial importance. Both times there were substantial allied fleets in service which, within some limits and with some difficulty, could be used on a joint basis. Both times the starting point for the United States was grossly inadequate by the standards of preparation now being discussed. And in both wars, although there were serious difficulties that one would certainly not willingly and unnecessarily accept again, the American maritime industries, and the American economy and government as a whole, rose to the occasion.

With all these cautions, and in the face of these uncertainties, one is still driven to the conclusion that as a matter of military prudence the United States needs a peacetime merchant fleet, even if it is uneconomic. Moreover, it will have to be an active fleet, not just a reserve one. Otherwise it would be immobilized for some period at the beginning of a war and would lack the nucleus around which rapid expansion could take place. In addition, national security would appear to dictate that in addition to ships and management under the jurisdiction of the United States, the merchant marine should contain a nucleus of American seagoing, operating personnel. This will facilitate the wartime expansion of the merchant fleet. It is also important for effective wartime services. The ability to operate the ships may depend upon the tractability of their crews. Many operating problems will arise if the crews consist of citizens of neutral, much less enemy, nations. Thus, at least some portion of the United States merchant marine should be "all-American" for military reasons though this is not necessary for commercial purposes.

If it is accepted that the United States needs a merchant marine for defense, the question becomes, "What should be the size and composition of the merchant marine and how should it be supported?" Two reports of rather different origin accept this view. The *Gray Report* said:

It should become a basic principle of United States shipping policy that governmental protection and subsidy measures will not be used to maintain in operation a merchant fleet or any class of vessels in excess of the size authoritatively determined to be required for the purposes of national defense.[5]

The Postwar Planning Committee of the Maritime Commission put it this way:

The question therefore is not whether we should have a merchant marine but the number of vessels, both active and laid-up, considered necessary to protect the national welfare.[6]

Since the commercial reasons for having a merchant marine are not compelling and the military reasons are, evaluation of the 1936 Act should be based upon its efficiency as an instrument to develop a merchant marine for national defense use and only incidentally or secondarily for commercial purposes. This view casts doubt on the declaration of policy of the Act. Certainly national defense does not require a merchant fleet "sufficient to carry . . . domestic water-borne commerce and a substantial portion of the water-borne export and import foreign commerce of the United States and to provide shipping service on all routes essential for maintaining the flow of such domestic and foreign water-borne commerce at all

---

[5] *Report to the President on Foreign Economic Policies* (Washington: GPO, 1950), p. 89.
[6] *The Postwar Outlook for American Shipping,* cited, p. 5.

times." Military considerations should be based upon estimates of military contingencies and the potential ability to handle them successfully. Such estimates must necessarily include judgments regarding the possible types of war to be fought, the expandability of the merchant fleet, the size of the reserve fleet, and the potential output of shipyards. Only by a lucky coincidence would estimates based upon the volume of water-borne commerce and the adequate servicing of essential trade routes be the same as those derived from military considerations.

There would be general agreement that the vessels to be operated under provisions of the Act should be capable of conversion to military use in time of war. Further, it is consistent with military preparedness to have some, if not all, the vessels owned by United States citizens so far as practicable. Thus items "(b)" and "(c)" of the policy statement of the 1936 Act (p. 68) are wholly consistent with it national defense objectives.

However, all the ships in the fleet need not necessarily be manned with "citizen personnel" as indicated in part "(d)" of the declaration. The essential nucleus of "citizen personnel" may be larger or smaller than can be employed to operate the essential fleet.[7] The nucleus of "citizen personnel" is required to facilitate expansion of the fleet in time of war. The nucleus fleet, in turn, provides necessary tonnage immediately available at the first stage of a major emergency or to cope with a minor one. It also provides training and practice for citizen personnel. If a large nucleus fleet of vessels is decided upon, it may not need to be manned entirely by citizen crews because, relative to the nucleus, the required expansion may not be large. The minimum size of this fleet would appear to depend upon the personnel-expansion factor. It would never be so small that there would be insufficient numbers of seamen to accommodate the anticipated expansion of the fleet in time of war.

If we agree that at least some part of the American mer-

[7] The construction provision of point "(d)" also fails the test of military preparedness. As indicated in Chapter III, the number of ships built in United States shipyards should not exceed that necessary to maintain an essential nucleus of the shipbuilding industry. This number may be larger or smaller than the essential merchant fleet requirements.

chant marine (the national defense nucleus) must be all-American, largely privately-owned (to provide for flexibility, the benefits of individual initiative in adjusting to rapidly changing conditions, and the bearing of much of the risk and cost of operation by private enterprise rather than by a government agency), and active despite its competitive disadvantages, then government intervention becomes necessary. This brings us to a consideration of the operating-differential subsidy provisions of the Merchant Marine Act, 1936.[8]

OPERATING-DIFFERENTIAL SUBSIDY PROVISIONS OF THE MERCHANT MARINE ACT, 1936

Briefly stated, the major features of the operating-differential subsidy provisions of the 1936 Act are as follows.[9]

1. *Eligibility*. The government will grant a subsidy if it finds that subvention is required to meet foreign-flag competition and to promote the foreign commerce of the United States on an essential trade route. The applicant-operator must offer (or propose to offer) service with American-built ships (or vessels documented under United States laws not later than February 1, 1928, or ordered or under construction for a United States citizen prior to that date). The operator must either own or agree to purchase or build vessels approved by the government as suitable for the trade routes over which they will sail. The operator must also meet certain standards of competence and have adequate financial resources. (This is to protect the government against operators who are inexperienced or incapable.)

2. *Amount of subsidy*. The government will pay the difference between the foreign and domestic ship operators' costs of insurance, maintenance, repairs not compensated by insurance, wages and subsistence of officers and crews, and any other items it may designate. Only "fair and reasonable" costs are included in the calculations. Foreign costs are estimated.

[8] Other forms of intervention—e.g., the restriction of the coastal trades and the "fifty per cent" aid cargo provision—are discussed in Chapters V and VI.
[9] Unless otherwise noted, statements of the major provisions of the subsidy are based upon Title VI of the Merchant Marine Act, 1936.

3. *Essential trade routes.* To be subsidized, shipping companies must operate vessels on essential trade routes. The Maritime Administration has defined an essential trade as a "route between ports in a United States coastal area or areas to foreign markets which has been determined by the Maritime Administration to be essential for the promotion, development, expansion, and maintenance of the foreign commerce of the United States."[10] Thirty-one essential routes have been designated on the basis of considerations involving economics, "geopolitics," national defense, and steamship economics.[11] Using these criteria, new routes can be added or old ones changed or dropped.

4. *Number of voyages subsidized.* The 1936 Act does not limit the number of voyages to be subsidized each year. Under present practice, Congress specifies this number, leaving it to the Federal Maritime Board to allocate the total among the subsidized lines.[12] So far, Congress has authorized more voyages than the subsidized operators applied for.

5. *Age of subsidized vessels.* Unless the Federal Maritime Board decides that the public interest will be served by the employment and subsidization of a vessel more than 20 years old, the ship will not be subsidized. Normally, then, only vessels up to twenty years old will be eligible for operating-differential subsidies.

6. *Recapture of excess profits.* After ten years of subsidy payments (or sooner if the contract between the subsidized operator and the government is terminated) the subsidized operator must pay the government one-half of his profits in excess of "10 per centum per annum upon the contractor's capital necessarily employed in the operation of the subsidized vessels, services, routes and lines. . . ." if the operator's profits have averaged more than 10 per cent annually for the period considered. No more than the amount of the operating-differential subsidy paid out by the government to the operator may be recaptured.

[10] United States Department of Commerce, Maritime Administration, *Review of Essential Foreign Trade Routes* (Washington: GPO, 1953) p. 14.
[11] Same, p. 6. The authority and duty to determine essential trades is found in Sec. 211 of the 1936 Act. See Chapter VIII for a fuller discussion.
[12] See for example, *Public Law 195*, 83rd Cong., 1st sess.

7. *Capital reserve fund.* Out of gross earnings the subsidized operator must establish a capital reserve fund. In this fund he must annually deposit his depreciation allowance on vessels operating under subsidy contract. If earnings do not cover depreciation the deposit may be deferred until earnings rise sufficiently to permit appropriate supplementary payments to the fund to compensate for earlier deficiencies. The contractor must also deposit all proceeds from insurance and indemnities in this fund.

8. *Special reserve fund.* "If profits, without regard to capital gains and capital losses, earned by the business of the subsidized vessel and services incident thereto exceed 10 per centum per annum and exceed the percentage of profits deposited in the capital reserve fund . . . the contractor shall deposit annually such excess profits in the reserve fund."

Generally speaking, the contractor can make only three types of disbursement from this fund in addition to the recapture payments to the government as described above. First, he may reimburse his general funds for losses on the operation of subsidized vessels after he has signed an operating-differential subsidy contract. Second, he can reimburse his general funds for current operating losses on completed voyages of subsidized vessels if the government determines that these losses will not be made up by profits on other voyages during the current year. Third, if after reimbursing the general fund for his losses and fully meeting all his obligations under the recapture provisions, the amount remaining in the special reserve fund is more than five per cent of the capital necessarily employed in the business he may, if the government approves, withdraw all or part of the excess into his general fund. He may then distribute this excess as a special dividend, or as a bonus to officers and employees of his firm.

9. *Tax status of reserve funds.* All deposits in the reserve funds of the subsidized operators are exempt from federal taxation. However, withdrawals from the special reserve fund transferred to the general fund or disbursed as bonuses and dividends are taxable as though they were earned during the year withdrawn.[13]

---

[13] This provision of the 1936 Act has been the subject of considerable controversy. Much of it is not germane here. Interested readers may wish to

Analysis

These provisions, while inevitably a bit complicated, seem clear enough. A few features may be noted before appraising their results.

Subsidized ship operators rightly point out that the operating-differential subsidy scheme does not insure a profit. *Costs* are subsidized. The operator must struggle for revenues. Furthermore, under some circumstances, costs are ultimately not subsidized either. If the profits are sufficiently greater than 10 per cent per year during the life of the subsidy contract, the government may recapture all its subsidy payments.

Under the reserve funds' provisions, contractors (subsidy receivers) are forced to provide for the future continuation of their companies. This has made the subsidized group of operators a stable element in the industry. And this, of course, has contributed to the national defense posture of the United States.

The operating-differential subsidy provisions of the 1936 Act clearly show that three convictions probably guided the authors of the Act. The first grew primarily out of the mail pay scandals that occurred under the provisions of the Merchant Marine Act of 1928. The authors were convinced that by imposing stringent accounting and financial requirements they could prevent financial malpractice and insure, so far as legislatively possible, that the subsidized lines would adopt sound business practices consistent with the public interest. The second was that national shipping policy should not unduly embarrass the government in its negotiations under the Reciprocal Trade Agreements Act. Under this trade program, adopted in 1934, the United States government trades reductions in its import tariff rates for equivalent reduc-

---

study *Communication from the President of the United States Relative to Tax Deferment and Tax Exemption Benefits to the Maritime Industry, Together With a Report to the President on Government Assistance Necessary to Maintain a Merchant Marine Adequate to the Commercial and National Defense Requirements of the United States, Submitted by the Secretary of Commerce, and a Supplementary Report Submitted by the Treasury Department Entitled "Scope and Effect of Tax Benefits Provided the Maritime Industry"* (Washington: GPO, 1953). Hereafter called *Communication from the President.* Under Section 511 of the 1936 Act, any ship operator may establish a construction reserve fund that entitles him to limited tax deferment.

tions in the rates applied by other countries. Only under special circumstances does it raise rates. The operating-differential subsidy scheme "protects" United States-flag lines from the full effects of their foreign rivals' lower costs. However, it does so without directly impeding foreigners' sales of shipping services. Thus, after passage of the 1936 Act, the tariff negotiators representing the United States were not handicapped by the development of a new trade restriction by the United States at the time they were pleading for lower tariffs all around. Given the conflict between military and peacetime economic considerations, a policy of operating-cost equalization on a limited scale can be readily defended. The third conviction was that an overt, calculable subvention is preferable to a hidden subsidy. The cost to the taxpayer can be determined and those needing and receiving aid can be identified.

RESULTS OF THE
OPERATING-DIFFERENTIAL SUBSIDY PROGRAM

Given the important military and somewhat doubtful commercial reasons for government action to insure the existence of an adequate American merchant marine, what has the operating-differential subsidy program contributed to the development of that merchant marine?

This question cannot be answered with assurance. The program was hardly under way before World War II began. During the war it was suspended. It was resumed again in 1947. For a while after its resumption, foreign trade shipping boomed under the combined impact of the war-deferred demand for American products and the large volume of commerce stimulated by the foreign aid and loan programs of the United States. Shipping prospered. The absence of strong, modern, foreign-flag merchant fleets also contributed to the favorable earnings records of American operators. Only recently has foreign competition, coupled with declining aid cargoes, brought distress to American-flag companies. Perhaps the next few years will provide an adequate testing period for the efficacy of the operating-differential subsidy policy.

Meanwhile, only preliminary evaluation is possible from the data at hand.

Table 9 shows the composition of the active, American-flag, foreign-trade, dry-cargo merchant marine on December 31, 1954.

Table 9

PRIVATELY-OWNED ACTIVE UNITED STATES-FLAG DRY-CARGO
SHIPS OF 1,000 GROSS TONS AND OVER OWNED BY
SUBSIDIZED AND NONSUBSIDIZED COMPANIES IN
FOREIGN TRADE AS OF DECEMBER 31, 1955

	Subsidized		Unsubsidized		Total	
Type of vessel	No. of vessels	Per cent	No. of vessels	Per cent	No. of vessels	Per cent
Passenger and comb.	19	6.4	0	0	19	3.4
C Type	249	84.4	110	42.3	359	64.7
Libertys	0	0.0	81	31.2	81	14.6
Victories	25	8.5	37	14.2	62	11.2
All other types	2	0.7	32	12.3	34	6.1
Total	295	100.0	260	100.0	555	100.0

Source: Special tabulation for the author in a letter from Irwin M. Heine, Chief, Statistics and Special Studies Office, Maritime Administration, April 27, 1956.

As Table 9 shows, more than half the dry-cargo vessels engaged in foreign trade were owned by subsidized companies as of the end of 1955. If the domestic trades are included, there were 39 combination passenger-freighters, and 679 dry-cargo vessels in the active merchant marine of the United States at the end of 1955.[14] So subsidized vessels accounted for 41 per cent of this fleet, about 49 per cent of its combination ships, and roughly 41 per cent of its freighters. If tankers are included—none of them subsidized—the active ocean-going merchant fleet of the United States totalled 1,072 vessels of

[14] U.S. Department of Commerce, Maritime Administration, "Employment of United States Flag Merchant Fleet Seagoing Vessels 1,000 Gross Tons and Over, as of December 31, 1955," *Report #300* (Washington: January, 1956). The exact number of "subsidized" vessels cannot be accurately stated, since voyages and not vessels are subsidized. Thus the term "subsidized" is loosely used here and provides a rough estimate of the extent to which the voyages of American-flag vessels are subsidized.

13.6 million deadweight tons at the end of 1955.[15] About 28 per cent of these were subsidized.

As measured by type of ship, the fleet owned by the subsidized operators is better than the unsubsidized dry-cargo and passenger fleet in the foreign trade merchant marine of the United States. This is probably attributable to (1) the use of Liberty ships in the tramp services provided by the unsubsidized operators, and (2) the requirements of the Maritime Administration regarding the types of vessels to be used in the subsidized services. If we assume that the subsidized lines would be unable to operate all their vessels without the aid of operating-differential subsidies, then we must conclude that the quality of the American merchant marine has been improved by the subsidy program.

THE SIZE OF THE ESSENTIAL NUCLEUS

How does this active fleet compare with what is needed for national defense purposes? A few guesses can be made. We must recognize that recommendations regarding the minimum size of the active merchant marine consonant with the needs of national defense will vary from time to time. Aside from the assessment of the world military situation, the size, composition, and condition of the government's reserve fleet are important factors in the estimated necessary size of the active fleet for military purposes. If the reserve fleet were to be modernized by reconstructing the ships now in it, one set of estimates would be appropriate. Another would be appropriate if this fleet were to be left alone and augmented by vessels retired from the active fleet. At present, the reserve fleet consists primarily of very slow Libertys, whose potential usefulness declines each day as the world's active merchant fleet becomes more modern. This means that, other things being equal, the estimate of an adequate national defense active merchant marine must rise each year to compensate for the declining usefulness of the reserve fleet. Thus a wide

[15] These figures exclude vessels in the inland waterways and Great Lakes, and those owned by the United States Army and Navy, and special types of vessels such as cable ships and tugs. Data taken from *Report #300*, cited.

range of recommendations is to be expected from year to year and, indeed, at any particular time.

For example, in 1947, the President's Advisory Committee on the Merchant Marine assembled estimates on the recommended size of the postwar American merchant marine. The estimates came from the *Harvard Report*, the Maritime Commission, the Department of Commerce, the Navy, and the War Department. The Advisory Committee reported as follows:

It is at once apparent from an examination of this table that there is surprisingly close agreement among the estimates. All fall within the lower limit of 860 ships of 8,900,000 dead-weight tons and the upper limit of 1,325 ships of 13,350,000 dead-weight tons given in the report prepared by the Graduate School of Business Administration, Harvard University. The mean of all these estimates lies slightly above 1,000 ships of between 11,000,000 and 12,000,000 dead-weight tons. The Committee submits its belief that under current conditions this mean represents a reasonable minimum size of an active seagoing merchant fleet to meet the country's security requirements, providing that it is kept at a high pitch of efficiency by being composed of fast modern ships; is properly balanced as to type between passenger-carrying vessels, dry-cargo vessels, and tankers; and is backed up by a reserve of inactive ships also balanced as to type and kept in a state of reasonable preservation and readiness.[16]

On June 16, 1953, Rear Admiral R. E. Wilson, Deputy Commander and Chief of Staff, Military Sea Transport Service, said that the Department of Defense minimum requirements called for an "active operating United States merchant marine" that included (1) 1,287 notional dry-cargo ships of 13,899,600 deadweight tons, (2) 26 notional troop-ships of 250,900 gross tons, and (3) 428 notional tankers of 7,062,000 deadweight tons.[17]

[16] *Report of the President's Advisory Committee on the Merchant Marine* (Washington: GPO, 1947), p. 52.
[17] U.S. Senate, *Merchant Marine Studies*, Hearings before a Sub-committee of the Committee on Interstate and Foreign Commerce, 83rd Cong., 1st sess. (Washington: GPO, 1953), pt. 1, p. 67.
"Notional" is a unit of measure. For cargo ships it is defined as 10,800 deadweight tons at 10 knots per hour. For troopships it is 2,400 troops at 15 knots per hour. For tankers it is 100,000 barrels of fuel oil, or 115,000 barrels of diesel oil, or 130,000 barrels of gasoline, with a deadweight capacity of 16,500 tons at 15 knots per hour.

The following informal table compares the various estimates and the active fleet at the end of 1954. Admiral Wilson's gross tonnage figures for troopships are converted to deadweight tonnage by a crude method.[18]

	Minimum	Maximum
Harvard Report (1945)	8,900,000 Dwt	13,335,000 Dwt
Maritime Commission (1947)	11,140,000	—
Department of Comm. (1947) (Excludes passenger & tanker vessels in foreign trade)	8,500,000+	10,000,000+
Department of Comm. (1952)	17,234,000	—
Navy Department (1947)	11,400,000	—
Department of Defense (1953)	21,181,000	—
Active Fleet, incl. MSTS nucleus fleet (Dec. 31, 1954)	15,736,000	

Note that Admiral Wilson's estimate is nearly two-and-one-half times the minimum estimate of the *Harvard Report*. Though the active fleet at the end of 1954 was 70 per cent above the 1939 level it would have to be increased by about one-third—adding 5.3 million deadweight tons—to reach

[18] Gross tons were converted to deadweight tons by multiplying by 0.87. This was the ratio of deadweight to gross tons of all combination passenger and cargo ships (active and inactive) in the American ocean-going merchant fleet on December 31, 1953, as reported in Maritime Administration, . . . *Report #300*, cited. The estimates in the informal table (except for 1952, 1953, and 1954) are from *Report of the President's Advisory Committee. . .*, cited, p. 53. The 1952 Department of Commerce estimate was for a "projected American merchant marine adequate for United States . . . ocean-borne trades." Passenger and combination gross tonnage converted to deadweight tonnage by the method described above and deducting 4,650,000 deadweight tons from their figure. This represents 465 freighters in the "ready reserve for foreseeable future." It was taken from *Communication from the President*, cited, p. 34. MSTS tonnage taken from worksheet records of John McCarron at the headquarters of the MSTS, Washington, D. C. According to these records, the MSTS nucleus fleet included 210 vessels (including service and miscellaneous craft) totalling approximately 1.7 million dwt.

the state of readiness recommended by the Department of Defense.

Estimates of the Department of Defense are subject to change as military plans are modified in the light of world military and political developments. Further, the military estimates of shipping requirements will not necessarily be the same as the amount of shipping tonnage finally deemed essential by the government. The final decision rests upon political as well as military considerations. We should expect, therefore, that the government will probably set its sights somewhat, perhaps much, lower than the Department of Defense has. How much, remains in the realm of conjecture.

The *Murray Report*, prepared several months after Admiral Wilson's appearance before the Senate subcommittee investigating merchant marine policy, apparently confirmed the Admiral's views. It noted that the "Joint Marad-Navy Planning Group which was formed to study this problem has concluded that as of December 31, 1952, the active merchant fleet under United States control was deficient by 261 notional dry-cargo freighters of 10,000 cargo measurement tons and 10 knots (equivalent to 69 mariner-type and 127 Bland-type ships); 26 notional tankers of 16,500 deadweight tons and 15 knots (equivalent to 6 T-5 type and 10 commercial type vessels operating at 18 knots); and 8 passenger-carrying ships of the *Independence* type." [19]

Converting these figures to deadweight tons yields a total of 3.3 million. [20] Adding this to the total deadweight tonnage of the active United States-flag merchant marine on December 31, 1952 (18.0 million or 20.0 million if the MSTS nucleus fleet is included) gives totals of 21.3 and 23.3 million dead-

[19] P. 15.

[20] The deadweight tonnage of freighters was obtained by using the previously stated definition of a notional dry-cargo vessel. The deadweight tonnage of the *Independence*-type vessels was computed by taking the gross tonnage (approximately 29,000 tons) and multiplying by 0.87 (see above, fn. 18). The source of the gross tonnage figure was U. S. House of Representatives, *Redetermination of Vessel Sales Prices of S. S. Independence and S. S. Constitution,* Hearings Before the Special Subcommittee to Review Redetermination of Vessel Sales Prices of S. S. Independence and S. S. Constitution of the Committee on Merchant Marine and Fisheries, 82d Cong., 2d sess. (Washington: GPO, 1952), p. 123. Deadweight tonnage of active merchant fleet as of December 31, 1954 taken from the *Murray Report,* Table 2, Appendix.

weight tons. The lower figure is very nearly the same as Admiral Wilson's estimate. We should note that the Marad-Navy statement referred to vessels under United States "control." This means the American-flag merchant marine plus vessels controlled by United States citizens but registered under the flags of Panama, Honduras, Liberia, and Venezuela. (See p. 14). Thus, expansion of these other fleets would reduce the need to expand the American merchant marine for defense purposes.

After having apparently sided with Admiral Wilson, the *Murray Report* expressed doubt that "any substantial number of ships in addition to the number already in operation can be operated profitably under the United States flag even with subsidy." It then concluded "that on December 31, 1952 . . . the size of the active United States merchant fleet was very close to adequate, for initial mobilization requirements. While there is no margin of safety, the ability of the active fleet to meet more fully the requirements of defense planning will be enhanced as new and more efficient ships take the place of old and obsolete units."[21]

The *Murray Report* also stated that this conclusion would not be altered significantly if the December 31, 1953 inventory of United States-flag vessels were used instead of the earlier year's. However, this is not borne out by the facts. The deadweight tonnage of the active fleet was 18 million tons in 1952 and 15 million (or roughly 17 million including the MSTS nucleus fleet) in 1953. The apparent discrepancies in the *Murray Report* were certainly not clarified by a statement made by the Deputy Maritime Administrator. In February 1955, he testified that the active fleet as of January 1, 1954 was "about 200" ships short of immediate mobilization requirements. This could amount to about 2 million deadweight tons—a sizeable deficiency.[22]

If we knew the assumptions behind the military estimates and had access to all the information upon which the final

[21] P. 16-17. It should be noted that though the number of vessels may be considered as satisfactory, their quality and distribution among types is not.
[22] U.S. House of Representatives. *Study of the Operations of the Maritime Administration and the Federal Maritime Board,* Hearings Before the Committee on Merchant Marine and Fisheries, 84th Cong., 1st sess. (Washington: GPO, 1955), p. 20.

decision (if, indeed, there is such a decision) rests, we could appraise the soundness of these estimates and perhaps arrive at an independent view of the size merchant marine required for defense. One suspects that the military estimates are on the high side, for safety's sake. They may be based on the assumption that massive movements of men and material will be required very soon after the outbreak of hostilities. If so, they may be out of line with more recent developments in American military policy. Perhaps changed estimates will be forthcoming. Meanwhile, lacking the data necessary to make an independent assessment of defense requirements in the merchant marine, let us take the military policy as given and adopt for working purposes the most recent estimate given above—that the active fleet should come to about 21 million deadweight tons.

On this assumption, the entire merchant marine policy of the United States, as distinct from the shipbuilding policy,— not the operating-differential subsidy program alone—has not succeeded. About two million more deadweight tons should have been employed to provide adequately for national defense. This would be roughly one-eighth more shipping than is included in the active merchant marine of the United States (including the MSTS), and an amount roughly equal to the whole Danish merchant marine in 1954. Clearly an attempt to add this tonnage to the merchant marine of the United States would create difficult international and domestic problems.

If the military estimate of 1953 is accepted as a goal—over 21 million deadweight tons—then the active merchant marine would have to be expanded by one-third from its size at the end of 1954. This would mean adding about 5.4 million deadweight tons. Part of this apparent deficiency between the estimates and the actual size is overcome by the existence of ships flying foreign flags but owned by the subsidiaries of American companies. As indicated earlier (see p. 14), these vessels total about 6 million deadweight tons. However, most of the tonnage consists of tankers while the need is for freighters and passenger ships. The "ultimate" goal today is probably an expansion of between 2 million and 5 million deadweight tons— surely a large volume of tonnage to add.

THE COMMERCIAL RESULTS OF OPERATING-DIFFERENTIAL SUBSIDIES

The results of the operating-differential subsidy program should also be examined in the light of its "commercial" goals as distinct from the military requirements. In 1952 the Maritime Administration prepared estimates of the size and composition of an American merchant marine "adequate" to handle a "substantial portion of the foreign commerce of the United States in the foreseeable future." According to these estimates, this fleet should contain 630 cargo ships (approximately 6.3 million deadweight tons) and 62 passenger and combination vessels (roughly 583,000 dwt.).[23] The active, dry-cargo foreign trade merchant marine of the United States was well short of these estimates on December 31, 1955. It would have required an additional 117 cargo vessels of 800 thousand deadweight tons capacity and 24 passenger-freight combination ships (224,000 dwt.) to have brought this fleet up to the levels projected by the Maritime Administration.

Obviously, the operating-differential subsidy program alone cannot be blamed for this failure to create a dry-cargo foreign trade merchant marine as large as projected by the Maritime Administration. After all, the Maritime Administration was merely estimating the size of the fleet in the "foreseeable future." Perhaps several more years must elapse before the "foreseeable future" has become history. Only then can the Maritime Administration estimates be properly judged. We should also recognize that other policies and factors should share the credit or blame for the present size of this fleet. Certainly, in the last two years the effects of overriding economic, political, and military factors (e.g., cessation of armed conflict in Korea) must have outweighed the influence of continuing factors such as the operating-differential subsidy. How else can we explain the decline in the dry-cargo foreign trade merchant marine? It fell from 884 vessels (9.2 million

[23] *Communication from the President*, cited, p. 34. Cargo ship deadweight tonnage estimated by assuming that the average cargo ship planned for this fleet would have a capacity of 10,000 deadweight tons. (The Maritime Administration proposed a total merchant marine cargo fleet of 1,300 vessels totalling 13,600,000 deadweight tons.) Passenger-combination vessel gross tonnage converted to deadweight tonnage by method explained in fn. 18.

deadweight tons) on June 30, 1952 to 576 ships (6.2 million deadweight tons) on December 31, 1955.[24]

At this stage of our attempt to determine the results of the operating-differential subsidy program we can conclude that (1) the privately-owned subsidized fleet is of better quality than the unsubsidized, (2) more than half the dry-cargo foreign trade fleet of the United States is supported by the sub-

Table 10

TOTAL UNITED STATES OCEAN-BORNE FOREIGN TRADE CARGOES CARRIED BY DRY-CARGO SHIPS ON ESSENTIAL AND OTHER FOREIGN TRADE ROUTES, 1948, 1950-53

[In millions of tons of 2,240 lbs.]

Coverage	Year				
	1948	1950	1951	1952	1953
All trade routes					
All flags	78.6	68.7	114.7	103.1	85.9
U.S. flag	37.0	23.4	44.7	34.0	22.9
Per cent U.S. flag	47%	34%	39%	33%	27%
Essential trade routes					
All flags	70.5	57.6	103.6	92.3	78.6
U.S. flag	34.6	21.3	43.5	32.3	22.3
Per cent U.S. flag	49%	37%	42%	35%	28%
Other trade routes					
All flags	8.1	11.1	11.1	10.8	7.3
U.S. flag	2.0	1.8	2.1	1.6	0.7
Per cent U.S. flag	25%	16%	19%	15%	10%

Note: The trade routes covered include only *ocean* routes. This excludes the Great Lakes-Canadian trade. The inclusion of this trade would lower the percentage carried by American-flag vessels. Figures exclude military or "special category" items. In-transit cargoes included.

Source: For 1948-52, U.S. Department of Commerce, Maritime Administration, Office of National Shipping Authority and Government Aid, Division of Trade Routes, *United States Ocean-borne Foreign Trade Route Traffic Carried by Dry Cargo Ships, Calendar Years 1948, 1950, 1951 and 1952* (Washington: December 18, 1953), pt. 2. For 1953, Maritime Administration, Forms 7801-2 as cited in *Study of the Operations of the Maritime Administration . . .*, cited, p. 282-283.

[24] 1952 figures from *Annual Report of the Federal Maritime Board, Maritime Administration, 1952* (Washington: GPO, 1952), p. 64. 1955 figures from Maritime Administration, . . . *Report #300*, for December 31, 1955. This includes 25 vessels engaged in "other U.S. agency operations."

sidy program, (3) one-half of the passenger-combination foreign trade merchant marine requires subsidy support, and (4) the currently active merchant marine is smaller than the minimum recommended by the Department of Defense.

Before rendering final judgment on the efficacy of the operating-differential subsidy program, three other items deserve attention. Admittedly, none can be considered as a consequence solely of the program. However, an examination of each will be informative. The three are (1) the percentage of water-borne foreign trade carried in American-flag vessels, (2) the profits of subsidized companies as compared with non-subsidized operators, and (3) the cost of the operating-differential subsidy scheme.

Share of trade

The reader will recall that, according to the 1936 Act, one of the objectives of United States maritime policy is to have a merchant marine "sufficient to carry . . . a substantial portion of the water-borne export and import commerce of the United States and to provide shipping service on all routes essential for maintaining the flow of such . . . foreign water-borne commerce at all times." Over the years, industry spokesmen and others have informally defined a "substantial portion" as at least half of the commerce.[25] This view seems also to have been shared by many government officials who were highly placed in matters of maritime policy, though there is no formal sanction for it.

Our evidence suggests that on the essential trade routes the share of cargoes carried by American-flag vessels not only failed to reach fifty per cent, but declined markedly during the period 1948-53. This is shown in Table 10. Unfortu-

[25] For example, Maitland S. Pennington, Vice President, Pacific Transport Lines, made the following statement to the Magnuson Committee: "The term 'a substantial portion' has generally been recognized as meaning at least 50 per cent. This is, of course, an over-all percentage. It cannot be achieved on some trade routes but may be exceeded on other trade routes so as to bring about a general over-all accomplishment of the goal." (U.S. Senate, *Merchant Marine Study and Investigation* [*Government Aid to Shipping*], Hearings on S. Res. 50, Subcommittee of the Committee on Interstate and Foreign Commerce, 81st Cong., 2d sess. [Washington: GPO, 1950], pt. 7, p. 1636.)

nately there are no precisely camparable data for earlier or later years. However, there is little doubt that since the end of World War II the portion of United States foreign trade dry cargoes moving aboard American-flag vessels has been declining. During 1954, about 26 per cent of the dry-cargo *ocean-borne* foreign trade was lifted by United States-flag ships. For 1955 the figure was 23 per cent. This compares with 66 per cent in 1946. In 1938 it was also 26 per cent.[26] However, though the *share* has dropped to near prewar levels, the absolute volume carried by the American merchant marine will probably remain substantially above what it was prewar. Although the operating-differential subsidy program is not the only one affecting operations in the foreign trade of the United States, it is clear from the data presented thus far that the aid given to American shipping companies has not helped to increase their share of postwar cargoes. It may have arrested the decline that was taking place before the war. We cannot be sure.

From the foregoing analysis we can conclude that United States shipping policy has not succeeded in enabling operators generally to retain a "substantial portion" of the available foreign commerce. Yet there is some additional evidence which indicates that the subsidization of *liner* operators may have been quite helpful to them. They have consistently captured a higher percentage of foreign trade cargoes than have all United States operators (liner and non-liner) combined, as the following figures show:[27]

[26] 1954 figure from U.S. Department of Commerce, Bureau of the Census, "United States Water-borne Foreign Trade," *Summary Report FT 985* (Washington: June 24, 1955), p. 10. For 1946 and 1938, U.S. Maritime Commission, Research Division, *U.S. Foreign Trade Route Traffic—1946*, prepared by W. G. McLennan (Washington: June, 1947). 1955 figure from Bureau of the Census, "Water-Borne Foreign Trade Statistics," monthly issues.

[27] Liner data for 1938 and 1948 are from U.S. House of Representatives, *Long Range Shipping Bill*, Hearings on S. 241, Committee on Merchant Marine and Fisheries, 82d Cong., 2d sess. (Washington: GPO, 1952), p. 470-472. Liner statistics for 1950-52 computed from U.S. Department of Commerce, Bureau of the Census, "Water-Borne Trade by Trade Area," *Summary Report FT 973* (Washington: Nov. 16, 1951, June 17, 1952), Tables 1 and 3; U. S. Department of Commerce, Bureau of the Census, "Water-Borne Foreign Trade Statistics," *Summary Report FT 985* (Washington: Jan. 4, 1954), Tables 3 and 4. For 1953-54, *Summary Report 985,* cited, (Washington: June 15, 1954 and June 24, 1955), p. 9 and 10 respectively.

	1938	1948	1950-52	1953-54
Per cent of U.S. dry-cargo foreign trade carried by U.S. vessels	26	47[a]	35	26
Per cent of U.S. liner-cargo foreign trade carried by U.S. liners	37[b]	55[b]	45	37

Notes: [a] On essential trade routes this figure was 49 per cent.
[b] Trade on essential routes.

Clearly, subsidies were not alone responsible for the better record of the liner operators. Nor were these subventions the only factor in the better showing of liners on essential trade routes. After all, the essential trade routes include those having the greatest traffic. On these routes, the regularly scheduled sailings that liners provide offer the best way to attract cargoes. Subsidies, nevertheless, must be given some credit for the showing of American-flag liners. They enabled the operators to offer the service. Without subsidy the number of sailings on these routes would have been smaller. The superior performance of American-flag liners on essential trade routes (the only routes served by subsidized operators) suggests that the operating-differential subsidy was undoubtedly an important element in their success.

Given the percentage of liner foreign trade dry cargoes handled by United States-flag liners, it seems fair to say that they carry a *fairly* "substantial portion" of *this* traffic. A combination of subsidies and other policies has contributed to this result. Since the United States merchant marine's share of all foreign trade dry cargoes is well below the liners' share on both essential and all trade routes, it is valid to contend that the absence of subsidies or equivalent aid is in part responsible for this result. Therefore, though we lack (and indeed can never obtain) clear proof of the effectiveness of the operating-differential subsidy scheme, we can conclude that it is helpful to American-flag operators.

Alternatively we can say that the reasons for the failure of the American merchant marine to fulfill the commercial and military goals set in the Merchant Marine Act, 1936, must be sought largely outside liner operations. This does not mean that liner operations should not be expanded. Perhaps they can be.

Profits

In view of the findings regarding cargoes lifted by liners, it is not surprising that subsidized operators appear to have made higher profits (as a ratio to net worth) than their unsubsidized United States-flag competitors. The figures in Table 11, should be accepted with at least four reservations in mind. First, the period covered is short and does not include recent years. Second, the number of nonsubsidized operators reporting earnings varied from year to year. Third, the profits of

Table 11

COMPARISON OF RATE OF RETURN ON NET WORTH OF
SUBSIDIZED CONTRACTORS AND 16 NONSUBSIDIZED
OPERATORS, 1946-51

(Per cent)[a]

Year	Subsidized Companies			Nonsubsidized Companies[b]
	Total	Before Subsidy	Net Subsidy	
1946	19.5	19.5	—	9.2
1947	27.1	25.8	1.3	13.0
1948	14.7	10.0	4.7	3.3
1949	14.8	7.0	7.8	8.6
1950	10.1	−.6	10.7	10.8
1951	15.7	7.3	8.4	18.3
Average 1946-51	16.5	10.5	6.0	10.7

Notes: [a] Percentage of operating earnings (exclusive of capital gains) to average of net worth at beginning and end of year. Earnings of subsidized lines are after estimated recapture accrual. Percentages are before taxes.

[b] Nonsubsidized operators include: Alcoa S. S. Co., Inc., American Hawaiian S. S. Co., Arrow S. S. Co., A. H. Bull S. S. Co. and subsidiaries, Isbrandtsen Co., Isthmian S. S. Co., Matson Navigation Co., Pacific Far East Line, Pope & Talbot, South Atlantic S. S. Lines, Standard Fruit & S. S. Co., States Marine Corp. of Delaware, States Marine Corp. (N.Y.), Victory Carriers, Waterman S. S. Co. Reports are available for 12 of these companies in 1946 and for 14 companies in 1947 and 1948.

Source: Reports to Maritime Administration as reported in *Communication from the President*, cited, p. 145.

subsidized operators are in part estimated because the amounts of subsidy to be recaptured cannot be finally determined until the expiration of the subsidy contract. Fourth, the earnings of some of the nonsubsidized companies include an "appreciable amount of income from other than shipping operations." Nevertheless, the figures are instructive.

The Treasury Department noted that the federal tax liabilities of these two groups of operators differed. Federal taxes took about 46 per cent of the operating profits of the nonsubsidized companies as compared with 26 per cent of the subsidized during 1946-51. This meant that after taxes the nonsubsidized earned 5.7 per cent on their net worth while the subsidized averaged 12.3 per cent. However, not all the difference should be ascribed to benefits under the operating-differential subsidy program.[28] In an earlier report the Treasury Department found that between 1937 and 1948 the subsidized lines' profits averaged 19.8 per cent of net worth while the nonsubsidized companies averaged 17.4 per cent. As Figure 5 indicates, during some periods nonsubsidized lines

Figure 5
RATIO OF PROFITS TO NET WORTH (BEFORE TAXES)
SUBSIDIZED AND NONSUBSIDIZED UNITED STATES-
FLAG LINES, 1937-49

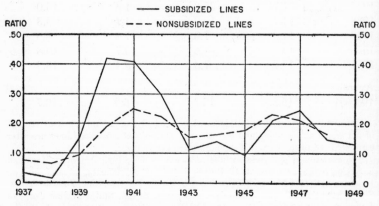

Source: "Scope and Effect of Tax Benefits Provided in the Maritime Industry" (A report of the Treasury), Exhibit B as reproduced in U.S. Senate, *Long Range Shipping Bill*, cited, p. 65-67.

[28] *Communication from the President*, cited, p. 145.

earned larger profits than their subsidized competitors. Thus, though the 1946-51 figures show that the subsidized operators were ahead on profits, this should not be taken to mean that they will always lead.

In 1946-51 the subsidized operators paid out about one-third of their net profits in dividends as compared with nearly one-half by the nonsubsidized. As a result of these differing policies and experiences the net worth of the subsidized companies increased by nearly 60 per cent from 1946 to 1951. while that of the nonsubsidized operators rose by only 20 per cent.[29]

One further observation regarding the "profitability" of the operating-differential subsidy is in order. The 1946-51 figures in Table 11 show that the average difference in net returns during the six-year span was largely attributable to the net subsidy payment (subsidy after estimated recapture). This finding warrants the inference that the subsidized lines have derived financial advantage over their nonsubsidized rivals. A continuation of their relatively stronger position may adversely affect the competitive position of the nonsubsidized operators. Eventually this could lead to a verification of the old contention that the effect of subsidy is to make more subsidy necessary.

The cost of subsidies

One of the advantages claimed for subsidies over indirect support is that the cost to the government and hence to the people can be easily computed. This is not entirely true as regards operating-differential subsidies. The figure is elusive. It can be accurately calculated only at the end of the contract period and after the amount of recapture has been determined. Most contracts run for ten years. Meanwhile recapture must be estimated. Until the amount of recapture is known, the cost of operating-differential subsidies can only be estimated. With these warnings in mind, let us look at the figures.

According to the 1952 *Annual Report* of the Maritime Administration, the estimated cost of the operating-differential subsidy program at the end of the first recapture period (con-

[29] Same.

tracts expiring from 1942 to 1950) was $21 million.[30] Subsidies were suspended during World War II (1943-46) and resumed in 1947. The total estimated accrual of operating-differential subsidies for the prewar and postwar years falling within the contract periods ending in 1950 or earlier amounted to about $70 million. Thus $49 million represents the estimated recapture.

The Maritime Administration has estimated the annual subsidy payable after deducting estimated recapture as follows:[31]

1947	$ 4.1 million
1948	17.7 million
1949	28.7 million
1950	48.3 million
1951	43.2 million
1952	61.1 million
1953	63.0 million
1954	61.6 million

Certainly these outlays do not bulk large in the total of government expenditures. Nor are they very impressive when compared with the vessel-operating expenses and revenues of the subsidized companies. In 1951, for example, the combined income statement of the subsidized lines revealed that net operating-differential subsidy receipts (after estimated recapture) equalled 8.2 per cent of vessel-operating revenue and 10.0 per cent of vessel-operating expense.[32] However, when compared with profits from shipping operations, the amount of subsidy becomes quite impressive. The subsidized com-

[30] *Annual Report,* cited, p. 63.

[31] U. S. House of Representatives, *Departments of State, Justice, and Commerce Appropriations for 1955,* Hearings Before the Subcommittee of the Committee on Appropriations, 83rd Cong., 2d sess. (Washington, GPO, 1954), p. 384. These figures total $327.7 million for eight years— roughly $40 million annually. A more recent estimate by the Maritime Administration shows a total of $550 million for the period January 1, 1947 to June 30, 1956, an annual average of $57.9 million. This rise is attributable to revised estimates of recapture and payment accruals. See U.S. House of Representatives, *Department of Commerce and Related Agencies Appropriations for 1956,* Hearings Before a Sub-committee of the Committee on Appropriations, 84th Cong., 1st sess. (Washington: GPO, 1955), p. 441.

[32] Computed from figures above and those appearing in the *Annual Report of the Federal Maritime Board, Maritime Administration, 1952,* cited. The 1954 rather than the 1952 estimate of the subsidy has been used on the grounds that it is probably more accurate.

panies reported net profits (before taxes) of $70.3 million
($76.0 million if the revised subsidy figure is used). The
operating-differential subsidy amounted to 57 per cent of
the $76 million net profit from shipping operations in 1951.[33]

The small ratio of operating-differential subsidies to vessel-
operating expense should dispel the commonly held belief that
American-flag vessel operators are grossly inefficient. Despite
labor costs that are about three times higher than their foreign-
flag competitors', apparently the American operators can compete successfully with a rather modest subsidy. There are, of
course, other government aids to shipping such as cargo
preferences that help to make this modest subsidy adequate.

We must, however, guard against the complacent acceptance of the operating-differential subsidy that could result
from focussing attention primarily on the ratio of the subsidy
to operating expense. Any industry dependent upon direct
subsidy for half of its profits can hardly expect to escape the
searchlight of critical inquiry. Such an industry, no matter how
small, may rightly be accused of being a public charge. Certain questions should be asked. After all, the relative smallness
of a subsidy is no justification for its continuation. Alternatives
should be explored.

COMPARATIVE WAGE COSTS

Without operating-differential subsidies many ships in the
foreign trade merchant marine of the United States would be
unable to continue sailing. The differences between foreign-
flag and American-flag wage costs are substantial. This is true
even after allowing for a large margin of error in the notori-
ously treacherous field of international cost comparisons.

Over the years these cost comparisons have told the same
dismal story from the American operator's point of view. For
1949, the Maritime Commission found that the total vessel

[33] Some readers may object to the revised profit figure used. Only the
amount of subsidy was changed. However, other adjustments might well
increase the net profit. Even using the 1951 estimate of net operating-differential subsidy and net profits, the subsidy amounted to 53 per cent of
the net profits. It is therefore safe to state that operating-differential subsidies equalled about one-half of the subsidized companies' net profits
before taxes.

Table 12

COMPARISON OF SELECTED OPERATING EXPENSES OF UNITED STATES AND FOREIGN-FLAG VESSELS, 1953

Countries	Wages			Subsistence			Stores		Maintenance and repair	
	Crew	Monthly costs	Differential	Crew	Ship-day costs	Differential	Costs	Differential	Costs	Differential
			Per cent			Per cent				Per cent
United States	48	$29,426	—	48	$81.60	—	$71,294	—	$65,403	—
Denmark	43	7,990	72.8	43	71.81	12.0	69,795	2.1	30,403	53.5
France	47	10,274	65.1	47	60.50	13.6	71,533	(.34)	37,680	42.4
Italy	41	7,713	73.8	41	41.82	48.7	91,722	(28.7)	32,753	49.9
Japan	56	6,273	78.7	56	30.24	62.9	78,202	(9.7)	33,850	48.2
Netherlands	55	7,567	74.3	55	58.30	28.6	64,711	9.2	29,641	54.7
Norway	43	7,145	75.7	43	68.80	15.7	63,427	11.0	38,941	40.5
United Kingdom:										
White crew	54	6,444	78.1	54	63.72	21.9	63,111	11.5	27,440	58.0
Mixed crew	80	5,541	81.2	80	60.80	25.5	63,111	11.5	27,440	58.0

Source: Division of Operating Costs, Office of Government Aid, Maritime Administration, as cited in *Study of the Operations of the Maritime Administration and the Federal Maritime Board*, cited, p. 281.

operating expense for a fifty-day voyage of a foreign-flag Liberty ship was from about one-third to one-half of the total for a United States-flag Liberty.[34] Table 12 shows comparative costs as estimated by the Maritime Commission for 1953. Note that the wages of crews aboard United States-flag vessels were three to five times higher than they were on the foreign-flag vessels.

The *Murray Report* noted that about 80 per cent of the operating-differential subsidy payments was required to overcome the wage cost handicap of American-flag operators.[35] The *Report* also states that the monthly wage costs of operating a C-2 type vessel under the United States-flag had increased by 384 per cent between 1937 and 1952. The breakdown of these increases is shown in Table 13. Increased manning scales, shorter work week before overtime, and fringe items such as vacation pay, welfare, and pension plans pushed the wage costs up. Foreign-flag operators, though experiencing some wage cost increases, did not fare nearly so badly as their United States rivals.

The *Murray Report* found that in 1951 the differences in wage costs between American- and foreign-flag vessels on "several subsidized . . . trade routes" amounted to 71 per cent of the Americans' wage costs. The differential increased steadily from a low of 54 per cent in 1948. The *Report* pointed out that one of the principal reasons for the large differential was the freedom of many foreign-flag operators to hire non-nationals as seamen. This enabled them to buy their labor in the cheapest market.[36]

At present the prospects for a competitively significant reduction in American-flag wage costs are dim indeed. The unions representing the shipboard employees are strong. They will not readily give up any of the gains of the past twenty years. Employers are no doubt also better organized than before World War II. However, the pressure of competition and the desire to avoid immediate losses, coupled with the knowledge that wage differences will be subsidized, certainly

[34] *A Study of Tramp Shipping Under the American Flag*, A report of the Tramp Shipping Committee, United States Maritime Commission (Washington: August 9, 1949), Table 3.
[35] P. 52.
[36] P. 54.

Table 13

MONTHLY WAGE COSTS FOR A TYPICAL UNITED STATES-FLAG
C-2 TYPE VESSEL, 1937 AND 1952

	1937		1952		
	Dollars	Per cent of total	Dollars	Per cent of total	Per cent increase over 1937
Base wages	4,543	91.0	15,736	65.2	246
Overtime	432	8.6	6,264	25.9	1,350
Fringe Items	20	0.4	2,152	8.9	10,660
Totals	4,995	100.0	24,152	100.0	384

Source: U.S. Department of Commerce, *Maritime Subsidy Policy* Washington: April 1954), p. 52.

does not strengthen their ability to resist union demands for higher wages, better working conditions, and a host of fringe benefits.

These demands in turn reflect wage and employment conditions in other industries in the United States. Many of these industries can afford to pay high wages and still compete effectively with their foreign rivals. High productivity per worker based upon the use of the latest technological advances accounts for this. Ship operators must pay wages equivalent to other American industries or they will be unable to retain or attract the required work force. But the high wages in shipping are not accompanied by sufficient technological superiority to offset lower foreign wages. Under these circumstances, if the United States wants the current or a larger merchant marine in the foreign trade, it must continue to subsidize wage costs. In sum, we cannot look hopefully to a lowering of wage costs as a practicable means to improve the competitive status of the United States foreign trade merchant marine.

CONCLUSIONS

The operating-differential subsidy program has not succeeded in its professed aims. It has failed to provide an all-American merchant marine large enough for defense purposes —according to the estimates of the Department of Defense. The active, foreign trade merchant marine does not carry a "substantial" part of the water-borne foreign commerce of the United States (if 50 per cent is taken as the mathematical equivalent of that adjective).

Still, as a means for insuring the existence of an American-flag merchant marine the operating-differential subsidy has the advantage of being relatively inoffensive. Foreign retaliation is not a great danger, given the current amount of subsidization. Competition, under the conference system, remains undisturbed. The shipper may benefit from the membership of American lines in the conferences. (See Chapter VII.) The rather slight commercial advantages of a national-flag fleet are probably obtained in large part.

If the operating-differential subsidy program were to be enlarged markedly (for instance, by including all vessels in foreign trade—a sort of general navigational bounty) in an effort to reach the national defense goals or to obtain 50 per cent of United States foreign trade cargoes, foreign dissatisfaction with United States shipping policy would grow. If other countries decided to respond in kind, with more subsidies and preferential treatment for their merchant fleets, the result would be an even greater economic surplus of shipping tonnage and an increased burden on the taxpayer.

An alternative means of increasing United States-flag merchant tonnage would be to subsidize intercoastal and coastwise vessel operators. Foreigners, already barred from these routes, would not protest, but the domestic railroad and trucking industries would, probably successfully. Still, there is undoubtedly a good case for the view that shipping subsidies in the coastal trades would bolster national defense. The ships attracted into the trades would expand the total United States fleet and would be easily available in wartime. It is possible, however, that if the coastal fleet were to be greatly expanded and if it did obtain a substantial share of domestic cargoes, the withdrawal of this fleet to other areas in time of war might throw an intolerable burden upon the truck and railroad companies. Thus the gain in shipping might be more than offset by the loss in domestic land transport. Of course, it is also possible, and perhaps more likely, that there could be a considerable expansion in coastal shipping without the danger of these potential adverse effects upon railroads and trucks. If on further examination this proved to be a sound assumption, and foreign ships continued to be excluded from the coastal trade, then a question would arise whether national defense considerations are really given the greatest weight in determining national shipping policy.

Granting that the expansion of operating-differential subsidies to include domestic operators is not likely and that extending their coverage in the foreign trade merchant marine leads to international complications, how can the minimum defense merchant marine requirements of the United States be attained?

Much of the world's merchant marine is controlled by nations banded together in NATO for their common defense. If for military reasons the United States needs a larger active merchant fleet than it has, the possibility could be considered of working out arrangements through NATO that would permit this with the smallest possible burden—economic and political—to the alliance. If it were agreed that a larger active merchant fleet were needed, then perhaps some international agreement would be required to prevent a subsidy or shipping-restriction war among the allies. A division of the financial burden of the surplus fleet might be part of such an agreement. Perhaps in the light of NATO discussions the United States would find that arrangements could be made with other shipping nations that would make it safe to reduce the size of the active merchant fleet considered necessary for national defense. There might be a number of other possibilities, but they remain to be explored. There is a Planning Board for Ocean Shipping under NATO. It has worked out arrangements for the pooling of merchant shipping in time of war and for the machinery of interallied control.[37] It does not seem to have dealt with the problem of pooling the burden of maritime preparedness for war. Perhaps this is because friction over shipping policy has not recently been troublesome. But it might become so if the United States were to decide it needed a larger active merchant fleet.

Secretary of State John Foster Dulles said in his address to the Council on Foreign Relations on January 12, 1954:

[37] Lord Ismay, *NATO: The First Five Years, 1949-1954*, (Paris, North Atlantic Treaty Organization, 1954), p. 145-6.

We need allies and collective security. Our purpose is to make these relations more effective, less costly. This can be done by placing more reliance on deterrent power, and less dependence on local defensive power.

This is accepted practice so far as local communities are concerned. We keep locks on our doors; but we do not have an armed guard in every home. We rely principally on a community security system so well equipped to punish any who break and steal that, in fact, would-be aggressors are generally deterred. That is the modern way of getting maximum protection at a bearable cost.

If these principles were applied to American shipping policy —insofar as it is an adjunct of military policy—some re-examination of present American assumptions would seem in order. Before additional subsidies or other types of aid are considered to bring the active United States fleet up to the levels set by the military, it would be well for those responsible for shipping policy to remember that coordination of national shipping policies of the western bloc as well as coordination of their national air, land, and naval plans and forces could be of substantial importance to the alliance, especially in peacetime.

V

CARGO PREFERENCES

No matter what the security size of the United States fleet should be, however, the device of cargo preferences is a highly undesirable means of achieving it.

Report to the President on Foreign Economic Policies ("Gray Report"), p. 89 (1950).

The Commission recommends that the statutory provisions requiring use of United States vessels for shipments financed by loans and grants of the United States Government and its agencies be repealed and that support sufficient to maintain a merchant marine adequate to our national defense requirements be provided by direct means, much as those provided for under the Merchant Marine Shipping Act of 1936.

Commission on Foreign Economic Policy, *Report to the President and the Congress*, p. 69. (1954).

THE POLICY

ON AUGUST 26, 1954 the President approved Public Law 664, an amendment to the Merchant Marine Act, 1936. It provides that "whenever the United States shall procure, contract for, or otherwise obtain for its own account, or shall furnish to or for the account of any foreign nation without provision for reimbursement, any equipment, materials, or commodities, within or without the United States, or shall advance funds or credits or guarantee the convertibility of foreign currencies in connection with furnishing of such equipment, materials, or commodities, the appropriate agency or agencies shall take such steps as may be necessary and prac-

ticable to assure that at least 50 per centum of the gross tonnage of such equipment, materials, or commodities (computed
separately for dry bulk carriers, dry cargo liners, and tankers),
which may be transported on ocean vessels shall be transported on privately owned United States-flag commercial
vessels to the extent such vessels are available at fair and
reasonable rates for United States-flag commercial vessels, in
such manner as will insure a fair and reasonable participation
of United States-flag commercial vessels in such cargoes by
geographic areas. . . ."

These provisions may be waived if the Congress, the President or the Secretary of State declares that an emergency
requires this. The law does not apply to cargoes carried by
the Panama Canal Company (United States government-
owned). Public Resolution No. 17 of 1934, concerning cargo
preferences related to Export-Import Bank loans, is unaffected
by the law. (See below.)

Clearly, Congress and the President ignored the recommendations of the Gray and Randall groups. There is, however,
considerable precedent for their action. Public Law 664
merely makes permanent provisions for cargo preference previously embodied in a variety of temporary legislation govern-
ing foreign aid and economic assistance. It is perhaps a
"natural" descendant of an act passed by Congress in 1904.
This provides that only United States-flag vessels (publicly
or privately owned) shall be used in "the transportation by
sea of coal, provisions, fodder, or supplies of any description
purchased pursuant to law, for the use of the Army or
Navy." [1] However, if the rates are "excessive and unreasonable," other vessels may be used.

In 1934, Congress passed Public Resolution No. 17 declaring
that in "any loans made by the Reconstruction Finance Cor-
poration or any other instrumentality of the Government to
foster the exporting of agricultural or other products, provision shall be made that such products shall be carried exclusively in vessels of the United States." Again exceptions can

---

[1] 33 *U. S. Statutes at Large* (1905), p. 518. With certain exceptions, employees of the United States government travelling on official business must,
in accordance with Section 901 of the Merchant Marine Act, 1936, travel
on United States-flag Vessels.

be made if the Maritime Administration certifies that "vessels of the United States are not available in sufficient numbers, or in sufficient tonnage capacity, or on necessary sailing schedule, or at reasonable rates."[2] In practice this has meant a roughly 50-50 division of these cargoes between United States-flag vessels and those designated by the loan-recipient.

The prevailing view has been that this 50-50 division is "fair" unless the borrowing country discriminates against American-flag companies. If it does, the United States government can bargain for a removal of the discrimination by threatening to invoke the 100 per cent provision of Public Resolution 17. Third countries, not involved in borrowing from the Export-Import Bank, have protested that this 50-50 policy discriminates against them since in practice the cargoes are shipped aboard vessels of the United States and the borrowing country only.

Cargo preference, argue its proponents, has long been a part of United States shipping policy, so why the strong opposition from the Gray and Randall groups, and many others? The answer lies in its greater importance today. Until the advent of the huge foreign aid programs and large-scale, worldwide military commitments, cargo preference applied to a relatively small portion of United States ocean-borne foreign commerce. Now, this is no longer true.

The stakes are high. Government-financed cargoes are substantial. Foreign and domestic shipping companies are fully aware of their importance and profitability. Governments, too, are vitally concerned. In the postwar years the United States government has urgently advocated the reduction of trade barriers and the removal of exchange restrictions. Though much has been accomplished, much remains to be done. Some foreign governments, reluctant to reduce their restrictions further, are quick to point out what they consider discriminatory acts by the United States. The United States, aware of the military importance of a large merchant marine, defends cargo preference as a way of achieving this end. As a result, cargo preference has become controversial both domestically and internationally.

[2] 48 *U. S. Statutes at Large* (1935), p. 500.

THE IMPORTANCE OF CARGO PREFERENCES

Advocates of the 50 per cent law have stressed its limited applicability. The Randall Commission, while recommending against the law, stated that the "importance of the matter will become more psychological than material as the scale of foreign aid declines."[3] This emphasis fails to direct attention to the importance of aid cargoes to the United States merchant marine. Both the advocates and the opponents of cargo preference have at times appeared to be arguing about a "fringe benefit." The facts show that at times the fringe was indeed a wide border.

Government-financed cargoes subject to cargo-preference rulings fall into four categories: (1) supplies and materiel for United States armed forces overseas, (2) military aid to allies, (3) economic assistance cargoes under the International Cooperation Administration (and its predecessors), and (4) shipments under Export-Import Bank loans.

With only minor exceptions (e.g. the use of foreign-flag vessels equipped with heavy lift gear) United States armed forces shipments are carried in American-flag ships both governmentally and privately owned. Military aid cargoes are subject to the 50-50 law. Currently, the Military Sea Transportation Service and the privately-owned United States merchant marine as well as foreign-flag vessels participate in lifting these cargoes. Economic aid shipments are nearly equally divided between United States and foreign shipping companies.

Unfortunately it is not possible to obtain a firm figure showing the amounts of cargo tonnage and dollar receipts obtained by American shipping companies from the government. Nevertheless, estimates can be made. If these estimates are used cautiously (i.e., allowing for a substantial margin of error), they can be taken to assess the importance of cargo preference to the United States merchant marine and its foreign competitors.

For the period 1952-54 I estimate that United States-flag vessels (including Department of Defense-controlled vessels lifting foreign aid cargoes but excluding these vessels when

[3] Commission on Foreign Economic Policy, *Report to the President and the Congress* (Washington: GPO, 1954), p. 69.

carrying troop-support cargoes) lifted about 30.5 million long tons of dry cargoes per year in the foreign export trade of the United States. Of this amount, approximately 1.3 million tons were attributable to aid shipments controlled by the Defense Department and 2.6 million tons to other foreign aid operations. About 9.3 million tons were troop-support cargoes handled for the Military Sea Transportation Service. If these estimates are correct, cargo preferences gave the United States dry-cargo, foreign trade merchant fleet about 13.2 million tons of cargoes per year during these three years, or more than two-fifths of its out-bound business.[4]

[4] These figures were derived as follows:

		(million long tons)
(1) Aid shipments controlled by Department of Defense and "special category" items		1.3
(2) Total foreign aid shipments	3.9	
(3) *minus* (1)	1.3	
(4) *Leaving* Other foreign aid shipments		2.6
(5) MSTS dry cargoes lifted by commercial vessels	10.6	
(6) *minus* (1)	1.3	
(7) *leaving* Other MSTS cargoes		9.3
(8) Total aid cargoes carried by commercial vessels		13.2
(9) Commercial cargoes		17.3
(10) Total dry cargo carried by commercial vessels		30.5

As indicated in the text, these figures must be used with caution. Department of Defense-controlled aid shipments include cargoes handled by MSTS vessels and regular commercial vessels. "Special category" items are strategically important and hence added to the category on line (2) for security reasons. They are carried by both private and other vessels. Thus the figure of 1.3 million long tons somewhat overstates the cargoes carried by the private merchant marine.

Item (1) had to be subtracted from both (2) and (5) because the data as given in the sources included the shipments carried in vessels controlled by the Department of Defense. However, the results are approximate. Item (8) includes special category items and aid cargoes carried by the MSTS nucleus fleet as well as by private vessels.

All MSTS shipments have been assumed to be outbound and handled by American-flag operators. Fiscal year data for MSTS and ICA average to obtain estimate of calendar years. MSTS measurement tons converted to long tons by method described on p. 172, below.

Sources: United States exports of domestic and foreign merchandise lifted by United States-flag dry cargo vessels,—U.S. Department of Commerce, Bureau of the Census, "United States Water-Borne Foreign Trade," *Summary Report FT 985* (Washington: June 15, 1954. June 24, 1955).

MSTS cargoes handled by commercial vessels,—MSTS, *Financial and Statistical Report* as transcribed for the author by Marie T. Van Horn of the MSTS and letter to author from H. E. Cole, MSTS, December 15, 1955.

From April 3, 1948 to June 30, 1954, the International Cooperation Administration and its predecessors paid a little over $1 billion for ocean freight services. Operators of United States-flag vessels received about $750 million of this total for transporting nearly 48 million long tons of cargoes—about 56 per cent of the shipments made.[5] In addition, the MSTS paid "commercial interests" $1.59 billion from fiscal 1951 through fiscal 1954[6] These figures alone should convince the skeptical that cargo preference is very important to the ship

[4] (cont.) Foreign aid shipments,—ICA, *Shipments on American Flag Vessels*, Special Report (Washington: July 1955), and letter to the author from A. G. Syran, ICA, October 11, 1955.

The calculations are based upon information in the Bureau of the Census, *Summary Report #985*, cited, and a letter to the author from J. Edward Ely, Chief, Foreign Trade Division, Bureau of the Census, April 4, 1955. Time has not permitted me to reconcile my estimates with those recently made by the Department of Commerce in *A Review of Direct and Indirect Types of Maritime Subsidies With Special Reference to Cargo Preference Aid* (Washington: Author, April 1956). My figures cover the period 1952-54, while its apply to 1953-54. The Department has included only civilian aid cargoes while I have tried to estimate military shipments as well. Information provided in *A Review* . . . suggests that I have understated the magnitude of civilian aid cargoes since I have not included figures for some items. For liner liftings of United States-flag dry-cargo exports alone, the Department estimated that 19.4 per cent consisted of civilian aid cargoes. My figure for *all* United States-flag dry-cargo exports is 18.4 per cent. However, combining the Department's tramp and liner data yields 33.6 per cent as the share of dry-cargo exports attributable to civilian aid programs. (See *A Review* . . ., p. 60-62.) Thus my figure of roughly 40 per cent for civilian plus military aid shipments *may* be conservative.

Nevertheless, both sets of figures indicate that as a percentage of United States-flag dry-cargo exports, aid cargoes were indeed significant between 1952 and 1954. Fairness demands that we recognize that aid cargoes were and are a significantly smaller percentage of total dry-cargo exports (about 16.3 per cent according to the *Review* . . ., p. 58) or any other more inclusive cargo tonnage figure. Still, for United States-flag dry-cargo vessels in the foreign trades, aid cargoes have been quite important.

[5] Computed from Foreign Operations Administration, *Allotments, Authorizations and Paid Shipments* (Washington: November 17, 1954), p. 20, 46, 53, 65 and International Cooperation Administration, *Shipments on American Flag Vessels*, cited, p. 1, 37.

[6] From the records of the MSTS as transcribed for the author by J. J. Floyd, and W. C. Willy (letter to author, January 28, 1955) and H. E. Cole (letter to author, October 10, 1955), of the MSTS. These payments cover the following items: (1) cargo—berth terms, space contracts, time charters, general agency agreements through the National Shipping Authority; (2) passengers—space contracts, time charters; and (3) petroleum—voyage charters, contract-operated tankers. A small part of this total covered payments to foreigners for vessels having heavy lift equipment.

operators in the United States. The stakes are well worth striving for and the shipping industry displayed noteworthy cohesion in pushing for permanent cargo-preference legislation.

While it is true that aid shipments have been declining, they are still substantial and military assistance, at least, may remain at an appreciable figure for an indefinite period. Transfers under military grants totalled $4.3, $3.1, and $2.1 billion in 1953, 1954, and 1955 respectively. Nonmilitary grants remained fairly steady at about $1.7 billion annually during these years.[7] Though not all the transactions attributable to the military and civilian grants benefit shipping, a very sizeable portion does. Given the world political and military situation, a sharp reduction in these grants appears unlikely.

Nonsubsidized vessel operators have been especially concerned about the future of cargo-preference legislation. After all, it gives them some assurance of cargoes and represents an indirect subsidy involving none of the obligations imposed upon operators receiving operating-differential subsidies. Unfortunately our data do not permit us to determine how much revenue and cargo the unsubsidized operators gain from the 50-50 legislation. However, the statistics do enable us to gauge the importance of cargo preference to those tramp operators who benefit from it.

Tramps have an advantage in carrying aid cargoes because regular sailing schedules are not of major importance. Some regularly scheduled liner companies chartered vessels for the express purpose of "tramping" aid cargoes. During 1952-54, United States-flag tramps lifted about 9.3 million long tons of cargo annually in the commercial export trade of the United States. In addition they transported roughly 2.4 million tons per year for the ICA. Thus aid shipments provided one-fifth of their total cargoes. Data published by the Department of Commerce while this book was being printed give substantially higher figures for 1953-54. According to these estimates, preferential cargoes—including surplus agricultural products and goods financed by Export-Import Bank loans as well as ICA shipments—accounted for about 78.5 per cent of the

[7] U.S. Department of Commerce, *Survey of Current Business*, March 1955 and 1956, p. 10 and 6, respectively.

export cargoes carried by United States-flag tramps, 60.1 per cent of their import cargoes (primarily strategic materials), and 73.6 per cent of their inbound and outbound cargoes combined. To keep these figures in perspective, we should note that civilian aid cargoes shipped aboard tramps of all flags made up 20.4 per cent of all tramp-cargo exports from the United States during this period and 2.9 per cent of their imports.[8] During the period April 3, 1948-June 30, 1954, American-flag tramps carried about 31 million long tons of aid cargoes—66 per cent of all these shipments made on United States-flag vessels.[9] Given the sometimes narrow profit margins of tramp operations, the absence of preferential, aid-induced, cargoes would no doubt be fatal to many tramp operators.

UNITED STATES TRAMP SHIPPING

Because cargo preferences are so important to tramp operators, we must examine this segment of the industry in more

Table 14

DISTRIBUTION OF MEMBERS OF AMERICAN TRAMP SHIPOWNERS
ASSOCIATION BY DATES OF INCORPORATION

Period	No. of companies incorporated	No. of vessels operated
Before 1941	9	14
1941-45	1	1
1946	1	1
1947	8	9
1948	8	13
1949	8	9
1950	16	20
1951	18	20
1952	1	1
Total, as of July 1953	70	88

Source: U.S. Senate, *Merchant Marine Studies*, cited, p. 368. Compiled from exhibit accompanying testimony of F. Riker Clark, President, American Tramp Shipowners Association.

[8] *A Review* . . . , cited, p. 62. Figures for 1952-54 come from sources cited in note 5 above.
[9] *Shipments on American Flag Vessels*, cited, p. 7.

detail before analyzing the arguments for and against cargo preferences.

The nature of this part of the industry makes it difficult to compile accurate statistics regarding it but the following estimates of American-flag tramp ships in operation give some idea of the postwar evolution.

At the time of this writing there are probably about 75 United States-flag tramp ships, most of them World War II Libertys. In 1948 it was estimated that there were as many as 700 or 800, including vessels chartered to subsidized lines. In 1950 the number was 125 and in July 1953 members of the American Tramp Shipowners Association operated 98 vessels. In April 1954 the president of the Association put the total of the tramp fleet at 125, of which 50 were currently employed. A year later his successor put the number of tramps operating at 75.[10]

There is reason to believe that the present tramp fleet is in good measure a creature of the 50 per cent provision. Congress first approved cargo preference on foreign aid cargoes on April 19, 1949. As Table 14 shows, about three-fifths of the companies in the American Tramp Shipowners Association were incorporated after 1948. In 1953 these new companies

[10] 1948 and 1950: U.S. Senate, *Merchant Marine Study and Investigation*, Hearings Before a Subcommittee of the Committee on Interstate and Foreign Commerce on S. Res. 50, 81st Cong., 2d sess. (Washington: GPO, 1950), p. 1402. Testimony of F. Riker Clark, president, American Tramp Shipowners Association.

1953: U. S. Senate, *Merchant Marine Studies*, Hearings Before a Subcommittee of the Committee on Interstate and Foreign Commerce, 83rd Cong., 1st sess. (Washington: 1953), p. 368; exhibit accompanying testimony of Mr. Clark.

1954: Author's conversation with Mr. Clark, April 9, 1954. A publication of the American Tramp Shipowners Association, *Tramp Shipping and the American Merchant Marine* (New York: Feb. 1954) states member companies "own and operate 108 Liberty ships under the American flag." (p. 10.)

Staff Papers Presented to the Commission of Foreign Economic Policy (Washington: GPO, 1954), p. 547, stated that there were "approximately 160 privately owned American vessels operating in tramp or non-berth service."

1955: U.S. House of Representatives, *Vessel Replacement Program*, Hearings Before the Committee on Merchant Marine and Fisheries on H.R. 4118 and H.R. 5959, 84th Cong., 1st sess. (Washington: GPO, 1955), p. 272; testimony of James B. Stuart, president of the American Shipowners Association.

operated nearly 57 per cent of the ships of the members of the Association.

The growth of tramp shipping after the war was an expected response to the tremendous demand for shipping space for the movement of bulk commodities. Tramps have traditionally filled the need for substantial seasonal and other movements of bulk cargoes. Adhering to no fixed schedules, usually sailing only when fully loaded, they have provided much of the needed flexibility in handling ocean commerce. Rates are determined on a competitive basis in a free market. Like subsidized ships, American tramps have higher operating costs than foreign tramps. Wage costs account for most of the difference. Exclusive of certain outlays for war area bonus, pension and welfare funds, and payroll taxes, the wage payments aboard a United States-flag Liberty have been estimated at about $15,000 per month higher than the salary and wage expenses of foreign-flag Liberties.[11] Nevertheless, in spite of their higher costs, American tramps can compete effectively with foreign tramps so long as rates remain high enough. In passing, we should note that while American tramp ship operators compete among themselves for United States foreign aid cargoes, they need not meet the rates offered by their foreign-flag competitors. The cargo-preference law provides that the rates the American operators may quote, and the United States government may pay, for their share of these cargoes should be "fair and reasonable for United States-flag commercial vessels."

Using the figures in Table 14 once more, an interesting comparison can be made between worldwide tramp rates and the incorporation of tramp shipping companies. Note that 50 per cent of the member companies were incorporated during 1950-52. They operated 41 of the 88 ships. Taking the rates of July-December 1947 as a base of 100, worldwide dry-cargo time charter rates rose from about 63 early in 1950 to a high of 250 late in 1951. Using the same base, trip charter rates moved from 69 to 182 during the same period. By contrast, in December 1953, the time charter rate was down to 65.7 and the trip charter rate stood at 84.4. The rate on coal for shipment from New York to Holland and Belgium provides

[11] *Merchant Marine Studies,* cited, p. 367.

a good example of the fall in a particular rate. In 1951 the rate was $11.50 per ton; in early 1954, $3.95. Further evidence of the fluctuations in rates is seen in the following figures for the week ending April 17, 1954, expressed as percentages of the average levels of 1951 when rates were high: coal, 37.0; grain, 48.8; sugar, 47.3; ore, 73.3; lumber, 41.6; general freight, 44.6. The time charter indexes in April 1954 were: less than one month, 35.3; 1 to 2 months, 34.8; 2 to 3 months, 37.0; over 6 months, 46.1.[12]

Inevitably in a free market some operators will occasionally be forced out of business. New ones will come in when rates are attractive. Only the best or the luckiest can survive year after year. Before World War II there was virtually no United States-flag tramp fleet. Foreign-flag tramp fleets declined in importance relative to liners.[13] The demand for shipping services has been gradually shifting away from irregular tramps to regularly scheduled liners. Bulk carryings, though substantial, are in many instances handled by specially designed industrial carriers. From the long-run view, then, the postwar-born American tramp fleet appears to be bucking increased foreign competition and perhaps a long-term tendency away from the use of tramp services as well.

If American-flag tramp ships were to be forced off the seas by the pressure of high costs upon low freight rates, American shippers would not be deprived of tramp services. Foreign-flag tramps would continue to operate. Given the character of the market for tramp shipping services there is

[12] Index figures for 1951 and 1953 are from chart and table prepared by the *Norwegian Shipping News* as reproduced in *The Journal of Commerce*, January 20, 1954. Coal rates are from the same article. Later figures, from the *North Atlantic Exchange Weekly Newsletter*, no. 41 (New York: Maritime Research, April 17, 1954).

[13] According to one estimate the ratio of tramp tonnage to aggregate tonnage of all types fell from .46 in 1914 to .33 in 1933. (Osborne Mance, *International Sea Transport* [London: Oxford University Press, 1945], p. 68.) Daniel Marx, Jr. in his *International Shipping Cartels . . .* (Princeton: Princeton University Press, 1953) noted (p. 227) that estimates such as Mance's based upon an earlier work by Franz Lohse, *Die Entwicklung der Trampschiffahrt in der Nachkriegszeit* (1934), had been challenged. However, he notes that there is reliable evidence that relative to liners tramp shipping declined slightly between 1914 and 1929 and then increased somewhat until 1936. Marx also indicates that since World War II tramp shipping appears to have declined. There is thus reason to believe that the long-term trend is against tramp operators generally.

little likelihood that American shippers would be the victims of discrimination by the tramp operators. Competition is keen among tramp vessel operators. True, rates would rise sharply under impetus of increased demand. This would happen even if United States-flag tramps were available. It is the possibility of occasional high rates that keeps some operators from leaving the industry during periods of low rates and scarce cargoes. We can safely conclude that American shippers would not be adversely affected by the disappearance of the United State-flag tramp fleet.

In contrast, some United States-flag tramp shipowners stand to lose substantially if the decision of the free market decrees their demise. This would indeed be unfortunate for them. However, with the story of tramp shipping between the wars before them they cannot claim that the risks of engaging in this business were unknown to them. And even if they could, it would be irrelevant. During the early postwar years the probability of making profits was great. Unfortunately the probability of *ultimate* failure and loss appears greater. Reasonable men can ask whether the tramp operator who eventually loses money while seeking the quick profits from postwar aid cargoes and the shortage of tonnage deserves any more public assistance than the Christmas tree seller left with a large stock of trees and a net loss the day after Christmas. The market has treated each impersonally. Why then should the tramp operator claim the right to public aid?

The answer of course is that he, too, claims to make an important contribution to national defense. The appraisal of this claim leads us directly into the first of the major arguments advanced in favor of cargo preferences.

THE PROS AND CONS OF CARGO PREFERENCE

Knowledge of the financial importance of the 50-50 and other preference laws and administrative regulations to the vessel operators tends to induce mental reservations about arguments advanced by the shipping industry that invoke the "public interest" as a justification for cargo-preference laws. With this in mind, let us examine some of the arguments in favor of cargo preferences.

The national defense argument

Spokesmen for the tramp shipping group contend that tramp tonnage contributes to national defense. Cargo preference, according to these spokesmen, is a legitimate means of aiding this otherwise unsupported fleet. Is this argument sufficiently powerful to warrant approval of the 50 per cent provision?

Certainly the existence of an active tramp fleet is useful to the military. Furthermore, tramp operators may have experience that gives them an edge over the liner operators in their usefulness to the armed forces. They are accustomed to irregular sailings to any port in the world. Their crews have wide experience on a variety of trade routes. Their administrative organization is flexible and accustomed to quick adjustment to changing conditions. We should note that all these attributes are not possessed exclusively by tramp operators. Many liner companies share them as well.

Against these "national defense advantages" of a United States-flag tramp fleet must be set certain important disadvantages. Most important of all, this fleet consists mainly of middle-aged Liberty ships built during World War II. They are a modified version of a British ship specifically designed for tramp operations. Relative to their length and beam they have large deadweight tonnage capacity (10,800), shallow draft (27 ft. 10 in. when loaded) and simple propulsion equipment. They are excellent vessels for tramping. For military operations during war they are too slow. Their top speed is about 10 knots per hour; this means that they must travel in convoys—and dangerously slow ones at that. Though these ships would undoubtedly be called to military duty should the United States become involved in a large-scale war, this would be through necessity and not choice. And they could just as well be reactivated from the government reserve fleets, if necessary.[14]

Without considerable financial support from the government, tramp operators will not be able to replace their ships

[14] There are about 1,500 Libertys in the 2,000-ship Maritime Administration reserve fleet at anchorages on the Atlantic, Gulf, and Pacific coasts, (See American Bureau of Shipping, *The Bulletin* [New York], monthly.)

when they wear out. Even the liner companies receiving operating-differential subsidies may find this difficult. And the latter have been forced by law to maintain what originally appeared to be adequate depreciation reserves. Furthermore, their competitive disadvantage has not been as great as that of the tramp operators. It may prove to be cheaper to modernize the reserve Libertys than to devise cargo-preference and other schemes to keep the middle-aged, obsolete tramp fleet in operation.[15]

Perhaps the greatest disadvantage of supporting the American-flag tramp fleet, by cargo preferences or otherwise, is that it tends to perpetuate a surplus of tonnage in operation. This is particularly unfortunate as regards tramp vessels because this segment of the merchant marine is supposed to be flexible. Its function is to stand ready to handle peak loads and to lay up when cargoes are scarce. It is a risky business with rewards to the clever and lucky. Clearly, the cost differential between American and foreign operators puts the former at a serious, if not fatal, disadvantage during periods of depressed rates. If private foreign companies can provide the necessary flexibility in tonnage, there is no reason to burden the American taxpayer to support an industry economically unjustifiable and militarily inefficient. The greater this type of support, the larger this fleet will tend to become and the more assistance it will need.

Suppose, however, that military necessity dictates that a large tramp fleet be on the seas at all times. This could mean that, relative to available cargoes, too many tramps would have to be in operation. Without government aid many would stop sailing. If the United States assists its own tramp fleet by cargo preference, foreign-flag tramps may be forced out of business. Since most of them are operated under friendly foreign flags, this would increase the number that need to be operated under the United States flag as a measure of military preparedness. Such a development would surely create diffi-

---

[15] Under the Emergency Ship Repair Act of 1954 (*Public Law 608*, Ch. 777, 83rd Cong., 2d sess.) Congress appropriated $25 million for "a program of repairing, modernizing or converting such merchant-type vessels in the national defense reserve under the jurisdiction of the Secretary of Commerce as may be necessary to provide for the purpose of national defense an adequate and ready reserve fleet of merchant and auxiliary vessels."

culties among the allies that could be avoided by another course. To some extent the United States and its allies have agreed upon a "military division of labor." These military accords are perhaps easier to reach than those involving commercial considerations as well. Commercial matters affect private interest groups and become matters of domestic political controversy.

If the United States adopted the policy of letting the nations able to provide the cheapest tramp tonnage do so, most, and perhaps all, of the American-flag tramp industry would be wiped out. But this economically sensible argument would also be justified on military grounds so long as the United States and its allies worked closely enough together. The alliance might be able to provide for a reserve fleet of suitable quality for wartime. If military considerations required a greater tonnage of tramps in operation than was commercially supportable, the cost of subsidizing foreign-flag tramps would be less than that of supporting the high-cost, American-flag tramp fleet. At present, United States cargo preference encourages the preservation of the high-cost vessels and discourages the development and use of lower-cost foreign tramp fleets. As a matter of military budgeting this policy is unwarranted, if a firm arrangement can be worked out between the United States and its allies.

The nonsubsidized liner argument

Because they do not sail regular schedules on essential routes, tramp ships are not eligible for operating-differential subsidies and rely on cargo preferences for assistance in battling with their foreign competitors. But there is another branch of the American shipping industry that benefits also from cargo preferences, although it could be eligible for subsidies. This is the group of liner companies operating in the foreign trade of the United States who do not want the operating-differential subsidy primarily because they do not want to submit to the regulations required by the Merchant Marine Act, 1936. They claim that without the substantial boost to revenues provided by aid cargoes under cargo preference, they would be in difficult financial circumstances. They contend that as an important part of the "fourth arm of defense" their support by cargo preference legislation is justified.

A complete evaluation of the nonsubsidized liner argument would take us over much the same ground covered in the tramp fleet national defense argument. This need not be repeated. The important difference between the two arguments is that the liner operators may be eligible for operating-differential subsidies if they sail on essential trade routes. They have chosen not to ask for subsidies. They justify cargo preference, in part, as a wholly legitimate way of helping a fleet of vessels that can do without operating subsidies.

The position of the nonsubsidized liner operators reduces to a preference for one kind of aid over another. Some of them, for example, favor a blanket labor-cost differential subsidy.[16] The common factor in their advocacy of both these policies is their unwillingness to submit to the degree of regulation required by the 1936 Act. Apart from this, the liner operators' position on cargo preference is subject to the same arguments examined elsewhere in this chapter.

The need for cargoes (i.e. revenue) argument

Subsidized companies also favor cargo preferences. Equalizing costs under the operating-differential program is not enough, according to this argument, since it does not provide the operator with revenue. Obviously, equal costs are of no value if insufficient revenues accrue to cover costs. Cargo preference thus provides some assurance that competition for some cargoes, at least, will be limited to United States-flag vessels.

At first glance it seems almost inconceivable that with costs equal to those of their foreign-flag rivals, United States-flag vessels should be unable to attract enough cargoes to provide adequate revenues. Yet this admission is implicit in this argument. Why is this so? The usual answer given is that without the protection of cargo-preference legislation most of the aid cargoes would move in foreign-flag vessels in order to save

---

[16] See *Minority Report of John Gammie* [*States Marine Line*] *of The Ocean Shipping Panel to the Transportation Council For the Department of Commerce* (New York: Oct. 8, 1953), mimeographed, p. 8.

dollars to buy more American goods or to add to monetary reserves. Furthermore, these advocates of cargo preference state that additional foreign discrimination against American-flag vessels occurs on shipments from foreign ports to the United States. Only cargo preference, they contend, prevents the situation from becoming intolerable. Evaluation of this argument depends in part upon findings regarding discrimination.

The foreign discrimination argument

Certain foreign governments have discriminated against the American merchant marine.[17] They have employed a variety of devices to accomplish this end. Among them are the following: exchange control, discriminatory fees and charges against United States shipping companies, preferential routing of shipments to foreign-flag liners, preferential berthing arrangements for foreign-flag vessels, discriminatory lighthouse and consular invoice fees, discriminatory pilotage dues, and regulations requiring the use of foreign customs brokers. This is not an exhaustive list but it illustrates the types of discrimination encountered by American-flag vessels. United States ship operators quite understandably object to these regulations. They have asked the United States government for help. They have suggested cargo preference as a suitable means to combat foreign discrimination against the United States merchant marine. For those who make policy, this has raised the question of the efficacy of this proposal.

A consideration of this question suggests a number of others. Are foreign governments less likely to increase the

[17] In 1952, the U.S. Department of State reported that the following countries had discriminated against American-flag shipping: Argentina, Brazil, Chile, Colombia, Ecuador, Uruguay, Venezuela, Canada, France, Italy, South Africa, Spain, Egypt, Turkey, Portuguese East Africa, and Kenya Colony, British East Africa. (U.S. Senate, *Discriminatory Acts of Foreign Governments Affecting Our Merchant Marine*, Hearings Before a Subcommittee on Merchant Marine and Maritime Matters of the Committee on Interstate and Foreign Commerce, 82d Cong., 2d sess. [Washington: GPO, 1952], p. 91-97.) In 1953, in a progress report to the Subcommittee, the Department noted that in the fifteen months between this report and the one rendered in 1952, only one new case of a "clearly discriminatory practice against United States shipping" had occurred. It also added the Philippines to the 1952 listing. (Letter to Senator Charles E. Potter from Thruston B. Morton, Assistant Secretary of State, August 4, 1953.).

area of discrimination because the United States has written aid cargo preference into its body of permanent law? Would foreign governments have reduced the area if the United States had not taken this action? Does cargo preference give the United States a useful weapon in combatting foreign discrimination? Unfortunately, we cannot provide universally acceptable answers to these questions. We can however, trace the possible consequences of mutual retaliation against discrimination.

Discrimination against a particular group of sellers, whether classified by product or country, fosters ill-will by arbitrarily shutting *special* groups out of markets. Then retaliation in kind commands popular though unthinking support. In shipping, this course of action is especially hazardous. Americans and foreigners are both buyers and sellers of shipping services. American discrimination against foreign sellers, though immediately beneficial to American sellers, can be quickly countered by foreign discrimination against American sellers. The retaliation hits the industry initially favored by the discrimination. As the Chamber of Shipping of the United Kingdom noted, "The desire of an ever-increasing number of countries to develop mercantile marines sufficient to carry at least 50 per cent of their own foreign trade would, if pursued through policies of flag discrimination, choke the whole system of international sea transport, with untold cost to the traders of the world and with no lasting benefit to the countries adopting those policies."[18]

In general, then, cargo preference as a retaliatory device against foreign discrimination is not likely to lead to a betterment of conditions for the United States merchant marine. If carried to its absurd extreme, cargo preference would give each merchant marine the exclusive right to carry its country's export cargoes. This would mean one-way cargoes only. No shipping company can long operate profitably while utilizing only half its cargo-carrying capacity.

In particular, moreover, there are other objections to the United States using cargo preference in aid shipments as retaliation against foreign discrimination. Even if we assumed

[18] *Annual Report and Report of Proceedings of the Seventy-Seventh Annual Meeting* (London: Witherby, 1954), p. 56.

that that type of retaliation were sensible, the cargo-preference policy of the United States would largely miss its targets. Most of the complaints about foreign discrimination against United States shipping have named countries in the western hemisphere and Africa as the offenders. Of the countries receiving substantial amounts of military and civilian aid, only France, Italy, Spain, and Turkey are listed.

The complaints against Italy cited a law that might hurt United States-flag liners in their carrying of third class passengers and a *possibly* discriminatory currency regulation. The complaints against France have been directed against the French requirement that foreign vessels entering French ports must use French *courtiers maritimes* (custom brokers) for entering and clearing their vessels. American shipping companies point out that this is an added expense because they already have branch offices capable of taking care of these matters. At one time Turkey discriminated in favor of a foreign line by permitting it to sell passages for Turkish pounds. This practice was stopped after representations by the United States government. Spain, another aid recipient, was reported as restricting the total amount of pesetas that could be collected by American shipping companies for freight services. The rest had to be paid in dollars and, since Spaniards could get few dollars, this further handicaped American-flag lines.

Fairness demands that the Spanish regulations be classified as "seriously discriminatory." The French *courtier maritime* regulation is undoubtedly annoying but hardly as crippling to American shipping companies as the Spanish exchange regulation. The Italian and Turkish discriminations are indeed minor. Thus, the discriminatory actions of government aid recipients, as reported by the Department of State, can hardly be termed important enough to warrant cargo preference for United States-flag vessels carrying aid cargoes.[19]

In 1954, the State Department reported that cargo-preference arrangements were included in trade agreements involving twenty countries. At that time a Pan-Arab merchant fleet,

[19] The Maritime Administration reported complaints about the same countries with the addition of Germany—"potential difficulties of exchange . . . and possible discrimination against United States shipping through currency regulations." This complaint was filed in 1950. (*Discriminatory Acts of Foreign Governments Affecting Our Merchant Marine*, cited, p. 84.)

assisted by a 50-50 provision for dividing cargoes between ships of this merchant marine and those of other nations, was under consideration. In addition, Saudi Arabia had granted cargo preference to a particular tanker company.[20]

Discrimination against United States shipping can best be countered by negotiations to eliminate it rather than by counter-discriminatory measures. This could be done as follows. The United States could grant exceptions to the cargo-preference law to any country that would agree not to discriminate against American-flag shipping in any way. To some extent a similar approach has been successfully used in connection with the approval of loans by the Export-Import Bank. Waivers of the requirements of Public Resolution No. 17 are granted in exchange for relaxation of shipping restrictions detrimental to the United States merchant marine. In essence, the emphasis should be upon granting a favor (e.g. loan, gift) in exchange for a concession.

Exchange control, often not listed as a specific complaint, adversely affects the American merchant marine. Foreign governments, anxious to conserve scarce dollars, undoubtedly discriminate against American-flag lines as much as possible. Every dollar saved by using their own flag ships can then be used to buy items they must purchase in the United States because of their unavailability elsewhere. American shipping is hurt by this.

Does cargo preference help overcome foreign exchange

[20] This agreement calls for the shipment of all petroleum out of Saudi Arabia on vessels of the Saudi Arabian Maritime Company, organized by Aristotle Onassis, except that the Arabian American Oil Company (Aramco) may give preference to those of its own vessels that were carrying Saudi Arabian petroleum before December 31, 1953. See *The New York Times*, January 20, 21, 1955. Aramco has protested and the contract is under further discussion. As this book goes to press, *The New York Times*, June 9, 1956, reports that the Chilean senate approved a "50-50" bill. The United States and European maritime countries protested. The Chilean government opposed the bill because there are not enough Chilean-flag vessels to carry one-half the country's foreign trade.

Other information on cargo preference from U. S. Senate, *Cargo Preference Bill*, Hearings Before a Subcommittee of the Committee on Interstate and Foreign Commerce on S. 3233, 83rd Cong., 2d sess., (Washington: GPO, 1954) p. 9-10. See also "The Arab World," *The Egyptian Economic and Political Review*, (Cairo: Industrial Research Organization, November 1954); U. S. Department of State, *The Department of State Bulletin*, July 12, 1954, p. 63-69; *A Review . . .* , cited.

discrimination? Hardly. It merely shifts dollar-economizing activity to some other area, thereby adversely affecting other American exporters of both services and goods. If their exports, in turn, are to be sustained at what they deem to be appropriate levels, either foreign aid recipients must be forced to spend their gifts of United States money on some of these items or the total amount of money granted to the foreigners must be increased. In the latter case, the taxpayer in the United States ultimately bears a greater burden. Thus, through cargo preference American-flag shipping companies may be compensated for losses in revenue attributable to discriminatory foreign exchange and trade controls, but at a loss to other Americans. And, ultimately, if retaliation follows upon counter-retaliation, ship operators themselves will lose.

The practice of negotiating the removal of foreign discrimination by concessions on cargo-preference policy, while it is promising where discriminations are peculiar to the shipping industry, does not offer a solution of the exchange control problem. At best it is likely only to shift the discrimination against other United States sellers. Only proper fiscal and monetary policies combined with improved and enlarged world trade can overcome the basic conditions requiring the operation of exchange control. These policies, too, should be advocated by the United States. Emphasis upon a variety of difficulties encountered by the shipping industry and others will probably help to emphasize the need for action to correct the fundamental conditions. But a shipping policy that hinders other countries from earning dollars works against this end.

The argument that some form of aid is needed

"Don't abandon cargo preference until an adequate substitute for this aid is found." This is the gist of an argument advanced by some shipping interests. Quite understandably, they have urged that cargo preferences remain an important aspect of United States shipping policy because they fear, and perhaps rightly so, that a precipitate abandonment of the 50-50 regulation would be disastrous to many shipowners. They therefore urge that nothing be done to rescind the law until provision is made to provide equivalent support in some other acceptable form. Evaluation of this argument depends on an estimate of the consequences of ending the 50-50 policy.

Elimination of cargo preferences would hit the tramp operators hardest. Since their contribution to a national defense fleet, given the type of vessels they operate, is of low priority, this loss cannot be considered as serious to the national interest even though about 70 vessels are involved. Some of the vessels would probably be transferred to foreign registry and operators in friendly nations would help fill in the gap left by the American tramp shipowners. (For data on United States-owned, foreign-registered ships, see p. 14). The net loss to the active merchant marine of the western bloc would probably be less than the decline in the number of United States-flag tramps.

Institutional carriers would hardly be affected. They are parts of integrated manufacturing and distribution operations. Their cargoes, sometimes largely one-way, are not primarily dependent upon the demands of government or commercial shippers.

Certainly it would be surprising if tankers were affected seriously. Only a very small fraction of aid cargoes consisted of petroleum and products. Some United States-flag petroleum tanker operators would be rather adversely affected if the 1904 military cargo preference were repealed. Some private operators have profitable contracts to transport petroleum for the MSTS. However, loss of this business would probably send them into either the domestic trade or to foreign trades under another flag. In either event it is unlikely that the net loss to the United States-controlled tanker fleet would be large.

Intercoastal and coastwise operators would not be affected unless some of the vessels displaced in the foreign trades were transferred to domestic operations. This is highly unlikely in the light of the unfavorable conditions in the intercoastal and coastwise trades. (See Chapter VI.)

The effect that the elimination of cargo-preference legislation would have upon United States-flag liner companies cannot be satisfactorily estimated. We cannot assume that "liner cargoes" have been the only preferential freight handled by the liner companies. As noted earlier, some of them chartered vessels expressly for "tramping" in aid and military cargoes.

The sums paid to these concerns by the government have been substantial. Their anxiety regarding possible loss of these revenues, as reflected in their intense activity in favor of permanent cargo-preference legislation, indicates clearly how important this aid is.

Should cargo preference be terminated, subsidized foreign-trade liner operators may well have less to worry about than have their unsubsidized United States-flag competitors. Theoretically, at least, the subsidized companies should be able to compete effectively with foreign-flag operators. Their costs are presumably the same and the rates, set by the shipping conferences, are identical. True, they may be victims of exchange control regulations but this is a problem not soluble in terms of shipping policy alone.

Nonsubsidized liner operators, without aid cargoes, would suffer a drop in revenue that might in some instances lead to substantial operating losses. Since their operating costs are not subsidized, they cannot as successfully weather drops in revenue as can the subsidized liners. We must remember, though, that some nonsubsidized operators have sound basic cargoes unrelated to military and aid programs. They can sustain losses in revenue and still continue operations. Again, the loss of American-flag vessels would be partially offset by a gain in the number of friendly, foreign-flag vessels.

All estimates of the effects of eliminating cargo-preference legislation should be examined in the light of the potential military importance of the American merchant marine. If *any* loss of American-flag tonnage is considered militarily undesirable, then the reductions that would follow from the elimination of cargo preferences would be intolerable.[22] Then, indeed, no step should be taken to remove preferences before substitute supports are provided. Unfortunately for the policy makers, this simple formula for action (or inaction) cannot be used.

Though the rescission of cargo preferences would lead to a reduction in the *number* of vessels in the active merchant

---

[22] This view is strongly put by the Department of Commerce in *A Review* . . . , cited, p. 28: "To assume that the United States war-time capability can be improved or even maintained by a reduction in its peacetime merchant fleet and shipbuilding capacity is a patent absurdity."

marine of the United States still further below what the military has publicly stated it would prefer, the net loss of tonnage in the merchant marine of the western bloc might be very small. If the volume of aid cargoes were to be maintained the number of friendly foreign-flag vessels would probably increase. Thus, from the standpoint of national defense, as viewed by those who advocate the collective approach as embodied in NATO, the risks of eliminating cargo preferences without immediately replacing this aid with some other form of government assistance may not be as great as the shipping industry would have us believe.

CONCLUSIONS

The cargo-preference legislation recently enacted into law is clearly inconsistent with the general aims of United States foreign economic policy. Along with agricultural price support schemes coupled with import quotas and export subsidies, cargo preference invites foreign criticism and retaliation. It also encourages surpluses—in this case, merchant marine tonnage instead of farm staples. It complicates negotiations with foreign countries by giving their diplomats and others reason to doubt the sincerity of the government's desire to reduce barriers to trade within the free world.

Foreign maritime nations may also be excused if they appear uncertain about what the United States means when it advocates that they work harder to support themselves. They could do a better job if permitted to sell their shipping services in open competition with the American merchant marine. While the addition to total dollar earnings would not solve their international financial woes, it would help some. About $125 million per year might have been added to foreigners' dollar earnings for the period 1948-54 if they had been able to compete openly for aid and military cargoes.[23] Perhaps they

[23] This estimate assumes that foreigners would have obtained one-half of the United States-flag operators' share of freight earnings on aid shipments and one-half of their earnings from Military Sea Transportation Service freight. This figure—$260 million ($60 million aid, $200 million MSTS)—was then deflated by the ratio of foreigners' port expenditures in the United States to their ocean shipping receipts in their trade with the United States—52 per cent.

should be permitted to compete for all and not merely half of the aid cargoes. It is well to remember that such a policy would reduce the cost of foreign aid to the taxpayer in the United States.

Cargo preference cannot be commended as a desirable way to build up and maintain a nucleus merchant marine for national defense. It seems clear that variations in foreign aid appropriations may result in a change in the size of the merchant marine not wholly consistent with military needs, although some observers claim, to the contrary, that aid appropriations "properly" vary with military and political conditions.[24] It is therefore perhaps unwise to rely upon cargo preference to support an important fraction of the militarily required nucleus fleet. In the interests of national security a firmer pillar of aid should be used if and when necessary.

---

[24] *A Review* . . . , cited, p. 28-29. The authors then add: "Who can gainsay that the preservation of the relatively small United States fleet, serving as it has as an instrument of United States foreign and military defensive policy, has not deterred other Koreas?"

VI

CABOTAGE RESTRICTIONS

ALMOST from its beginning as a sovereign nation the United States has restricted its intercoastal and coastwise trades to American-built, American-flag vessels. A law passed and approved in 1798 provided for discriminatory tonnage duties to be placed on foreign-operated vessels plying the coasting trades of the United States. Not only were the duties to be paid by foreigners higher but they had to be paid upon arrival at any United States port instead of once a year as required of United States-flag operators. In 1808 legislation was approved excluding foreign-flag vessels from the domestic trades. In 1817 another law was passed again excluding foreign-flag vessels from these trades. The Merchant Marine Act, 1920, applied similar restrictions to noncontiguous trades.[1] Today, unless especially authorized to do so, foreign-flag ships are not permitted to engage in the coasting or the noncontiguous (e.g. Alaska, Hawaii) trades.

The United States is not the only nation providing a domestic navigation monopoly to vessels of its own flag. In his concise monograph on international merchant marine problems, Osborne Mance, writing in 1945, noted that among others, France, Finland, Greece, Portugal, Spain, and the U.S.S.R. had reserved their coasting trades to the national flag. On the other hand, Germany, Great Britain, Italy, and the Scandinavian countries had permitted either vessels of all or certain other nations to ply these trades.[2]

Reserving the coasting trades to national-flag vessels is, of course, a protectionist measure of considerable value to do-

---

[1] *U. S. Statutes at Large* [1845], p. 27-28, 2 *U.S. Statutes at Large* [1845], p. 499-502. *U. S. Statutes at Large* [1846], p. 351.
[2] Osborne Mance, *International Sea Transport* (London: Oxford University Press, 1945), p. 112-113.

mestic shipping companies. In the United States, shipbuilders as well stand to gain because only ships built in domestic shipyards are eligible to sail in these trades.

Cabotage restrictions have also been defended as essential to national defense. According to this view, they permit the United States to build and maintain a merchant marine that will be immediately available (because of location) in time of war. Some observers also consider it wise to exclude foreign-flag vessels from the domestic trades because of the possibility of espionage and sabotage inherent in the presence of these vessels in the internal commerce of the United States.

THE RECORD OF COASTAL TRADE

In 1925, the efficacy of cabotage restrictions was evaluated as follows: "The extent to which the reservation of the coasting trade has been an aid to our shipping is shown by our tonnage figures. On November 30, 1924, the Commissioner of Navigation reported 4,138,417 gross tons of vessels in the coasting trades. One million and a half gross tons of our finest vessels today are engaged in our intercoastal trade through the Panama Canal."[3]

On December 31, 1955, the domestic trades employed 3,832,000 gross tons or 7 per cent less than in 1924. Total intercoastal trade used 440,000 gross tons or less than one-third as much as in 1924. Most of the gross tonnage in the domestic trades consisted of tankers (2.8 million gross tons). Of this amount 2.7 million gross tons were in the coastwise trade.[4]

The figures clearly show that employment of ships in the coasting trades failed to keep pace with the growth of population and trade in the United States. This failure adversely affects the national defense of the United States. For example, in 1939, the government could commandeer 468 dry-cargo vessels of 2.2 million gross tons from the intercoastal, coastwise and noncontiguous trades. As of December 31, 1955, it could

[3] H. C. Calvin and E. G. Stuart, *The Merchant Shipping Industry* (New York: Wiley, 1925), p. 283.
[4] 1955 figures from U.S. Department of Commerce, Maritime Administration, "Employment Report of United States Flag Merchant Fleet Seagoing Vessels, 1,000 Gross Tons and Over as of December 31, 1955", *Report #300* (Washington: January 1956).

have obtained only 142 dry-cargo ships of 1 million gross tons.[5] Admittedly, the vessels in the 1955 fleet were somewhat faster than those in the domestic merchant marine of 1939. However, this was probably not enough to offset the decline in cubic cargo capacity.

The 1955 domestic fleet was not as old as the 1939 model. This, too, partially offset its smaller capacity. However, if pre-World War II experience is a guide, this advantage will decrease every year. Prewar business conditions and cargo prospects apparently did not warrant adequate replacement of obsolete or old vessels. An inventory taken on January 1, 1940 revealed that about 80 per cent of the coastwise and noncontiguous fleet was over 19 years old. About 96 per cent of the intercoastal merchant marine fell into this category.[6] Ships built during the World War I boom were put into these trades. Following World War II, the newer vessels turned out by the shipyards during the war were placed in service. Prospects for their eventual replacement are, as we shall presently see, not encouraging. And again, national defense will suffer.

As indicated earlier (see p. 24-25), dry-cargo coastwise and intercoastal traffic is far below prewar. Even during the thirties dry-cargo operators in these trades encountered declining cargoes. Why? Foreign competitors are nonexistent and therefore cannot be blamed; nor can subsidized American-flag lines, for when they enter these trades they forfeit (under the Merchant Marine Act, 1936) proportionate operating- and construction-differential subsidies in order to put them on competitive par with the nonsubsidized coastal operators. World War II, the efficiency of trucks and railroads, and the high cost of ocean transportation must share the blame.

World War II virtually halted the coasting trades. Vessels were pressed into military service. The trucks and railroads picked up the cargoes formerly moved by vessel. However, as indicated in Chapter II, there is strong evidence showing that intercoastal and coastwise dry-cargo trade began to decline before World War II. Rail and truck competition

[5] Same, for 1955 figures. Appendix Table 3, for 1939.
[6] Sixty-six per cent of the coastwise and noncontiguous vessels were between 19 and 24 years old. Eighty-four per cent of the intercoastal ships were in this group. Data from National Resources Planning Board, *Transportation and National Policy* (Washington: GPO, 1942), p. 362.

coupled with sharply rising vessel-operating and cargo-handling costs took their toll in the form of lower profits and smaller water-borne cargoes. Intermittent labor troubles disrupted sailing schedules causing further loss of trade for the shipping lines.

Rail competition has always been an important factor in coastal vessel operations. Before World War II, the railroads were sometimes permitted to charge low long-haul rates to meet vessel competition. This put vessel operators in a difficult position as the following illustration shows. In the thirties, low-rated commodities such as flour, wood pulp, copper, tinplate, coal and coke bore intercoastal rates of from $6 to $8 per net ton. Water carrier costs then totalled about $8 per ton. Nevertheless, during slack periods intercoastal operators accepted this freight and the attendant losses because laying up or running empty vessels would have meant even greater losses. After the war, rates rose to about $16 per net ton but cargo handling costs alone were $16 per net ton—an impossible situation for the vessel operator.[7]

Shipping companies still complain of rate reductions by the railroads. The railroads, favored by a heavy volume of traffic, have been able to cut some water-competitive rates and still convince the Interstate Commerce Commission that the new rates cover all expenses. The traditional relationship between rail and water rates has been reversed. Vessel operators complain about noncompensatory rail rates and contend that these low rates are harmful. They have asked that their (water) rates be raised to a compensatory level for shipping companies and then a suitable differential be added to establish railroad rates.[8]

Labor costs, which have risen more in shipping operations than in railroading and trucking, have been primarily responsible for the ship operators' being squeezed between costs and revenues despite large increases in freight rates. One analyst has estimated that crew wages and benefits plus cargo handling

[7] San Francisco Bay Ports Commission, *A Report on Intercoastal Shipping with Special Reference to the San Francisco Bay Ports Area*, by J. S. Stumpf (Sacramento: California State Printing Office, 1953), p. 14-15.
[8] For a statement of the request see I.C.C. Docket No. 29721, *All Rail Commodity Rates Between California, Oregon, and Washington*, 277 I.C.C. (1950), p. 558.

amount to about 70 per cent of total vessel-operating expenses. He found that crews' wages, benefits, and subsistence had increased by 357 per cent between 1938 and 1952. They amounted to $15,800 per intercoastal voyage in 1938 and $72,200 in 1952.[9] Meanwhile, though freight rates increased, operating ratios remained unfavorable. During 1934-38 operating expenses divided by operating revenues averaged 103.3. Only 1936 was below 100, and it was 99.7. In three postwar years 1950-52, the operating ratios were 104.8, 97.4, and 102.4 in order—hardly a record to inspire new ventures in the field.[10]

A further indication of the plight of intercoastal and coastwise operators was provided by Clarence G. Morse, Maritime Administrator, who presented profit figures for "10 representative coastal and intercoastal operators." The group as a whole lost $2.3 million in 1953 and $778,000 in 1954. Two of the companies sustained losses in both years, six had profits in both years, and the remaining two each lost money in one year, one in 1953 and the other in 1954. These figures taken alone do not prove that coastal shipping opportunities necessarily are relatively poor. However, combined with the other evidence at hand, they do warrant that inference.[11]

The growth of population and the industrialization of the West changed transport needs in favor of the short-haul and against the long-haul. As interior distribution and manufacturing points and population centers have grown in number and importance, the old port-to-hinterland routes of waterborne shipments have become more expensive. Though many

[9] Same, p. 15, 20. In their study of the Pacific Coast shipping industry, Gorter and Hildebrand found that in 1948 maritime wage rates on the Pacific Coast (longshore and offshore combined) were 185.2 per cent higher than in 1935 while straight-time hourly earnings of railroad employees were only 93.6 per cent higher. They also found that between 1937 and 1947 the hourly wage of truck drivers increased 69.2 per cent while Pacific Coast maritime wage rates went up 158.3 per cent. (W. Gorter and G. H. Hildebrand, *The Pacific Coast Maritime Shipping Industry, 1930-1948*, v. 2, [Berkeley: University of California Press, 1954], p. 137.)

[10] *A Report on Intercoastal Shipping. . . .*, cited, p. 37.

[11] U. S. House of Representatives, *Vessel Replacement Program*, Hearings Before the Committee on Merchant Marine and Fisheries in H. R. 4118 and H.R. 5959, 84th Cong., 1st sess. (Washington: GPO, 1955), p. 186; U.S. Department of Commerce, Maritime Administration, *A Review of the Coastwise and Intercoastal Shipping Trades*, (Washington: Author, 1955), p. 24-29.

water rates have remained below rail and truck rates, the *total* costs to the shipper have risen to equal and in some cases to exceed the cost of movement by rail and truck. Thus, given slower ship schedules, it is hardly surprising that traffic has tended to shift from ships to their land-based competitors.

Some evidence of the divergent developments in land and oceangoing domestic traffic appears in Table 15.

Table 15

ANNUAL AVERAGE CARGO TONNAGE HANDLED BY UNITED STATES RAILROADS, AND BY INTERCOASTAL VESSELS VIA THE PANAMA CANAL
1936-40 AND 1946-52
[In millions of tons]

| Period | Railroads[a] | | Intercoastal vessels[b] |
	Originated	Carried	
1936-40	986.1	1,778.7	7.0
1946-50	1,466.1	2,781.6	3.6
1951-52	1,497.0	2,855.0	5.0

[a] Revenue tons of 2,000 lbs.
[b] Tons of 2,240 lbs.; fiscal years.
Source: For railroads, 1936-40, 1946-50 Interstate Commerce Commission, *Statistics of Railroads in the United States,* annual report, as cited in U.S. Department of Commerce, Bureau of the Census, *Statistical Abstract of the United States, 1953,* (Washington: 1953), p. 550. For 1951-52, Same, 1954, p. 578. For intercoastal vessels, Appendix, Table 4, fiscal years averaged to estimate calendar year totals.

During the period 1951-53 intercoastal shipping via the Panama Canal averaged about 5 million long tons of cargo per year. This was an improvement, but still well below prewar levels and less than half the 1930 tonnage. In 1951-52 railroads exceeded their wartime (1941-45) averages by about 15 million short tons. Trucking operations have grown phenomenally during the postwar years. In 1946, Class I intercity carriers hauled 112 million short tons of cargoes while during 1951, 237 million short tons of freight moved on these carriers.[12] Thus intercoastal water-borne cargoes have declined

[12] For 1946, Interstate Commerce Commission, *Statistics of Class I Motor Carriers,* annual report, as cited in *Statistical Abstract of the United States, 1953,* p. 559. For 1951, Same, *1954,* p. 587.

both absolutely and relative to the volume of traffic carried by railroad and truck.

If the sheltered coasting trades are to be revived without subsidy or other government aid, the ship operators must find a more efficient way to handle long-haul general cargo. Trailer ships carrying loaded truck trailers or railroad cars appear to offer some hope. Putting cargo in larger packages may also help. Both approaches are still in the experimental stage. Though these developments are encouraging, they have been partially offset from time to time by some important obstacles. These include management inaction, brighter opportunities in other fields, and labor opposition. All have worked powerfully against innovations in shipping.

During the last thirty years the pattern of economic development in the United States has favored the growth of railroads and trucking concerns. Even if World War II had not occurred, general cargo would probably have moved increasingly by rail and truck. Only in long-haul, bulk, or large-lot cargo carrying would ships have competed successfully. From this we should not infer that the relative and absolute decline of coastal dry-cargo shipping will continue. A choking of rail and truck facilities, a rise in land-carrier costs and rates, a shift in the pattern of economic change, may encourage a revival of shipping. The recent interest in trailer ships may be the first sign of a trend back to domestic water transport. On balance, at present, the outlook for shipping companies is not bright, although not hopeless either.

Our examination of the record in the coasting trades hardly inspires confidence regarding the future of the American merchant marine in domestic seagoing commerce. And if this domestic trade fleet is to be an important element of the active merchant marine readily available in time of war, much will have to be done. Compared with 1939, even after allowance for the newer and faster vessels in the fleet, the 1955 coasting trades merchant marine would fail in its assigned wartime role.

As Table 16 shows, there was a substantial decline in the size of the fleet between 1939 and 1955, with dry-cargo vessels bearing the brunt of the reduction. The table also reveals the postwar reorientation of the United States merchant marine. It has become primarily a foreign trade fleet. Before the war

Table 16

TOTAL AND DOMESTIC TRADES ACTIVE MERCHANT MARINE OF THE UNITED STATES, 1939, 1954 AND 1955

Fleet and per cent of total[a]	1939		1954		1955	
	No.	Gross tons (thousands)	No.	Gross tons (thousands)	No.	Gross tons (thousands)
Dry cargo and tanker						
Total U.S.	1,092	6,399.3	1,123	9,432.0	1,163	9,768.0
Domestic trades[b]	772	4,298.0	398	3,428.0	425	3,779.0
Per cent domestic trades of total	70.7	67.2	35.4	36.3	36.5	38.7
Dry cargo						
Total U.S.	740	3,918.7	784	5,968.0	822	6,240.0
Domestic trades[b]	468	2,170.7	159	1,085.0	161	1,115.0
Per cent domestic trades of total	63.2	55.4	20.3	18.2	19.6	17.9

[a] As of June 30 in each year.
[b] Includes coastwise, intercoastal and noncontiguous trades.
Source: Computed from Appendix Tables 3 and 3a.

vessels were concentrated in the domestic trades (although nearly half the dry-cargo tonnage was in foreign trade service.) In 1955 the coasting trades used less than one-fifth of the dry-cargo merchant marine, whether measured by number or tonnage.

With part of the foreign trade fleet subsidized directly and much of it supported indirectly by cargo preferences, there appears to be little hope of expansion of that portion of the American merchant marine. Quite the opposite appears likely. If aid cargoes decline, and foreign competition becomes even more severe, this fleet will become smaller. And there appears to be only a slight chance that in the near future the coasting trades will require many additional vessels to handle their cargoes. What can be done, if one grants that the coasting trades' merchant marine should be maintained at current strength or greater?

SOME ALTERNATIVE POLICIES

An operating-differential subsidy for domestic vessel operators is an unlikely possibility. Railroads, trucking concerns, and airlines could almost certainly exert enough political pressure to defeat any attempt to extend subsidies to shipping companies in the coasting trades.

Rate adjustments that improve the competitive position of the shipping companies are also not likely. After World War II, the coastwise and intercoastal operators pressed the Interstate Commerce Commission for higher rates all around—both rail and vessel. Some upward adjustments were made. For the most part they were considered inadequate by the shipping concerns.

Cargo preference, or sharing of domestically consigned government shipments, would probably not be acceptable policy either. One argument that would no doubt be used to defeat it would be that such a policy would mean excessive government interference in the free, competitive market for transportation services. This would indeed be an interesting development in view of the cargo-preference law now applicable to government aid shipments to foreign countries. The distinction between foreigners and fellow citizens is apparently very important. It leads to un-economic decisions in the case of foreign trade and somewhat more rational economic ones in domestic trade.

It has been suggested by some observers that since unequal labor costs are primarily responsible for the weak competitive position of the ship operators, the wage rates in all domestic transportation industries should be adjusted to remove the discrepancies. This proposal, too, is impracticable. Equalizing wage costs is administratively impossible even though conceptually possible. Equalizing wage rates is equally difficult because of the differences in jobs performed. Attempting to get equal wage rates by encouraging the shipping, trucking, and railroad unions to combine for the purpose of collective bargaining involves many difficulties and dangers inimical to a sound transportation system.

Of course, equalizing wage rates would only be a poor substitute for equalizing wage costs—if indeed *that* is to be desired. Differences in cost generally reflect differences in efficiency. The economic use of men and natural resources requires that we employ the cheapest method for getting a job done. Economic competition should not be considered fair if the low-cost operator is handicapped so as to remove his advantage over his competitors. This procedure, as used in horse racing, insures a "fair" race with each horse presumably equally able to win the race. It does not insure that the cheapest (i.e. the fastest) horse will win. By handicapping the most efficient producer or seller we deny ourselves the most for the least cost. Surely, this is not desirable in the field of transportation unless other criteria, such as national defense, are more important.

One other proposal deserves attention. It, too, would encounter political opposition. Nevertheless, it has some merits that might give it an advantage over the other proposals thus far considered. Basically it is very simple. It merely calls for opening the domestic coastwise and noncontiguous trades to foreign-flag operators. Since their operating costs are lower, it seems reasonable to anticipate that they could operate profitably at lower than current rates. This would squeeze domestic-flag lines caught between higher operating costs and lower freight rates. To offset this they could be made eligible for operating-differential subsidies to put them on equal cost terms with their foreign-flag competitors.

There would be many objections to this scheme; enough no doubt to defeat its adoption. Consider some of them. It would be argued that foreign vessels would not be available to the government in time of war. This would not be true if the government license to operate in the coasting trades were to provide adequately for government control of foreign-flag vessels during a national emergency. Even without this provision, other arrangements could be made to use them. They might be more readily available than American-flag ships in foreign waters.

It would also be contended that though lower rates would encourage additional traffic, the increase would be insufficient to require many more vessels in these trades; and further, that the cost of the operating-differential subsidies would be excessive. Both these contentions might prove correct. However, even if the available fleet were to increase only slightly and the subsidy outlay were to be high, the savings to shippers and consumers might more than offset the higher subsidy bill. There are no reliable means of forecasting the outcome of the policy. Only actual experimentation can yield the answer.

Railroads and trucking companies would undoubtedly strongly object to the proposal. They would probably try to demonstrate that lower ocean freight rates would have to be met by lower rail and truck freight rates. This, they would argue, might increase total traffic only slightly. As a result they might have a bit more freight to handle but at lower rates. This could mean a reduction in profits or a loss. Again, we must note that there is no sure method by which the traffic, revenue, and cost patterns can be predicted.[13]

None of the policy suggestions appears to be politically feasible. In addition, there are important economic objections

[13] One student of maritime affairs has suggested that a drop in ocean freight rates in the coastwise and intercoastal trades would bring a large increase in revenues to shipping companies. He bases his suggestion upon the fact that freight costs are a large part of the final product costs of commodities carried in these trades and that rival forms of transport are highly competitive. J.G.B. Hutchins, *The American Maritime Industries and Public Policy, 1789-1914* (Cambridge: Harvard University Press, 1941), p. 43. This type of competitive condition has led to government regulation of rates. A fall in all rates might not benefit, and could harm, the competitors.

to each of them. As a result, United States maritime policy for the domestic trades will probably continue unchanged. If this happens, the coasting trade merchant marine will probably continue to play a minor role as a potential national defense auxiliary. The burden of maintaining an adequate "all-American" merchant marine will continue to fall largely upon the operators in foreign trade. And this will become increasingly expensive. Yet, political expediency dictates this course. Subsidies, cargo preferences, and the like are often condoned when foreigners are hurt. They are frequently not when Americans are the victims.

The intercoastal part of domestic shipping would be helped by a reduction of the tolls charged by the Panama Canal.[14] At current freight rates and with the current volume of cargoes this would obviously improve the financial position of the operators. Whether it would enable them to lower freight rates, increase their liftings, and profitably increase their fleets cannot be forecast.

Even under the unfavorable conditions prevailing in the coasting trades, innovations are being made. Trailer ships, carrying loaded freight cars and truck trailers, are being employed with some success. One tanker-operating company has modified a tanker to enable it to transport trailers on the ballast leg of its regular intercoastal trips. Special-purpose craft for lumber and other commodities have been introduced. The government has recently encouraged these developments by insuring, for the first time, a loan for the construction of a roll-on, roll-off trailer ship. All this might lead to a success that could markedly change the character of and prospects for domestic trade.[15]

[14] For an interesting discussion of this and other policy matters affecting coastal shipping see A Review of . . . Intercoastal Shipping Trades, cited, p. 30-43.
[15] The recent revival of river boat traffic provides an interesting example of the recovery of an industry once thought by many observers to be on its way to extinction. See "Resurgence of the River Boat," Monthly Business Review (Cleveland: Federal Reserve Bank of Cleveland, February 1955), p. 4-10.

For articles about recent developments in roll-on, roll-off vessels see The New York Times, April 4 and 27, 1956; The Wall Street Journal, March 26, April 20, 1956. See also A Review of . . . Intercoastal Shipping, cited, p. 32-33.

From the standpoint of economics, current cabotage policy is the best one, on the assumption that foreign-flag vessels are not to be permitted to ply United States domestic trades. Except for the regulatory functions performed by the Interstate Commerce Commission, the railroads, trucks, and ships compete freely. Within this restricted framework management is free to do what it wants. For the shipping companies this means considerable freedom because they are not as closely regulated and supervised as the trucks and railroads.

If shipping companies are unable to survive under these conditions then we must conclude that they are economically unjustified. We should not mourn their death, except perhaps as an item of passing cultural interest. If, however, military considerations demand the existence of a sizeable, active merchant fleet operating in the domestic trades, then perhaps one of the policy alternatives we have discussed should be adopted.

Among these, preference should be given to the policy of admitting the vessels of friendly nations to participate in these trades. This policy coupled with an operating-differential subsidy would be the next best alternative. It would probably bring about lower freight rates. It would involve a minimum of government interference with private enterprise. And it would enable foreigners to earn dollars while providing the United States with an adequate, active reserve fleet for emergencies. Some domestic interests would be hurt. In the interest of national security this may be acceptable.

In any event, if a domestic fleet is not considered essential to national defense, the present policy will suffice. If it is deemed essential, then a hard choice must be made. This is always true when national interest takes precedence over private interest.

VII

SHIPPING CONFERENCES

THIS AND THE TWO following chapters deal with certain aspects of the government's policies toward competition among ship operators: conferences,[1] essential trade routes, and the Military Sea Transportation Service.

To understand and properly to evaluate the policies of the United States government in these fields requires some knowledge of the prevailing competitive conditions. The following brief sketch of these conditions is therefore relevant to all three chapters.

CONDITIONS OF COMPETITION

Competition in the dry-cargo foreign trades involves basically three kinds of carriers—the tramp, the nonconference liner, and the conference liner. In the tramp market, rates are usually determined by the free play of the forces in the market. An exception occurs when American tramp operators bid for United States government foreign aid cargoes. In this bidding, foreign tramp operators are excluded. Nonetheless, within this restricted market United States-flag operators bid competitively. Under the impact of shifting demands for shipping space and varying quantities of cargo space available, freight rates fluctuate widely in these markets.

Nonconference liner operators offer much the same service as conference members, but they are not bound by conference rates. Ordinarily, nonconference liner freight rates fluctuate

---

[1] This chapter owes much to the excellent, authoritative study of shipping conferences made by Professor Daniel Marx, Jr. To avoid excessive footnotes acknowledgment of his contribution will not be repeated at every point. See Daniel Marx, Jr., *International Shipping Cartels: A Study of Industrial Regulation by Shipping Conferences* (Princeton: Princeton University Press, 1953).

less than tramp rates. Conference liner operators offer services at rates set by mutual agreement among members of the conference. Since conferences may require either unanimous or majority approval of rates, they are less flexible than tramp and nonconference liner rates.

Tanker operations will be omitted from discussion. Competition among tanker operators apparently does not generate the problems that characterize competition in the dry-cargo market. This is probably attributable to the existence of large fleets owned by petroleum companies, the type of shipping contract employed, the small number of commodities (i.e., types of petroleum and products) involved, and the role played by water transport in the petroleum industry.

Competition between conference and nonconference liners

Nonconference and conference liners, by offering substantially the same service, compete for similar cargoes. In some situations the competition is intense while in others a policy of "live and let live" prevails. If a shipping route is overtonnaged and the conference rates are low relative to costs, this competition is keen indeed. If the conference rates are high and the route is not overtonnaged, then neither conference nor nonconference operators are under pressure to draw freight and passengers away from their competitors.

Competition between tramps and liners

Tramps and liners (conference and nonconference) compete to a limited extent. Tramps ordinarily seek bulk cargoes such as coal, grain and ores. If possible they try to carry no more than one or two commodities on any leg of a voyage. Occasionally some of them will try to get cargoes usually handled by liners. This occurs when they have less than a full shipload of a bulk commodity and are anxious to top this off. Liners may try to obtain bulk cargoes if they have little general dry cargo booked for a given run. Basically, though, tramps and liners operate in different markets. The former move bulky, low value commodities in large single shipments on no regular schedule of sailings, while the latter contend mainly for high value cargoes picked up and delivered on regularly scheduled sailing dates. However, each offers potential and sometimes annoyingly actual competition for the other, usually over a limited range of goods during periods of distress.

Intraconference competition

If we assume, heroically, that the members of a conference adhere strictly to their agreement, then they must compete with each other on a so-called nonprice basis. Better service would appear to be the principal inducement to offer to shippers in an effort to obtain their patronage. This means offering faster, more convenient schedules, and special facilities for cargo handling—e.g., refrigerated space.[2] However, even speed may be ruled out as a competitive factor. In some conferences, rates have been geared to speed—the slower the vessel the lower the rates. Actually competition often goes beyond these theoretical confines. Violations of agreements occur and competition intrudes on rates. The abuses will persist so long as they are not flagrant or discovered by disadvantaged "clean" competitors. Such "shadings" of the rules are difficult to eliminate in an arrangement based upon self-interest but calling for self-discipline. Competition among conference members is often intense, depending upon conditions in the trade.

If the volume of business is substantial and the number of conference lines in operation small enough to permit adequate returns for all, the agreements usually stand in little danger of violation. Competition is then "gentlemanly." And even if business is poor there are circumstances under which cut-throat competition does not occur. If, for example, carriers on a given route have a pooling arrangement, then there is no private advantage to be gained from attempting to divert cargoes from one's co-operators in the trade. Thus, even

[2] Such competition is popularly called "nonprice" although actually it is not. A shipper may get more service from one company than from another at the same price or freight rate. Since the "package" of service includes more in one case than the other, the shipping line offering the greater amount of service actually charges a lower price for that portion of the entire "service package" which is the same for both competitors.

within conferences, competition among members may range from fierce to nonexistent.

Intergovernmental competition

In addition to the competition among private companies, there is another factor of overriding importance affecting the nature of the already vigorous competitive struggles. This is the desire of many nations to have merchant fleets flying their own flag. Some, such as the United States, deem it a matter of military security. Others, cut off from merchant shipping services during World War II, have resolved to maintain sufficient tonnage to prevent recurrence of such a shipping shortage. Then there are some countries, often newly independent areas, that want a merchant marine for prestige purposes.

The result of these nationalistic policies is that the decisions of governments replace those of the free market. Shipping tonnage is not adjusted to the demand for space resulting from commercial and governmental transactions. Some of it is kept in operation for other reasons. Yet governments generally try to operate as cheaply as possible. Maintaining a merchant fleet that carries little cargo is costly and may evoke protests from harried finance ministers as well as taxpayers. To reduce governmental expenditures, preferential schemes are concocted to provide cargoes for the underutilized vessels.

Under these conditions, competition is "nationalized." Political favor replaces better service or a lower rate as the prime way to gain traffic. Intergovernmental negotiation becomes necessary to avoid chaos. Considerations far from economic play an increasing role. Competition and rivalry among shipping lines remain important to be sure. However, their form and substance are different. Some nations have concluded that success in this kind of competition requires a nationalized merchant marine. This further complicates an already complex situation.

GENERAL CHARACTERISTICS OF MERCHANT MARINE COMPETITION

Rate wars, cutthroat competition, and the break-up of conferences are threats to the precarious competitive stability of the industry. The volume of traffic fluctuates widely and often suddenly. A sharp, quick decline in cargoes often creates what the industry calls an overtonnaged trade. Some operators will then feel compelled to cut rates in order to gain enough traffic to cover operating expenses. This will invite retaliation by rivals anxious to retain their share of the available cargoes. Deferable expenses will be temporarily ignored and rates driven down sharply.

The history of shipping is replete with such incidents. Every operator strives to get his ship "full and down," sometimes shaving rates to do so. Laying up or running a ship nearly empty are very costly alternatives. Anything earned over operating expenses is welcomed during hard times. And the ship operator need not be chided for short-sightedness. Losses in one period may be far more than offset by profits in a later period. Further, it must be remembered that an owner-operator cannot ordinarily sell his ship profitably if business is depressed. Unless he can shift it to another trade, he must often do the best he can where he is. In this respect, he is immobile. His immobility contributes to the instability of the shipping industry.

When the demand for shipping space is great relative to the amount available, rates, under conditions of uncontrolled competition, often rise rapidly and far (as evidenced by tramp freight rates, for example). More ships enter the trade. A surplus of tonnage may develop, and then the situation described earlier prevails.

As a member of the United States delegation to the Inter-American Maritime Conference reported: "The experience of the past has shown that lines operating without conference agreements or other stabilizing influences will inevitably engage in rate wars which are harmful to trade and destructive of services. The inherent difficulties of regulating an international business such as shipping makes the conference system an acceptable substitute for rigid government control of ocean rates."[3]

[3] "Ocean Freight Rate Problems—Self Regulation—Government Regulation," Summary of report presented by Lloyd Tibbett, Division of Regulation, United States Maritime Commission, as reproduced in *Proceedings of the Inter-American Maritime Conference* (Washington: Pan American Union, 1940), Congress and Conference Series No. 34, Vol. 2, p. 91.

As we noted earlier, shipping competition ranges from near monopoly and cartel-type arrangements on the one hand to free competition on the other. To this must be added that the entire competitive structure is highly susceptible to corrosive competitive practices that from time to time seriously weaken parts of this structure. Through shipping conferences the industry attempts to prevent this corrosion. Conferences, in turn, create some interesting and important problems of governmental policy.

THE OPERATION OF SHIPPING CONFERENCES

The Western Steamship Committee, an organization representing "major steamship lines . . . associated in 14 West Coast Conferences," describes the need and functions of a shipping conference as follows:

Ordinarily, an industry such as ocean shipping, where common carriers serve a vital public interest, would be subject to strict rate regulation by some governmental agency responsible to the public. The various state public utility commissions for intrastate commerce, and the Interstate Commerce Commission, for commerce between the states, perform such regulatory functions in the United States.

But over carriers who ply the open seas, transporting goods between sovereign nations, no such rate regulation is exercised. In the tangle of sovereign rights, none could function. To fill this need, most of the responsible ship operators of the world maintaining common carrier services have joined together to impose self-regulatory codes upon their operations; this they did in the interests of stability.

The associations of common carriers are known as Conferences, and their members voluntarily accept the conditions of the codes which, in other industries of similar nature, are usually imposed from outside. Acceptance of such regulation, naturally, is not without self-interest, for prior to the establishment of conferences devastating rate wars *were the rule rather than the exception.*[4]

Shipping conferences originated when the Calcutta Conference was formed in 1875.[5] The immediate impetus came from

[4] Western Steamship Committee, *The Steamship Conference System—And Your Stake in World Trade* (San Francisco: n.d.), p. 6-7.
[5] The material in this paragraph is based upon Osborne Mance, *International Sea Transport* (London: Oxford University Press, 1945), p. 95.

the increase in shipping tonnage around 1869, when the Suez Canal opened for traffic. Under the Calcutta Conference, the same rates applied from a number of ports of departure, and preferential rates and other concessions to privileged shippers were eliminated. However, shippers formerly accorded such favored treatment protested. In response, the conference originated the deferred rebate scheme. Under this, shippers who patronize conference members exclusively for a certain period are given a rebate provided they continue their exclusive patronage for some specified interval after the expiration of the period to which the rebate applies.

Hundreds of conferences operate today. Professor Marx listed 116 freight conferences in United States foreign trade alone, as of January 18, 1950.[6] Deferred rebates play an important part in many of the foreign conferences (carrying shipping between foreign countries or inbound from foreign countries to the United States). The dual rate system—a controversial feature of United States foreign trade conferences—is sometimes used as a substitute for the deferred rebate. This system provides that conference members grant lower rates to shippers who agree to patronize conference lines exclusively for a given period.

Government policy toward shipping conferences is in good measure based upon an evaluation of the arguments for and against the system. Fortunately, like tariff arguments, they have become fairly well standardized and can be stated briefly.[7]

The case for conferences

Those who favor conferences usually defend them as follows. First, freight rates tend to be more stable than they are without conference control. Though flexible, the rates will

[6] Marx, cited, p. 176-181.
[7] The arguments have been assembled from a variety of sources—Marx, cited; Mance, cited; Western Steamship Committee, cited; E. G. Mears, *Maritime Trade of the Western United States* (Stanford: Stanford University Press, 1935); *Proceedings of the Inter-American Maritime Conference*, cited; various government publications; newspaper reports; and personal interviews with ship operators and government officials. The arguments are so generally well known that no further source notations will be given.

not go up as much as uncontrolled rates during periods of shipping shortage. Forward contracts are feasible and this encourages international trade.

Second, conferences offer regular, dependable service. Since only nonprice competition prevails among members, the emphasis is upon frequency and quality of service. This benefits the shipper who can avail himself of the services of the most modern vessels and cargo-handling practices. Service is less likely to be suspended during times when demands for cargo space are low. Many conferences offer optional ports of discharge so shippers can reroute cargoes to take advantage of changes in market condition.

Third, all shippers of a given class—whether patronizing conference lines exclusively or not—are given equal treatment, i.e., shippers signing exclusive patronage agreements are all treated alike and those not signing such agreements are also treated alike without discrimination among members of each group of shippers.

Fourth, conferences reduce cutthroat competition. This benefits both ship operators and shippers. Operators gain because they avoid the losses that may accompany rate wars. Investors in shipping are protected and the managers of shipping companies find it less difficult to attract and retain the funds required to operate the lines. Shippers gain despite the absence of occasionally very low rates. If rate wars continue unabated for some time, only a few competitors might survive, possibly only one or two. They (or he) would be in a monopolistic position able to extract high rates from the hapless, unprotected shippers.

Fifth, by their effective use of various devices to secure steady, loyal customers for their services, conferences are able to obtain a relatively stable nucleus of cargoes so essential to the provision of regular, adequate service. This permits both shipping companies and shippers to develop long-range plans that are mutually advantageous to the parties concerned.

Sixth, conferences provide standardized methods for handling claims and other matters incidental to ocean-borne shipments.

Lastly, without some controls shipping competition degenerates into rate wars and other practices inimical to operators and shippers alike. Since national governmental regulation of international shipping is impracticable and no international governmental body exists to do the job, the shipping conference is the best means for establishing the necessary controls.

Mance suggests that an outstanding virtue of the steamship conference is its flexibility and adaptability to changing conditions. "In general, it may be said that conferences are essentially flexible and will adapt themselves to the circumstances of their trades rather than attempt to act on hard and fast lines. The result is that they have an infinite capacity to accept— and absorb—the inevitable."[8]

The case against conferences

Opponents of the conference system ordinarily counter the arguments of its supporters by contending that there are at least four important reasons for eliminating the conference system. First, shipping conferences are monopolistic arrangements that enable the ship operators to obtain higher rates than they would if free price competition existed among the conference members.

Second, the arrangements by which conferences obtain the exclusive patronage of "their" shippers discriminate against the nonconference ship operator attempting to compete by offering lower rates to potential shippers. They also discriminate against shippers who, having been "forced" to agree to ship their goods on conference lines exclusively (in exchange for either a deferred rebate or lower rates), are no longer free agents in the market for shipping services.

Third, since they lack the spur of price competition and operate at rates higher than those that would prevail in a free market, conference members can continue operations despite declines in the demand for shipping services that would drive them out in a freely competitive market. Conference practices therefore tend to preserve tonnage in excess of needs. This is wasteful of men and resources.

Fourth, shipping conferences, being monopolistic, enable their members to earn excessive profits.

[8] Mance, cited, p. 97.

The issues analyzed

Each of the arguments for or against conferences probably contains an element of validity. Some probably cannot be proved or disproved. Despite this, public policy toward conferences represents an implicit evaluation of conferences based largely upon judgments regarding the weight to be given to each of these arguments. This in turn, involves some difficult decisions regarding the criteria to be used.

Government policy toward shipping conferences must represent the best possible reconciliation of the interests of at least four important groups—conference members, nonconference vessel operators, shippers, and the government (representing the public interest). Though all four parties have common interests, they also have significantly conflicting views regarding the control of shipping competition. Effective assessment of governmental policy must therefore begin with an examination of the viewpoints of these groups.

With very few exceptions the members of all four groups agree that unregulated competition among liner companies is not desirable, even though temporary and occasionally lasting benefits accrue to some. Thus, basically, the differences in outlook involve varying views regarding the *control* of this competition. Only a small minority of those interested in liner operations favors unrestricted competition. The majority remembers well the disheartening disruptions that have accompanied such competitive conditions.

It is also generally agreed that frequent, dependable service provided by conference ships of modern design at rates that fluctuate within a narrow range is desirable. Not *all* shippers, however, require such service. Those who do not, agree that they need not patronize liner companies. The United States government, interested in an active merchant marine available for emergency use at all times, also favors regular liner service, even though some routes may be overtonnaged.

Much of the disagreement over conferences centers on the tying arrangements employed to insure exclusive rights to transport the shippers' merchandise. On this issue the conferences face opposition from the other interests—shippers, nonconference operators, and the government. Though we have touched upon this matter before, this disagreement warrants further attention. It lies at the heart of the conference system and thereby, as we shall presently see, confronts all the parties concerned with a common dilemma.

As Professor Marx has so ably demonstrated, to object to the tying arrangements is to object to the conference system itself.[9] An effective conference, with all its desirable features, cannot exist without binding agreements between shippers and the conference that incorporate undesirable features and opportunities for abuse of shippers. Unless the ship operators in a conference can prevent shippers from utilizing the services offered by their nonconference rivals, they are put at a crucial disadvantage by their agreement to adhere to the rates established by the conference. They would control only a portion of the supply and none of the demand in an industry in which the supply of shipping services offered on a given route can readily be increased by diverting vessels from other routes and in which the total number of ships in operation can be rapidly augmented by taking them out of private and government reserve fleets. This would give them no advantages and the disadvantage of relative price inflexibility in the face of competitors individually free to manipulate rates.

Two alternatives would be available under these circumstances. First, the conference operators could try to persuade all ship operators to join a conference. This would give them complete control over the supply of services and enable them to "market" these services in a manner designed to protect the interests of the operators. If the first approach were impossible because not all shipping lines would agree, then the second alternative would be for the conference operators to gain control over the demand for their shipping services for stipulated periods of time. This has proved to be the only feasible course of action open to them. They control part of the supply and part of the demand.

As many observers have emphasized, this rationalization of part of the market for shipping services is a mixed blessing. Shippers get regular service and steady rates (both of which can be provided by nonconference operators as well) but they pay a price in the form of a restricted range of choice of ship-

[9] Marx, cited, p. 218-221.

ping lines to carry their merchandise. For certain contractual periods they cannot, without penalty, choose to ship at the lowest rates quoted. This lack of freedom is irksome to the "captive customer" who at times may be treated rather summarily by his "captor-conference." Certainly these complaints of the shippers are important. Any buyer likes to be free to purchase what he wants as cheaply as possible.

Nonconference liner operators rightly claim that even though they can make attractive rate offers to prospective shippers, the tying arrangements—particularly the dual rate and deferred rebate schemes—prevent them from effectively competing with the conference members. Conditions change rapidly in the market for shipping services and the nonconference operators are thus sometimes frustrated in their attempts to obtain the accounts of new shippers during a period of business decline.

Conference members themselves sometimes chafe under the discipline required for an effective conference. Self-interest compels each member to submit to the rules of the organization. Yet there are times when a conference member must yearn for the freedom to operate independently. Sometimes the yearning gives way to action and the conference dissolves. So long as business conditions and individual company earnings are satisfactory, conference agreements on rates, schedules, and other matters are not oppressive. When profits decline this may no longer be true. We can safely assume that when conferences disintegrate, members have decided that the advantages of tying agreements are, temporarily at least, outweighed by the disadvantages of the intraconference restrictions just discussed.

The United States government, as a large shipper, shipowner, and operator, and as the agency responsible for the national welfare, is in an odd position as regards appropriate policy toward shipping conferences. It wants competition to be free enough to insure rates near those that would be established in a free competitive market. It also wants stable rates, which can best be obtained by permitting ship operators to form monopolistic combinations. However, the formation of such groups is not ordinarily favored by the government. Still, the overtonnaging of some trades, often a concomitant of the monopoloid combinations, may be in the interest of national defense. Are these conflicting desires effectively reconciled in the policy of the United States government toward steamship conferences?

UNITED STATES POLICY TOWARD SHIPPING CONFERENCES

The limited power of any national government prevents it from effectively controlling international shipping competition. For the United States this has been particularly vexing because of the anti-monopoly and anti-cartel bias of government policy. For the most part, other important maritime nations do not share this bias. They accept cartels with little official animosity. The United States government accepts conferences but it puts restrictions on their American members. Much of the United States policy on conferences appears in the Shipping Act, 1916. As the following passage shows, United States-flag ship operators are not forbidden to join conferences but they must not engage in certain practices engaged in by some conferences.

SEC. 14 . . . That no common carrier by water shall, directly or indirectly, in respect to the transportation by water of passengers or property between a port of a State, Territory, District, or possession of the United States and any other such port or a port of a foreign country—

First.   Pay, or allow, or enter into any combination, agreement, or understanding, expressed or implied, to pay or allow, a deferred rebate to any shipper. The term "deferred rebate" in this Act means a return of any portion of the freight money by a carrier to any shipper as a consideration for the giving of all or any portion of his shipments to the same or any other carrier, or for any other purpose, the payment of which is deferred beyond the completion of the service for which it is paid, and is made only if, during both the period for which computed and the period of deferment, the shipper has complied with the terms of the rebate agreement or arrangement.

Second.   Use a fighting ship either separately or in conjunction with any other carrier, through agreement or otherwise. The term "fighting ship" in this Act means a vessel used in a particular trade by a carrier or group of carriers for the purpose of excluding, preventing, or reducing competition by driving another carrier out of said trade.

Third. Retaliate against any shipper by refusing, or threatening to refuse, space accommodations when such are available, or resort to other discriminating or unfair methods, because such shipper has patronized any other carrier or has filed a complaint charging unfair treatment, or for any other reason.

Fourth. Make any unfair or unjustly discriminatory contract with any shipper based on the volume of freight offered, or unfairly treat or unjustly discriminate against any shipper in the matter of (a) cargo space accommodations or other facilities, due regard being had for the proper loading of the vessel and the available tonnage; (b) the loading and landing of freight in proper condition; or (c) the adjustment and settlement of claims.

Any carrier who violates any provision of this section shall be guilty of a misdemeanor punishable by a fine of not more than $25,000 for each offense.

In reading this law one must remember that the government cannot directly regulate the rates and services established by international shipping conferences. Though the law may appear to give the government the right to regulate rates, this applies only to domestic operations. The United States government can exert *indirect* control over international conference agreements by refusing to approve the participation of American-flag vessels under the agreement, by penalizing them if they do so, and by refusing certain port privileges to foreign-flag vessels.

The 1916 Act (Section 14a) also provides means of disciplining foreign lines participating in steamship conferences affecting United States foreign trade. If they use deferred rebate schemes or other "unfair practices" they can be refused entry to American ports. The same penalty can be invoked if a conference excludes United States-flag lines from joining the organization on "equal terms" with other members. In this way conferences can be kept open to new members, thus overcoming one of the objections to a cartel-type organization.

Further safeguards are provided in Section 15 of the 1916 Act. All conference agreements affecting American-flag lines in United States foreign trade (and "every common carrier by water, or other person subject to this Act") must be filed with the Federal Maritime Board. The Board "may by order disapprove, cancel, or modify any agreement or any modification or cancellation thereof" if it finds the agreement "to be unjustly discriminatory or unfair as between carriers, shippers, exporters, importers, or ports, or between exporters from the United States and their foreign competitors, or to operate to the detriment of the commerce of the United States, or to be in violation of this Act. . . ." Violators of any provision of this section are liable to penalty of $1,000 for each day the violation occurs.

Section 15 also provides that shipping conference members shall be exempt from prosecution under certain antitrust laws. This constitutes official recognition of the need for cartel-type organizations in ocean shipping.

Section 16 of the Shipping Act, 1916, forbids "unreasonable" discrimination for or against persons, localities, and classes of traffic. Under this section it is also unlawful to grant preferential rates through false billing, classification, and other similar means, or to induce marine insurance companies to grant less favorable rates to competitive ship operators. Anyone violating Section 16 is liable to a maximum fine of $5,000 for each offense.

If rates are "unjustly discriminatory between shippers or ports or unjustly prejudicial to exporters of the United States as compared with their foreign competitors" the Federal Maritime Board may alter the rates to eliminate this unfairness and order the carrier to discontinue his unduly discriminatory practices. The Board has some authority as regards carrier regulations and procedures, for receiving, handling, storing or delivering cargoes. (Section 17.)

The Merchant Marine Act, 1920, empowers the Federal Maritime Board, "to make rules and regulations affecting shipping in the foreign trade not in conflict with law in order to adjust or meet general or special conditions unfavorable to shipping in the foreign trade, whether in any particular trade or upon any particular route or in commerce generally and which arise out of or result from foreign laws, rules, or regulations or from competitive methods or practices employed by owners, operators, agents, or masters of vessels of a foreign country. . . ." (Section 19.)

Two other features of United States policy toward shipping competition deserve mention. Both appear in the Merchant

Marine Act, 1936. Under Section 205 it is unlawful for any "common carrier by water," acting on the basis of a conference agreement or any other arrangement, to prevent any other common carrier from servicing a United States-controlled port improved by the use of funds appropriated by Congress at "the same rates which it charges at the nearest port already served by it." This provision was designed to help newly developed ports in their struggle for traffic and appears to be a case in which reasonable or not undue discrimination is forbidden.

Under Section 212e of the 1936 Act the Maritime Commission studied differences between inbound and outbound United States foreign trade rates and practices that were alleged to be discriminatory. It concluded that the two types of trade (inbound and outbound) were very different. This precluded recommendations regarding discrimination, pending further investigations.[10]

To summarize, the United States policy toward shipping conferences is one of recognizing their uses while trying to guard against their abuses. American operators are permitted to participate, despite the cartel-like features of conferences, and they get government support if conferences deny them membership on equal terms. At the same time, American operators participating in conferences are subject to a code of rules intended to protect shippers and the public interest against undue discrimination and the exploitation of monopolistic advantages. Foreign ship operators engaging in "unfair practices" are also subject to punitive action by the United States. By this combination of policies, the United States government seeks to balance the interests of ship operators in and out of conferences, of shippers, and of the country as a whole.

CONCLUSIONS

United States policy toward shipping conferences is based on the assumption that regulated competition is preferable to unregulated. The same assumption lies behind government control of competition in aid and land transport. It reflects the

[10] See United States Maritime Commission, *Report to Congress* (Washington: GPO, 1938), p. 17.

view that intergovernmental agreements and agencies are unsuitable for dealing with the complexities of many aspects of international shipping. It represents a neat solution to the problem of reconciling domestic anti-trust policy with the necessity for cartel-type organizations in foreign trade shipping. These are all important advantages of the policy.

Some features of the policy are not advantageous. So far as conference rate practices keep rates above the level that would obtain in a more competitive market, the shippers are not benefited and trades may be overtonnaged. Chronically overtonnaged trades entail a waste of men and equipment, but economic considerations may be outweighed by considerations of national defense. Though it is often asserted that stable rather than fluctuating rates are more conducive to a high volume of trade, the proof offered in support of this theoretically acceptable statement is not impressive. Further, proof is lacking that the *average* rates paid by shippers in the absence of conferences would be either higher or lower than the average under conference regulation. Thus, while United States policy helps to preserve conferences and their obvious advantages to ship operators, it is not clear that the policy is equally advantageous to shippers and those interested in attaining a close relationship between the quantity of shipping available and the quantity needed. Certainly, monopolistic abuses unfavorable to these two groups do occur under the conference system.

The alternatives to current United States policy regarding steamship conferences are not promising. Surely United States-flag vessels should not be forced to "go it alone" outside the conference system. In the freely competitive market in which they would find themselves, they would require additional subsidies and other governmental aid or they probably would not survive. And if they were adequately supported, foreign-flag merchantmen would no doubt seek and obtain governmental assistance, too. Rate wars could readily ensue, not only among nonconference operators but between conference operators and subsidized nonconference companies. This would soon amount to intergovernmental competition. Embittered economic and diplomatic relations would ensue. So, this alternative is unwise.

An international agency to control shipping competition is also not desirable today. Many problems now handled under relatively simple administrative procedures would no doubt become ensnared in bureaucratic "red tape." Some ship operators, provided with a "court of appeals," would be prone to let this "court" adjudicate conflicts best settled by the interested parties themselves. If governmental representatives became involved in the administration of conferences, political considerations might well interfere with economic decision-making. Thus, on administrative grounds alone, this alternative must be rejected.

United States policy falls between these extremes in the range of alternatives. By insisting upon "open" conferences, "fair" discriminatory rates and practices, and the protection of nonconference operators, it fosters its own self-interest without damaging its relations with other nations. So long as a sizeable volume of the world's shipping tonnage operates under private ownership, the conference system, faced with actual and potential competition from industrial carriers, tramps, nonconference lines, government-operated ships, and the vessels in the United States reserve fleet, appears to serve United States requirements best under the kinds of safeguards provided by federal maritime legislation. It is not a *wholly* satisfactory arrangement from all viewpoints but it is better than the feasible alternatives. However, should government ownership of national merchant marines become widespread, an international agency such as the Intergovernmental Maritime Consultative Organization (IMCO) might be a better means for regulating ocean shipping.[11]

---

[11] At the time of writing IMCO has not been established. Only 17 of the necessary 21 ratifications have been obtained. One of the principal objections to IMCO is the fear that it may concern itself with non-technical matters involving economic and commercial issues. There is widespread agreement that IMCO could perform valuable services in bringing about agreement on various technical aspects of ocean shipping. However, some of its proposed statutes would permit IMCO to examine the nontechnical aspects of shipping mentioned above. (See United Nations, General Assembly, *Official Records, Tenth Session, Second Committee. 384th Meeting* [December 2, 1955], p. 175; Same, Economic and Social Council, *Official Records, Nineteenth Session, Supplement no. 4* [New York: 1955] p. 3.)

VIII
ESSENTIAL TRADE ROUTES

THE *Murray Report* declared that "the essential trade route concept is sound and has contributed to the economic stability of the liner segment of our merchant fleet in the foreign trades. However, constant scrutiny of all trades should be given in order to assure that the granting of subsidy aid is in keeping with the traffic needs of each essential route." [1]

As noted in Chapter IV, operating-differential subsidies are granted only to companies that schedule sailings on one or more of the thirty-one essential trade routes of the United States. These routes were designated as essential by the United States Maritime Commission on May 20, 1946.[2] They were found to be, in the language of the Merchant Marine Act, 1936: "essential for the promotion, development, expansion, and maintenance of the foreign commerce of the United States."

Under Section 211 of the Act, the Maritime Commission was instructed to "give due weight to the cost of maintaining each of such steamship lines [on essential trade routes], the probability that any such line cannot be maintained except at heavy loss disproportionate to the benefit accruing to foreign trade, the number of sailings and types of vessels that should be employed in such lines, and any other facts and conditions that a prudent business man would consider when dealing with his own business, *with the added consideration, however, of the intangible benefit the maintenance of any such line may afford to the foreign commerce of the United States and to the national defense.*" (Italics mine.)

In reviewing the essential trade routes in 1953, the Maritime

[1] P. 121.
[2] U.S. Department of Commerce, *Review of Essential United States Foreign Trade Routes* (Washington: GPO, 1953), p. 4. This action was authorized under section 211 of the Merchant Marine Act, 1936.

Administration noted that "present day influences in the world are different from those influences which exerted force in 1936 when the initial concepts regarding trade routes were established." [3] It then continued, "As a result of recent world events other factors in line with Congressional intention must be considered, for the reason that their influence is of increased importance to the national welfare of the United States." The Maritime Administration listed four "basic areas of consideration [as] . . . paramount" in the determination of essential trade routes: economic, "geopolitical," national defense, and steamship economics.

Under "economic" the Maritime Administration considers the following: (1) comparison of the trade area with total trade as to exports, imports, dollar balance exchange, and post-war and prewar trends in these items; (2) significance of the trade to the economy of the United States as measured by such factors as the importance of exports and imports to the United States economy, the competition between American and foreign goods, and raw materials and resource potentials; (3) domestic industrial relocation and development as they are related to trade; and (4) trade inhibitors—tariffs, currency restrictions, quantitative restrictions, and licensing systems.

The "geopolitical" factors include (1) climate, geographical position, and strategic position; (2) aid programs; (3) importance of route for movement of materials vital to the United States and its defense; (4) political effect of United States-flag shipping on the route; (5) influence of the trade route on "so-called 'Fringe Nations'"; (6) development of trade possibilities because of political status; and (7) competitive position of products of the United States because of changed political status of foreign areas.

"Military" considerations involve these factors: (1) direction of movement of military cargoes; (2) stock-piling activities; and (3) advantages of increased exports to areas near trade routes essential to national defense.

"Steamship economics" encompasses judgment about many matters. Included are (1) delimiting the trade area to conform with economical ship operating practices; (2) the service requirements of the areas; the characteristics of vessels to be

[3] *Review of Essential . . . Trade Routes*, cited, p. 6.

employed; and (3) the type of foreign competition to be encountered.[4]

The postwar criteria developed by the Maritime Administration indicate clearly that the military benefits are no longer "intangible." Combined with the "geopolitical" gains to be obtained from the establishment and development of essential trade routes, they are probably sufficient in some instances to overcome the ordinary considerations of the "prudent business man." They will also outweigh the purely economic. The revised statement of criteria brings out more clearly than ever the mutual inconsistency of objectives that has plagued United States shipping policy. However, before reaching the conclusion that this conflict has produced deleterious effects upon the economy of the United States and the prosperity of foreign merchant fleets, we should examine the record.

Unfortunately, though figures exist, it is not possible to determine with acceptable accuracy the effects of the policy of fixing "essential trade routes" upon the United States merchant marine and its foreign competitors. The Maritime Administration will not release data that will reveal the percentage of cargoes carried by subsidized operators on each trade route. This proscription is applied because of the small number of American-flag rivals on some trade routes. By simple subtraction competitors would be able to find out how well their rivals were doing. Nevertheless, some data are available. They permit apparently sound inferences.

For 1952 it is possible to estimate the importance of subsidized operators on the essential trade routes. During that year, liners of all flags lifted about 35 million long tons of dry cargo on the essential trade routes of the United States. United States-flag vessels carried 35 per cent of dry cargoes (liner and nonliner) on these routes. If we assume that this figure also applies to the share of the total dry-cargo trade carried aboard United States-flag liners on these routes, it appears that these liners handled roughly 12.4 million long tons. In 1952, subsidized sailings accounted for 11.2 million tons or a little over 90 per cent of the dry cargo handled by

---

[4] This condensed list of criteria was taken from *Review of Essential . . . Trade Routes*, cited, p. 6-7. In some cases paraphrasing has been employed; in others direct quotation.

United States-flag liners on these routes.[5] At least for 1952, then, subsidized liners were overwhelmingly important in carrying the United States share of liner-lifted dry cargoes on essential trade routes. At this writing there are no comparable data for other years.[6]

Table 17 summarizes the findings of the Maritime Administration about the amount of cargo carried by United States-flag ships on essential and other trade routes. The period covered is too short to warrant any inferences regarding long-term trends. The figures do illustrate the wide year-to-year fluctuations in the amount of cargo handled by United States-flag vessels. When used in conjunction with the figures in Appendix Table 2,[7] they confirm the tendency of the share of foreign trade cargoes lifted by American-flag vessels to decline. Even here, though, there are marked yearly departures from the apparent trend.

The American-flag vessel share of dry-cargo tonnage on essential trade routes is far higher than on the other routes. The small absolute volume of tonnage carried on the latter lowers the United States-flag share of total dry cargoes only slightly. The data do not permit the inference that the establishment of certain routes as essential has attracted American lines to them. The much larger American-flag share of the

[5] Total liner and United States-flag liner cargoes on essential trade routes, from United States Department of Commerce, Maritime Administration, *United States Ocean-borne Foreign Trade Route Traffic Carried by Dry Cargo Ships, Calendar Years 1948, 1950, 1951 and 1952* (Washington: Maritime Administration, December 18, 1953), pt. 2, p. 5. Cargo tonnage carried on subsidized sailings, from records of the Maritime Administration as transcribed for the author by W. B. Harmon. Figures exclude all military and special category cargoes.

[6] One other bit of evidence indicating the greater relative importance of United States-flag liners on essential trade routes appears in the informal table on p. 94. For 1953 and 1954, United States-flag liners lifted a total 27.2 million long tons of dry cargoes in foreign trade. Subsidized sailings accounted for 22.1 million tons. (Figures from U.S. Department of Commerce, Bureau of the Census, "United States Water-Borne Trade," *Summary Report FT 985* (Washington: June 24, 1955), p. 10; tabulation cited in n. 5, above, and letter to author from W. B. Harmon, Maritime Administration, January 6, 1956.

[7] The differences between the totals in Table 17 and those in Appendix Table 2 are attributable to differences in coverage. Since the exact magnitude of the absolute totals is not important in the context in which this table is being used, the figures have not been reconciled with those in the appendix.

Table 17

UNITED STATES WATER-BORNE FOREIGN TRADE DRY-CARGO TONNAGE LIFTED BY UNITED STATES-FLAG VESSELS ON ESSENTIAL AND OTHER FOREIGN TRADE ROUTES, 1948, 1950-53

Part A.—*Percentage carried in United States-flag vessels*[a]
Year and Type of Trade Route

Direction of trade	1948			1950			1951			1952			1953		
	Essential	Other	Total	Essential	Other	Total	Essential	Other	Total	Essential	Other	Total	Essential	Other	Total
Imports	55	26	49	38	16	37	42	21	39	41	15	37	33	9	30
Exports	46	24	45	36	18	34	42	15	41	31	12	30	24	12	23
Total	49	25	47	37	16	34	42	19	39	35	15	33	28	10	27

Part B.—*Cargo tons carried in United States-flag vessels*
[In millions of long tons]

Direction of trade	1948			1950			1951			1952			1953		
	Essential	Other	Total	Essential	Other	Total	Essential	Other	Total	Essential	Other	Total	Essential	Other	Total
Imports	13.7	1.5	14.9	11.6	1.2	12.6	14.2	1.4	15.8	13.7	1.0	14.9	12.6	0.5	13.1
Exports	21.0	0.6	21.7	9.7	0.6	10.3	29.3	0.6	30.3	18.2	0.5	18.9	9.7	0.2	9.9
Total[b]	34.6	2.0	37.0	21.3	1.8	23.4	43.5	2.1	44.7	32.3	1.6	34.0	22.3	0.7	23.0

a The percentage of dry cargoes carried by United States-flag vessels as shown here differs somewhat in magnitude from those appearing in Appendix Table 2. However, the direction of year-to-year change is the same.

b These totals do not add properly because subtotals were rounded and because the absolute tonnage figures were derived by multiplying total essential and other trade route cargo-tonnage figures by the percentage (as computed by the Maritime Administration) of these cargoes carried aboard United States-flag vessels.

Source: For 1948, 1950-52, U.S. Department of Commerce, Maritime Administration, *United States Oceanborne Foreign Trade Route Traffic Carried by Dry Cargo Ships, Calendar Years 1949, 1950, 1951 and 1952* (Washington: December 18, 1953), pt. 2, p. 2-5. For 1953, U.S. House of Representatives, *Study of the Operations of the Maritime Administration and the Federal Maritime Board, Hearings Before the Committee on Merchant Marine and Fisheries,* 84th Cong, 1st sess. (Washington: GPO, 1955), p. 282-283.

dry cargoes is probably attributable to the greater traffic density, the types of cargoes available, the institutional arrangements between carriers and shippers (e.g. ore movements by company carriers), and many additional factors other than the designation of the trade routes as essential.

Even the presence of subsidized liners on essential trade routes does not appear to assure a high degree of United States-flag vessel participation in the traffic available. In 1953, for example, the average share covering all essential trades was 28 per cent. The American-flag share of dry cargoes ranged from 1 per cent on trade route 26-A—Pacific Coast, United Kingdom, and Eire—to 68 per cent on trade route 15-B—Gulf Coast, South and East Africa, and Madagascar.[8] This does not mean that the absence of subsidized liners would not lower the *total* share significantly. Nor does it mean that on given routes, where subsidized liners offer considerable service, their withdrawal would have only an insignificant effect on the American-flag share. Our findings merely indicate that designation of a trade route as essential, plus the presence of subsidized operators, does not necessarily lead to United States shipping companies' gaining a large share of the available dry cargoes.

This brief examination of the essential trade route scheme yields no startling or unusual conclusions. Their mere designation as essential by the Maritime Administration does not adversely affect foreign shipping lines. When the government grants operating-differential subsidies to liner operators on these routes, the division of cargoes among carriers undoubtedly shifts some. Thus, indirectly, the essential trade route designation affects foreigners. Nonsubsidized American as well as foreign carriers are affected. However, under the criteria titled "steamship economics" the government tries not to overtonnage a route more than the criteria of national defense and "geopolitics" demand. This, coupled with acceptance of the conference system, minimizes the harmful effects upon foreign shipping lines.

[8] The volume of cargoes lifted by American-flag vessels on each of these routes is not large. On 26-A it amounted to 4,000 long tons, the lowest of any trade route. On 15-B it totalled 315,000 tons, well below the 3.0 million tons (41 per cent of the total) carried on route 4— Atlantic Coast, Caribbean. Data from source for 1953 as stated in Table 17.

Further we should note that the granting of operating-differential subsidies only to liner operators on essential trade routes leaves a substantial area of shipping open to private competition free from direct governmental assistance. This would not be true if the United States government were to pay a general navigation bounty. Then *all* United States-flag vessel operators would be subsidized, regardless of route or type of operation. This would surely increase the competitive difficulties of foreign-flag shipping companies since more excess tonnage could be kept in operation.

IX

THE MILITARY SEA TRANSPORTATION
SERVICE

AMERICAN SHIPPING COMPANIES have complained bitterly
about the operations of the MSTS. This agency of the Department of Defense is responsible "for providing all ocean-
going transportation for the Armed Forces." [1] It operates its
own vessels and assigns space on private vessels for cargoes of
the military establishment. The Space Assignment Committee
(composed of representatives of the MSTS and the military
services shipping personnel or freight) determines how the
shipping requirements will be handled.[2] The Committee administratively determines whether space in the MSTS nucleus
fleet, privately-owned, or National Shipping Authority ships,[3]
or space obtained in some other way by the MSTS, will be
used for transporting armed services personnel and freight.

The MSTS nucleus fleet and private shipping offer dupli-
cate service on some trade routes. Needless to say, the existence of the MSTS fleet carrying items that could be moved
aboard ships of the privately-owned merchant fleet creates

[1] Memorandum from Secretary of Defense, Subject: "Relationship Between
the National Shipping Authority and the Military Sea Transportation Service" (May 10, 1951), as reproduced in *Statement Concerning the Organization and Operation of the Military Sea Transportation Service and its
Relationship With the U.S. Private Shipping Industry, by Vice-Admiral
F. C. Denebrink, USN, Commander Military Sea Transportation Service
before the Sub-Committee on Operations of the Military Sea Transportation Service (House Merchant Marine and Fisheries Committee) on 26
March 1954* (mimeographed), p. 13. (Hereafter referred to as "*Statement.*")
[2] If this committee cannot agree on priorities, when space requirements
exceed the shipping space available, the Joint Military Transportation Committee makes the decision. *Statement*, cited, p. 30-31.
[3] The National Shipping Authority is the agency of the Maritime Administration responsible for the government-owned commercial fleet.

political and administrative problems for the government, as well as financial problems for private vessel operators short of cargo. It may also arouse complaints from foreign-flag shipping companies who believe that their vessels should be used to service United States military installations in their countries. The functions, operations, and policies of the MSTS are therefore important aspects of the maritime policy of the United States.

FUNCTIONS OF THE MSTS

"The mission of MSTS . . . consists basically of three elements—to provide sea transportation for personnel and cargoes of the Department of Defense—to plan and negotiate for use of commercial shipping to augment the MSTS fleet as necessary—to plan for and be capable of expansion in time of war as directed." [4] This brief statement suffices to give meaning to a list of sixteen specific functions and responsibilities assigned to the MSTS. These range from the control, operation, repair, alteration, maintenance, and administration of government-owned vessels assigned to the MSTS to the "control of all passengers on MSTS vessels." [5]

Contrary to the belief of many, the MSTS is not primarily a transport-operating organization. True, it does operate a number of vessels. But this is only incidental to its principal functions. As the statement of its mission indicates, it provides sea transportation. This provision can be made either by using its own nucleus fleet or vessels of the privately-owned merchant marine. The larger the MSTS nucleus fleet, the less likely that private shipowners will get MSTS cargoes.

The MSTS was established to eliminate the unnecessary duplication of shipping facilities by the different branches of the armed services. It also prevents competitive bidding by these branches for the shipping services of the privately-owned merchant marine. Both of these objectives could have been achieved without the formation of a nucleus fleet. Why then, was this fleet established?

Fulfilling the mission "to provide sea transportation for per-

[4] *Statement*, cited, p. 20.
[5] Same, p. 9-10.

sonnel and cargoes of the Department of Defense" requires that the transportation be available when the armed forces want it. Without its own fleet, the MSTS would be entirely dependent upon private shipping. This would mean that the operating personnel aboard all ships carrying MSTS cargoes and passengers would be hired by private industry and be partly subject to the regulations of the relevant maritime unions. Under these conditions, a strike by unionized waterfront or shipboard employees could seriously cripple effective military operations. Military prudence demands a hedge against this risk.

Admiral F. C. Denebrink, Commander of the MSTS, testified: "Private American shipping, over the past 20 years, has been subjected to cessation of operations due to many factors beyond its control, such as work stoppages. On the other hand, military operations are continuing, as evidenced by United States Armed Forces overseas. The national security must not be compromised by major dependence upon private shipping when it is continuously subjected to cessations of operation . . . . While unions, in the past, have moved essential military cargoes, many complications arise when ships have both military and commercial cargoes. This situation can, and has, resulted in ships not sailing, or the military bearing the cost of handling commercial cargoes before military cargoes can be loaded or discharged." [6]

Though seldom mentioned in writing, there is a good disciplinary reason as well for maintaining a MSTS nucleus fleet. There were instances during World War II when the crews of privately-operated vessels were unwilling to sail their vessels into certain dangerous areas or when they refused duty, or were grossly undisciplined. This experience, combined with the fact that some maritime unions have been infiltrated by communists, has made the Department of Defense unwilling to relinquish its merchant marine. [7]

[6] U.S. Senate, *Military Sea Transport Service*, Hearings on S. 1439 and S. 1881 Before a Subcommittee of the Committee on Interstate and Foreign Commerce, 83rd Cong., 1st sess. (Washington: GPO, 1953) p. 69.
[7] These observations were made by Hanson Baldwin of *The New York Times* during a personal interview on May 17, 1954. See also articles by Mr. Baldwin in *The New York Times*, October 9, 1946, January 9, 1947 and December 30, 1948.

OPERATIONS OF THE MSTS

Basically, the MSTS acts as the sea transportation agent of the armed services. It handles all requests for military sea transport. It estimates the amount of cargo space required and then determines how this space will be supplied. The next step is to allocate cargoes to the vessels, both private and government-operated.

In fulfilling its mission the MSTS engages in large-scale operations. For example, in fiscal 1953 it arranged for the transportation of 28.8 million measurement tons of dry cargo (about 16.5 million long tons).[8] Private (nonmilitary) foreign trade dry cargo lifted by American-flag ships totalled about 29.7 million long tons. The MSTS also shipped about 17 million long tons of petroleum in 1953 as compared with a total of 22.1 million tons for private shipments aboard United States-flag vessels.

Private carriers lifted much MSTS cargo. For fiscal years 1953-55, the annual average was 22.3 million measurement tons or about 12.7 million long tons of dry cargoes (using a stowage factor of .70, or 1.75 measurement tons per long ton). In fiscal 1955 the amount of MSTS cargo carried by private operators was 9.1 million long tons, well below the average for the three years. For comparison, commercial foreign trade dry cargoes lifted by American-flag vessels during 1953-54 averaged 29.2 million long tons a year. Commercial ship-operating interests received nearly $466 million or about 67 per cent of the total outlays of the MSTS.[9]

As of January 1, 1954, the MSTS nucleus fleet consisted of 255 ships totaling a little more than 2 million deadweight tons.[10]

---

[8] A measurement ton is a cubic measure that has a different weight equivalent according to the type of cargo.

[9] The MSTS cargo and financial statistics cited in this section were obtained from the MSTS. J. J. Floyd and Marie T. Van Horn transcribed the data from their office copies of MSTS, *Financial and Statistical Report.* H. E. Cole, Comptroller, MSTS, in a letter to the author, Oct. 10, 1955, also provided information. The nonmilitary figures are for calendar years.

[10] Figures from Appendix Table 10. In addition to the ships listed on the next page, the MSTS operated 6 service craft—lighters. On January 1, 1955 the nucleus fleet consisted of 211 vessels of 1.7 million dwt.

The breakdown of this total was as follows:

	Commissioned	Contract-Operated	Civil Service	Total
No.	26	100	129	255
Dwt (Thousands)	272	1,000	743	2,015

The commissioned ships were military-manned. The contract-operated vessels were run by private crews under contract to the MSTS. The civil service ships were operated by civil service as distinct from nongovernmental employees and military personnel. All three types of ships are government-owned, under the custody of the Navy.

Augmenting the government-owned nucleus fleet were two other sets of vessels. Privately-owned, privately-operated ships were under time and voyage charters to the MSTS. In addition, government-owned ships, under Maritime Administration custody, were privately-operated under general agency agreements. There were forty-six ships in the latter category on January 1, 1954.[11]

Judged by commonly accepted standards, the MSTS fleet looms large on the shipping horizon. Its 255 ships equalled one-fifth of the total active merchant marine of the United States on January 1, 1954. It controlled, in its nucleus fleet, about 13 per cent of the active deadweight tonnage. On January 1, 1955, the figures were 18 and 12 per cent, respectively. Small wonder, then, that private shipping companies, despite their earnings from the MSTS, should be concerned about its policies.

POLICIES OF THE MSTS

The MSTS has established the following order of priority in the uses of shipping methods:
1. Ships of the nucleus fleet of the MSTS.

[11] This figure is from the worksheet records of John McCarron of the MSTS. Mr. McCarron had no records covering time and voyage charters. His tabulation covered only vessels in the custody of the Maritime Administration. Data presented by the MSTS to the Congress indicated that on March 1, 1954, the MSTS had 65 privately-owned ships under time charter and 25 under voyage charter. (March 1, 1954 statistics from *Statement*, cited, p. 27.)

2. Available berth space—i.e. space aboard regularly scheduled liners—to the maximum extent consistent with military requirements.
3. Time charters of privately-owned merchant vessels on a voluntary basis.
4. Shipping obtained from the National Shipping Authority under general agency agreement.
5. Foreign-flag shipping when United States-flag vessels are unavailable or unsuited to military requirements.[12]

Though commercial carriers handled about four-fifths of the dry-cargo tonnage shipped by the MSTS during the years 1951-53, they are not satisfied. This is understandable. The prize that remains outside their grasp is valuable. In fiscal 1953, for instance, the MSTS nucleus fleet lifted nearly 6 million measurement tons (about 3.4 million long tons) of dry cargo.

The shipping industry has challenged the MSTS to prove that it is cheaper to use MSTS rather than commercial vessels.[13] Unfortunately, the cost data for industry and government are not comparable, thereby precluding fruitful comparisons. However, even if it could be proved that private industry could do the job at lower cost, compelling reasons would dictate that the MSTS continue to handle a significant volume of its own shipments.

In this regard, the forthright testimony of Admiral W. M. Callaghan, the then Commander of the MSTS, warrants direct quotation. It clearly indicates the Navy's prime economic reason for employing the MSTS nucleus instead of the private merchant marine to lift MSTS cargoes.

[12] These priorities are based upon a "Memorandum of Agreement" between the Department of Defense and the Department of Commerce, August 15, 1951. The statements above paraphrase those found in *Statement*, cited, p. 30 and exhibit A-7.
[13] See, for example, U.S. House of Representatives, *Study of Operations of Military Sea Transportation Service*, Hearings Before the Special Subcommittee to Consider Operations of the Military Sea Transportation Service of the Committee on Merchant Marine and Fisheries. 83rd Cong., 2d sess. (Washington: GPO, 1954), p. 295. See also U.S. Senate, *Merchant Marine Study and Investigation (Transportation of Cargoes by the Military)*, Hearings pursuant to S. Res. 50, Subcommittee of the Committee on Interstate and Foreign Commerce, 81st Cong., 2d sess. (Washington: GPO, 1950), p. 1098. Testimony of Frazer A. Bailey, president, National Federation of American Shipping.

Senator Warren Magnuson was questioning Admiral Callaghan:

Senator Magnuson. Now supposing that you have 10,000 tons of cargo on the dock in Seattle, pure military cargo, to be shipped to Japan and there is a commercial line or there are commercial lines available. What is the practice as to whether you would put it in a military ship or a commercial ship?

Admiral Callaghan. My practice is to put that cargo in the military ship.

Senator Magnuson. Why is that?

Admiral Callaghan. Because I think it is indefensible to run a military ship without cargo in it to give business to a private ship. If the military ship is scheduled to make that run it is an indefensible policy not to put military cargo in that ship in order to afford business to a commercial operator.

Senator Magnuson. Is that because you maintain the cost is cheaper to put it in a military ship than to put it in a commercial ship?

Admiral Callaghan. I do not necessarily maintain that, but I think we would incur a double cost if we ran a military ship partially loaded and then increase the charter miles, or space charter miles in commercial shipping.[14]

Admiral Callaghan also clearly stated the position of the Navy regarding the military usefulness of the peacetime MSTS. Again, Senator Magnuson asked the questions.

Admiral Callaghan. . . . It is the daily operating experience that our Navy gets with auxiliary vessels of the merchant type that enables us to develop the skills and the techniques to carry on that type of mobile logistic support in time of an emergency.

Senator Magnuson. And you do not think it could exist with a private merchant marine?

Admiral Callaghan. It was markedly deficient in that respect.

Senator Magnuson. You do not think it could exist with a private merchant marine in this case?

Admiral Callaghan. I do not; no, sir.

Senator Magnuson. You feel that the Navy must continue to operate a certain portion of military merchant marine.

Admiral Callaghan. I do, definitely.

Senator Magnuson. How long would you say that should continue?

Admiral Callaghan. I should say that should continue until

[14] *Merchant Marine Study and Investigation,* cited, p. 1060.

the world situation approximated that perhaps in the early twenties or early thirties before the threat of a second world war faced us.[15]

In passing we should note that Admiral Callaghan's defense of the peacetime MSTS closely parallels the national defense argument used by the privately-operated shipping interests.

EVALUATION OF MSTS POLICIES AND OPERATIONS

If we assume that it would cost less to have the privately-operated American-flag merchant marine transport MSTS cargoes (and indeed this may be true), it still follows that, as Admiral Callaghan said, the *total* outlay by the government would be less if it was shipped via MSTS ships. That is to say, if the military are going to maintain and operate a merchant fleet, it is cheaper to use it to carry goods than to sail it empty and pay commercial operators for carrying cargo.

The choice offered the MSTS commander would look different if the commercial merchant marine demonstrated over a long period that it could offer dependable, uninterrupted service. Then, perhaps, the Department of Defense could reduce its estimate of the risk involved in greater dependence upon private merchantmen for lifting military supplies. Only then will private shipping companies have a sound case for recommending the increased use of their vessels for moving military cargoes. This, of course, assumes that the active capacity of the private merchant fleet can be economically kept at levels consistent with the needs of the MSTS.

Another question is suggested by this discussion. Should foreign-flag operators be permitted to transport American military supplies? So long as the United States had no military alliances, this question could be answered negatively, and that answer has been embodied in legislation. Now the system of alliances, forged primarily by the United States, has increased dependence upon foreign military assistance, and at the same time greatly increased the volume of peacetime overseas military cargoes.

Most MSTS cargoes are sent overseas to support military installations operated by the armed forces of the United

[15] Same, p. 1071.

States. Many of these bases are located in foreign countries. For the most part, these posts rely upon local sources for food, shelter, utilities, and other services. To this extent, then, American military activity abroad does not rely exclusively upon American men and supplies. One may well wonder why, having gone this far, the United States insists on the near-exclusive reliance upon American shipping to handle the overseas movement of men and materiel to these bases.[16] Our activities already depend on the skilful integration of foreign and United States activities in many fields. A collective defense arrangement presumably draws strength from permitting each partner to perform the tasks it can do best and cheapest. Denying each the opportunity to do so may needlessly warp the posture of mutual defense while increasing the cost.

Part of the answer to these questions is implied in the policy of refusing to rely entirely on private American vessels. But to the extent that the military do use private vessels, why not those of allied countries as well as of the United States? MSTS officials may answer by pointing to the tradition of all military services. Self-supply and reliance upon one's own materiel and manpower are fundamental to national safety. Plans must always be based upon the assumption that "going it alone" will be the final alternative. Perhaps a civilian is not qualified to challenge this line of reasoning. Yet, sometimes, the layman unhampered by tradition or the preachments of military schools may usefully bring a fresh challenge to accepted dogma. The dogma may escape unchanged after the encounter or it may require modification. Here the crucial issue is whether a strictly national policy in this sphere is appropriate to defensive arrangements based on alliances.

CONCLUSIONS

Given the responsibilities of the Department of Defense and the sporadic interruptions of service experienced by the American shipping industry, the MSTS nucleus fleet is a

---

[16] In March 1954, the MSTS had four special heavy-lift, foreign-flag vessels under time charter. It also had four Canadian-flag EC2 (Liberty-type) cargo ships under time charter. (*Statement*, cited, p. 27.)

necessity. Without it, the military could be fatally hampered in attempting to provide adequate defense for the country. True, the government has enough power to cope with interruptions in maritime services. It is not desirable, though, for the government to *have* to interfere in disputes between management and labor. This inserts government into an arena where many believe employers and employees should bargain freely. Deliberately creating an administrative arrangement which forces government to enter this arena is not desirable. It infringes on important rights and may be the forerunner of other more onerous and less justifiable restrictions. The existence of the MSTS fleet gives the government needed leverage in dealing with both private shipowners and labor.

So far as can be determined, the MSTS uses the private United States-flag merchant marine to the fullest possible extent consistent with its directives and mission. The shipping industry as a whole has little justification for complaint regarding the volume of dry cargoes, although it appears possible (as of 1953) that more petroleum could safely be entrusted to private shipping. Certainly the amount of money disbursed to commercial interests has been substantial. While it is true that ship charterers have perhaps been favored over those offering berth space, we can hardly blame the government for seeking the cheapest way to transport its men and materiel.

On the matter of permitting foreign-flag vessels to carry MSTS cargoes, strange as it seems, in the light of the discussion of cargo preferences, it might be desirable, on military grounds, to divide shipments destined to be handled by commercial carriers between foreign and domestic-flag lines. This would call for a rearrangement of the priorities list. It would meet the united opposition of all American shipping interests. Still, as indicated earlier, this proposal may well be sound from the military viewpoint. In addition, it would do much to strengthen the position of United States diplomats. Concessions in this area could be used to gain trade concessions from foreigners. This in turn, might lead to increased trade. Needless to say, United States shipping companies would gain from this. (Sometimes the bird in the hand may be worth less than the two in the bush!) Expanded world trade, based not only upon increased exports from the United States (attributable to concessions) but also upon increased imports (of shipping services) could yield greater benefits to United States shipping than the present policies do. All factors considered—political, military, and economic—the suggestion to share MSTS cargoes more fully with foreigners appears to warrant serious consideration.

X
CONCLUSIONS

> The ship owner is enthroned on an empire of
> anxiety. As the master of sea captains, he rules
> men who themselves know few peers in absolute
> authority. Yet he is the servant of millions who
> ship or travel by sea.
>
> From an advertisement in *The New
> York Times*, January 17, 1955.[1]

WERE the above quotation to be revised, most readers would
agree that for American shipowners, at least, a sentence should
be added. It would state that actual or merely contemplated
shifts in the maritime policies of the United States add to the
anxiety of the shipowners. Having approved this revision,
these same readers would probably concede that another additional sentence would not be amiss. It would call attention to
the anxiety of government policy makers attempting to determine the best maritime policies for the United States. Nothing
would need to be said about shipbuilders. They suffer mainly
from "derived" anxiety based upon the experience of shipowners and the actions of policy makers.

"Anxiety" is certainly an appropriate description of the
emotional state of those engaged in maritime activities—
whether productive, regulative, or promotive. The preceding
chapters have revealed multiple causes for this condition.
There is therefore no need to recount them in detail. Let us
only recall major developments as background for the assessment of maritime policy as a whole.

The United States seagoing merchant marine includes more
than twice as many vessels and three times the gross tonnage
it did in 1939. The active merchant fleet is a bit larger portion

[1] Written by Guild Copeland, Biow Advertising Agency, for Frank B. Hall
and Co., New York.

of the world's fleet than it was in 1939 (13 per cent), but its importance has declined from nearly 22 per cent of world tonnage in 1949 to about 14 per cent in 1955.

The age distribution of merchant vessels favors foreign-flag fleets. In 1954, 26 per cent of the ships (by gross tonnage) flying foreign colors were under five years old. For the United States, 4 per cent fell in this category. Nine-tenths of the sea-going American merchant fleet was between 5 and 15 years old as compared with about two-fifths of the vessels registered under foreign flags. There is good reason to suspect that the presence of more modern foreign-flag vessels adversely affects the American ship operator.

Nonetheless the postwar years have been generally prosperous ones for the American shipowners. Until relatively recently foreign-flag fleets had not been fully reconstituted, and the foreign aid programs of the United States supplemented sizeable commercial shipments. In 1950, when American ship operators were becoming concerned about the build-up of foreign merchant fleets and the nearing end of Marshall Plan aid, the Korean conflict gave shipping another reprieve from the drastic postwar readjustments anticipated by many.

In 1955, the commercial dry cargoes lifted by the foreign trade segment of the American-flag merchant marine were nearly two-and-one-half times the 1939 volume. This was a sharp gain over 1954 and may presage some upturn in annual cargoes although to date there appears to be a downward trend in the volume of these cargoes carried by the United States merchant marine. The experience of 1955 and the prospects for 1956 bear out the observation that there have also been sharp year-to-year fluctuations in both share and absolute volume of cargoes handled by American merchantmen. This means that in addition to the apparent longer-term decline in their cargo volume and their share of world shipping, American ship operators face the hazard of instability.

In the coastal trades the total volume of postwar cargoes was above prewar levels but the dry-cargo volume was far below. These trades were almost completely shut down during the war, and shipping companies have been unable to regain traffic lost to their land-based competitors. Noncontiguous trade, according to my estimates, has increased steadily over the years. Its volume is not large enough to offset losses in the coastwise and intercoastal traffic.

According to estimates based upon appraisals by responsible governmental officials, the active American-flag merchant marine is from about 2 to 5 million deadweight tons (roughly one-eighth to one-fourth of the active fleet) short of the militarily desirable figure. And even though foreign-flag vessels owned by subsidiaries of United States companies totalled 5.9 million deadweight tons, this tonnage consisted preponderantly of tankers while the deficiency in the United States-flag fleet was primarily in freighters and passenger vessels. With the prospects for increased foreign trade cargoes at best showing little gain and in the recent past generally declining, the coasting trades failing to recover to prewar status, the noncontiguous trade too small to help much, the problem of meeting this particular military requirement is far from solved.

United States shipbuilders, obviously dependent upon the fortunes of vessel operators, and the action of Congress, have no doubt become inured to extreme fluctuations in the demand for vessels. One need only recall that about nine-tenths of their output of merchant vessels since 1914 has been crowded into approximately eight years clustered about World Wars I and II. Though they have been somewhat busier during the years following the recent war than they were after World War I, they have recently experienced a pronounced slump in activity. Prospects for the immediate future are somewhat better. However, for the longer run, they cannot be deemed bright.

THE WEAKNESSES OF POLICY

These facts certainly support the conclusion that ship operation and shipbuilding have not kept pace with the American economy. Indeed, they have declined, both absolutely and in their relative place in the world. They have suffered from instability.

The great expansion in the American merchant fleet and in the output of American yards that took place during the war carried the industry to heights it could not hope to retain in peacetime. The wartime situation was, to some extent, projected into the peace by the inevitable delay in the recovery of foreign fleets and yards. The Korean War, emergency demands for coal and other supplies for Europe, and the expansion of shipping needed to sustain American troops abroad, have all helped to keep up the level of demand for American ships and shipping service. Even so a decline has set in.

This diagnosis of delayed readjustment to the changes from wartime conditions provides little comfort for the industry. The facts of decline and instability cannot be changed. The implication of levelling-off that the diagnosis contains tells little about when and where this might happen. From a broader point of view than that of the industry one can sympathize with the troubles of operators, builders, and maritime labor without implying that the shrinkage of the industry has harmed the American economy. But one cannot use so simple a criterion. Shipbuilding and operation receive government aid. There is a national policy of providing continuing assistance to these industries because it is judged to be in the national interest that they remain larger and more active than they would if purely commercial considerations governed.

The purposes in giving this aid are mixed. Insofar as they are "commercial," the only clear criterion set out in the law is that the United States should have a national-flag merchant marine sufficient to carry all its domestic water-borne commerce and a "substantial portion" of its foreign trade. If the general interpretation is accepted and a "substantial portion" is taken to mean 50 per cent, then government aid has not achieved its purpose. Not only has the American merchant fleet been carrying less than half of American foreign trade in most postwar years, but its share has been declining. To the extent that one would be justified in reading a broader commercial purpose into the policies of government aid, this purpose would presumably be to maintain a sound and thriving industry. The experience of ship operating and shipbuilding in the last few years would raise questions whether such a purpose had been achieved.

The main criterion for judging shipping policy must be its contribution to national defense. This motive has had the greatest stress in official formulation of policy, and undoubt-

edly accounts for the general acceptance of government aid
for shipping and shipbuilding. The national defense criterion
is not easy to apply to national shipping policy. Lacking essential classified data on war plans, one cannot make a sound,
independent judgment of the real importance of shipbuilding
facilities and a national merchant marine to defense. Much less
can one estimate the proper size that these industries should
have to provide for rapid expansion in wartime. One can
reach some tentative conclusions by accepting the military
necessity of shipping and shipbuilding and by using public
statements to indicate the size merchant fleet and shipyard
capacity that the military planners deem necessary. By this
latter standard the American-flag active merchant marine is
perhaps some 2 million tons smaller than it should be for
defense purposes. The level of output in shipyards is also too
low. Thus, by the criterion of defense—so far as the outsider
can judge it—shipping policy has not succeeded.

Still another approach to the assessment of shipping policy
is its relation to the general foreign economic policy of the
United States and to this country's diplomatic relations. Much
of the United States' foreign economic policy can be summarized by saying that ostensibly it aims to further the expansion and enhancement of international economic activity by
the removal of barriers to trade and other transactions, to
promote the best international division of labor, to stimulate
competitive private economic activity, and to minimize interference with the operations of the price system. Much of
United States shipping policy works contrary to these ends.
An important aim of United States foreign economic policy
since the war has been to enable other countries to earn their
own way in the world, and in particular to overcome the so-
called dollar shortage. United States shipping policy has
worked in a contrary direction. Subsidies, and especially cargo
preferences, have reduced the opportunities of foreign shipping countries to earn dollars, thus increasing the need for
direct aid from the United States.

Of course, United States foreign economic policy is not a
consistent, coherent, and unqualified effort to pursue the general principles already mentioned. There are many exceptions,
discrepancies, and failures. These may be regarded as blem-

ishes, but they may also be the result of a deliberate pursuit of other aims, such as national defense. Insofar as defense requires the kind of shipping policy the United States has pursued, then its failure to conform with the aims of foreign economic policy is secondary. But if commercial aims are mixed in with those of defense, or if defense aims could be achieved by other means more harmonious with the aims of foreign economic policy, then there are weaknesses in shipping policy. Subsidies and preferential treatment for American shipping certainly provide cause for friction between this country and those with merchant marines that would otherwise have gained the business. In recent years such complaints have been relatively subdued and the friction has not been great. Foreign merchant marines, rebuilt since the war, have been able to make progress in competition with the American merchant fleet in spite of United States policies. International trade has been expanding and generally buoyant. And further, there has been recognition of a common military interest in pursuit of which American merchant marine policy plays a part. But the friction is not entirely absent. Most of the major shipping nations affected are allied with the United States. Attempts should be made to eliminate this friction, unless the means of eliminating it entail sacrificing a greater national interest. Shipping policies made necessary by considerations of national defense should find acceptance and understanding on the part of allies. Friction arising from unnecessary measures, or measures motivated by various elements of economic nationalism, is an additional weakness of United States shipping policy.

Judged, then, by commercial, military, and diplomatic criteria, as well as by consistency with general foreign economic policy, this country's postwar shipping policy does not come off very well. What have been the causes of these weaknesses?

First, much of the difficulty results simply from the central fact that a substantial part of the industry is an uneconomic one requiring subvention from the public purse and continual shoring-up in other fashions as well. Even when there is little serious political challenge to the main direction of policy, such a situation is likely to be troublesome. Motives become mixed;

national interest and private advantage are intermingled in ways that make it hard to judge rights and wrongs, sound and unsound reasoning, real and fictitious needs. Those responsible for asking and giving government aid may hesitate to pursue their reasoning to its logical conclusion.

Second, the mixture of commercial and national defense aims tends to make policy internally inconsistent. Not only are the two aims different, but they require quite different sets of criteria; only by luck can both objectives be attained. The problem is exemplified most neatly by the difficulties arising from concern over the disposal of new ships—a legitimate commercial concern—resulting from maintenance of a minimum level of activity in national shipyards—a necessary part of the defense policy. Cargo preferences and subsidies demonstrate another conflict; the latter permit international competition for cargoes, the former restrict it.

Third, in spite of the primacy usually given to national defense in explanations of shipping policy, there has been an official unwillingness to accept defense as either the sole or at least the overriding purpose and to shape policy accordingly. There has been no clear-cut acceptance of the view that, in the absence of ability to compete successfully in the free markets of the world, the *only* justification for the continued existence of United States maritime industries is military. As a result, time, effort, and money have been wasted discussing and considering irrelevant issues. The only sound opportunity for reconciling shipping policy with the aims of foreign economic policy generally has been foregone. In consequence, shipping policy unnecessarily irritates relations with other countries.

Finally, even to the extent that defense has dominated shipping policy, the needs of defense have been left lamentably but perhaps understandably unclear. Indications have been given of the size merchant fleet and the volume of shipbuilding capacity judged necessary by military planners. But when shipping policy has failed to produce these results, there has not been the strong reaction that could be expected if defense were really imperilled. There is not much evidence of a forceful drive to remedy the omissions. So the requirements themselves become suspect. Doubt regarding their validity arises, too, from the apparent failure to adjust standards to the changing art of war. Nor is there much reason to believe that full account has been taken of the implications for shipping policy of the United States' commitment to some degree of collective security through alliances. As a result, unreal problems may be at the center of some of our apparent dilemmas in shipping. Unnecessary expenditure and irritation of other countries may be resulting from a lack of cogency in the military approach.

Some may think that these weaknesses are largely inescapable in the formulation of shipping policy in the American way. National defense is not the clear-cut set of requirements and responsive actions that a layman may think it to be (or as some examples of the military man's exposition may represent it). Consistency in foreign economic policy and smooth harmony in foreign relations are not to be had in the real world. Above all, the political process—in its broadest sense—does not permit rigorous application of neatly-defined principles or firm exclusion of the logically extraneous satisfaction of a group interest. We cannot escape from this process; it is the way policy is created and executed in the American democracy. I have not tried, in this book, to trace the way shipping policy has emerged from the political process, to assess the strengths of shipping, shipbuilding, and maritime labor groups, or the extent to which the sanction of military necessity helped gain them support. Such an account would undoubtedly help to explain important parts of the present state of United States maritime policy. Nevertheless, accepting the idea that policy is compromise does not imply that policy can be no different from what it is nor does it make irrelevant the effort to show the inadequacies of policy from the economic, military, and foreign policy points of view and to suggest means of rectifying them.

PRINCIPLES OF POLICY

A principal conclusion of this study is that in the light of officially stated objectives United States policies regarding shipping and shipbuilding have not been successful. Shipbuilding output is below national defense levels; American-flag vessels are carrying less than the "substantial portion" of foreign trade cargoes called for by the basic legislation; military goals have not been met; shipping policy is an irritant in our foreign relations. For the most part these policies have been judged in their own terms, performance being gauged by the purposes set out in legislation or other official statements. This seems appropriate, but it is only one part of the analysis. The criteria themselves need to be examined to see if *they* are appropriate.

Current maritime policy objectives apparently differ little from those set forth in the preamble to the Merchant Marine Act, 1936. Should they? The answer to this question depends in good measure upon one's assessment of the position of the United States in the world today as compared with its status in 1936. Do the appropriate conditions today differ enough to warrant changes in policy objectives? If they do, how should they be changed? What are the implications of these changes for the carrying out of policy? What economic and political repercussions may be anticipated? Those suggesting a shift in objectives or even a shift in emphasis among present objectives must address themselves to these queries.

Certainly all would agree that the world of 1956 differs markedly from what it was in 1936. And surely no one would dispute that the position of the United States has changed. Its economic relations with other nations have altered substantially in the last twenty years. Its military and diplomatic status has shifted. In short, conditions relevant to foreign economic policy and hence shipping policy have changed enough to warrant careful review of national objectives in both areas.

The American economy is not depressed, as it was in 1936. Concern with the economic welfare of the rest of the world has been recognized in foreign economic policy and, in good measure in its own interests, the United States has made substantial efforts to help other countries earn their way in the world. National defense is of much greater urgency than it was in 1936, and is a daily problem, not just the preparation for a rather remote contingency. The United States is engaged in a struggle for political power far different in character and with a different degree of consciousness than in 1936. As the most powerful member of an alliance which has more than military functions, the United States must now concern itself much more directly with the impact of its national decisions upon other countries. There can be little doubt that a shipping policy appropriate in 1936 may not be so in 1956.

In seeking a sound shipping policy we can begin with fundamental considerations that are rather simple—however complicated their translation into practice may prove. From a strictly economic point of view, the United States would be best served by a policy of no aid to shipping and shipbuilding and no restrictions on the competition of foreign vessels for American cargoes. The evidence at hand supports the conclusion that American shipbuilding and ship operation would decline markedly under the impact of foreign competition. There might be some exceptions in shipbuilding, especially in periods of high demand, or in orders for certain specially built vessels. In ship operation, American firms might well compete successfully in international trade if they were free to buy their vessels and hire their crews in the cheapest markets, free of the all-American restrictions they now must abide by. A change in technology in ship operation and shipbuilding might alter the balance of competitive advantage in favor of the United States. But even if a large number of the companies in the American maritime industry went out of business, the American economy would benefit, once an effective readjustment had been made. The men, capital, and resources that are now engaged in a largely uneconomic activity that has to be supported by the taxpayer and by restrictive legislation would be transferred to lines of work not requiring governmental support.

This picture of a purely "economic" policy is simple, but it is also unrealistic. Such a clear-cut "sacrifice" of an American industry is almost certainly beyond the bounds of political possibility. Moreover, such a single-minded policy is probably also not in the national interest. Existing policy is not wrong in stipulating that the needs of national defense must take precedence over strictly economic considerations in the formulation of shipping policy. On the basis of experience in two world wars, we must assume that the maritime industries have an important role to play in national defense. The needs are well known: more ships than are operated in peacetime; a body of merchant sailors and officers which can be expanded to man the larger tonnage; the ability to produce ships and to expand output with some rapidity. To provide for these needs requires: a reserve fleet; an active fleet; shipbuilding capacity; a current output of ships sufficient to keep the essential nucleus labor force and organizations at work in shipbuilding. The maintenance of these features for national defense may require subsidies and protection if competition would otherwise reduce any one of them below the necessary level.

Adopting these principles implies acceptance of some assumptions that are subject to serious question. The principles are based on the experience of past wars when the United States was a rear area, when large quantities of supplies and many troops had to be transported to Europe or Asia by sea, and when the war lasted several years. Future wars may differ greatly in character and the significance of the merchant marine may also differ. Some observers wonder whether changes in strategy and the technology of war have been accorded due weight in military thinking about the merchant marine. But, as I pointed out at the beginning of this book, the only safe assumption for the present is that there may be a need for a merchant marine along the familiar and traditional lines (the Russians are, after all, building many submarines). How large a peacetime establishment may be necessary to provide the basis for wartime expansion is another unanswerable question, in terms of the scope of this book. We need hypothesize only that the minimum required by military prudence is larger than that which would be achieved if strictly economic criteria were allowed full play.

Accepting the need to maintain the maritime industries at some unspecified but at least uneconomic level for purposes of national defense still leaves the question, "How *national* must this defense be?" The elements of an answer have already been given in this book. They need only be briefly recalled.

The United States has sought allies for mutual defense. It has, to some extent, worked out with them a common strategy and some division of military tasks. It relies, to some extent, on bases in foreign countries and on the local military efforts of foreigners to hold forward areas. Among these allies are most of the principal shipping nations of the world, with merchant fleets and shipyards capable of producing and operating ships at lower costs than the United States can. Several of these countries count on their merchant fleets for an important part of their foreign exchange earnings. Healthy and prosperous maritime industries can contribute to their ability to support themselves economically and to the strength and stability of their societies. Thus, to the extent that the defense requirements for merchant marine service can be met on an inter-allied basis, and to the extent that the services can be supplied by other shipping nations, there are economic and political advantages to the United States in such a course.

Thus an important element in American shipping policy should be an effort to work out arrangements with allies that will serve the national defense purposes of shipping policy. How far it may prove possible to go in this direction cannot be estimated in the abstract. American strategy inevitably comprises not only a common effort with allies but an independent military capability. Moreover, the alliances—of which NATO is the significant one so far as shipping is concerned—are not global and American military responsibilities may be so. Always there is a problem of striking a wise balance between the independent and the collective capability, just as there is a balance to be struck between reasonable military preparedness and the long-haul of economic and political well-being. Even a complete "alliance policy" for shipping might leave the United States with the problem of maintaining surplus capacity in shipbuilding and ship operation as part of the combined mobilization base for wartime. In any case it is unlikely that an "alliance policy" can be pushed to its extremes in shipping since this has not been done in any other field of policy.

We must assume, then, that even if the United States should recognize the advantage of finding ways to let a larger part of its shipping be carried in foreign vessels, it will still be judged necessary to maintain an American-flag merchant marine of some size, and a minimum defense-essential production of ships in American yards. Moreover, within this framework it will be found necessary to keep at least a nucleus fleet on all "all-American" basis.

To recapitulate, the fundamentals of a wise shipping policy for the United States are fairly clear. It should aim at the greatest economic advantage for the nation, which means a minimum of subsidy and preferential legislation. This aim will have to be modified by the needs of national defense for keeping in existence a larger merchant fleet and shipbuilding capacity than is economically justified. To the extent that defense arrangements can be worked out with our allies, there are political and economic advantages for the United States as well. Whatever progress can be made in that direction, it seems prudent for the United States to maintain an independent military capability as well which may mean the maintenance of a fleet, yards, and crews at levels that are not economically justified.

THE ELEMENTS OF POLICY

Accepting these principles as guides, how should the formulation of American shipping policy be conducted?

A strong case can be made for basing maritime policy solely upon the desire to attain national defense objectives. This would help to strengthen the military coalitions in which the United States participates. It would also facilitate policy making. Administrative decisions would be easier to make because of the simplicity of policy objectives.

The primary advantage of this simplification of objectives would be that policy and administrative decisions would be based solely upon the technical requirements of national defense. Vessel operators and shipbuilders unable to exist without government aid would be helped only if military requirements called for their continued operation. Military requirements, in turn, would be determined after consultation with other members of alliances and organizations. The final decision would therefore reflect the contributions of allies as well.

In this connection we should note that economy would be an important product of this arrangement. If current cost figures are reliable, the government would find it cheaper to rely more heavily upon foreign-flag shipping for defense purposes. It would probably be less expensive to subsidize foreign-flag vessels if military policy dictated the maintenance of excessive merchant shipping. Admittedly, these are unpalatable observations for the Americans engaged in shipping operations. Yet, in the *national* as opposed to the *private* interest they should be considered. If indeed the free world must look forward to many years of cold war and international tension, it must seek the maximum military security. There would be little wisdom in paying more than necessary for this maximum. Since the military security of the United States necessitates a system of alliances, common sense suggests that, so far as military considerations permit, each member nation should contribute what it can produce cheapest. This is no more than applying the principles of practical economizing to a practical military defense problem.

What modifications in current maritime policies would be necessary if they were based upon purely military considerations? Many of the basic policies would remain unchanged. However, actual operation under these policies would differ in some important respects.

Shipbuilding

Since World War II, shipbuilders and others have emphasized the national-defense importance of shipyards in operation. Considerable progress has been made in estimating the shipbuilding facilities required for military purposes in time of war. Estimates have been made of the minimum strength below which they should not be permitted to fall. The "dilution rate" of skilled workers has been given careful attention. In short, in this regard the shipbuilding industry has been put in the same class as producers of armaments. And rightly so, for shipbuilding in the United States has been fundamentally a defense industry since at least just prior to World War I.

The minimum facilities needed for defense should be kept busy if the skills and teamwork required in shipbuilding are to be maintained. Here, present policy falls short. Consistent application of the policy of shipbuilding for national defense calls for a given volume of output from the key yards. This production need bear no relation to the needs of ship operators. It is merely exercise for some of the muscles of national defense. The types of ships to be built may depend upon the needs of the reserve fleet and the demands of operators. However, in no case should the defense-minimum volume of production vary with the requirements of ship operators or the managers of the reserve fleet. If the minimum output and the requirements of private fleet operators happily coincide, this must be viewed as fortunate but not essential. The shipyards exist primarily for national defense and their output must always be high enough to preserve what are essentially, for the United States, military skills.

The Merchant Marine Act, 1936 provides for maintaining shipyard output at any given level. Congress must, of course, approve the necessary expenditures. Recently the government has indirectly encouraged the production of ships by offering private operators favorable long-term charters on the condition that the tankers be newly constructed. Certainly this legislation helps to keep some shipbuilders busy. It also helps to improve the reserve fleet by retiring some serviceable tankers from active duty and replacing them with new ones. It also makes immediate use of the new tankers, thus overcoming a deep-seated, widespread prejudice against building something commercially usable and then not employing it.

However, the tanker charter program, the trade-and-build legislation, the mortgage insurance regulations, the construction-differential subsidy scheme, and other laws to encourage private operators to order ships from domestic shipbuilders do not currently result in an output of sixty ships per year—the minimum prescribed in the *Murray Report*. We must therefore conclude, unless the *Murray Report's* figure is not to be accepted, that the indirect means adopted have failed to maintain the minimum output of seagoing merchant vessels needed for defense.

Only by considering shipbuilding as a purely defense industry will the appropriate program be adopted. It may well be that this attitude toward the industry will reduce the evaluation of its importance to national defense. This would be unfortunate for those engaged and employed in the industry but it could be fortunate for the country. If public expenditures for merchant vessels were to be the responsibility of the Department of Defense, then the Department of Defense would be forced to decide just how important this "fourth arm of defense" was to it. It would have to allocate funds to shipbuilding that might otherwise go to the manufacture of airplanes and other defense supplies. This kind of arrangement might help to clarify some of the obscurities in present defense planning with regard to shipbuilding.

Ship operation

Shipowners agree that without government aid in its many forms much of the American-flag merchant marine would disappear. It suffers from a crucial cost disadvantage mainly associated with higher labor costs. However, unlike the shipbuilders, the vessel operators could make profits without government help. They need only to be freed from restrictions that prohibit or inhibit their buying the services of labor, the ships, and other necessary items and services where they could obtain them cheapest. We should frankly recognize that the biggest single cause of their high costs relative to their foreign rivals results directly from the necessity for hiring their crews in United States ports. Thus they are in competition with the rest of the economy, where commercial considerations and high productivity justify higher wages. The seagoing crafts in these ports are tightly organized.

Obviously an "internationalized" United States merchant marine would be cheaper to operate. Operating-differential subsidies would probably be unnecessary. Why, then, should the United States seek to operate an all-American merchant fleet? It does so for "national defense" reasons and possibly for economic and political reasons as well.

The national defense argument is simple. The nation needs a core of trained Americans to man its ships. In time of war these men can be depended on to provide crews, and are subject to American legislation. Requiring that the ships be built in the United States helps keep fundamentally uneconomic shipyards occupied and thus ready for a national emergency.

Domestic politics has no doubt influenced policy, partly through the desire of some politicians not to alienate organized labor. Internationalizing the merchant marine would affect a vociferous, well-organized though relatively small

segment of unionized labor. Other labor groups would undoubtedly support the maritime workers. Their combined
efforts could probably unseat some legislators and influence
political affairs accordingly.

The shipowners might be subjected to severe economic
pressure if an attempt were made to permit internationaliza-
tion of the United States-flag merchant marine. Resentful
unionized sailors and other shipboard personnel might enlist
the support of longshoremen and others. A prolonged waterfront strike could ensue. This could be very costly to shipping
companies. The prospect of such losses might well limit their
enthusiasm for a chance to operate under fewer restrictions.

In practice the economic and political factors are probably
less important than the military. After all, many basically
American companies operate under foreign flags. There are
legal advantages in remaining under the United States flag.
These probably offset some of the financial disadvantages.

Though a case can be made for complete reliance upon foreign sailors and merchant vessels, administrative caution probably requires that a nucleus all-American fleet be retained in
operation. The emphasis should be upon keeping this fleet as
small as possible. If the world military situation calls for the
operation of tonnage exceeding current demands, the surplus
should be provided and paid for under an arrangement mutually satisfactory to the members of the military alliances.

With this as the aim, it would be possible to get rid of cargo
preferences and limit government aid to subsidies limited in
scope and amount by agreement among the United States and
its shipping allies. Cargo preferences interfere with allocation
of cargoes among shipping companies while subsidies combined with the operation of shipping conferences do not interfere with the shippers' choice of shipping line, foreign or
American. Admittedly, from some standpoints subsidies are
not desirable but they are to be preferred over cargo preferences. Both economically and politically cargo preference
arrangements have greater disadvantages than subsidies in providing the assistance needed to keep afloat the minimum
American-flag merchant marine needed for defense.

Cabotage restrictions have a longer tradition and greater
general acceptance than cargo preferences. Yet they too need

re-examination. The foreign-flag vessels that are completely excluded from the coasting trades might, with their lower costs, be able to compete effectively with the railroads and trucks. Obviously, maritime labor unions and the trucking and railroad companies would oppose admission of foreign-flag ships to the coasting trades. Even the military might, on the grounds that the United States should not be dependent upon foreign vessels in domestic trade. Still, if national defense requires more immediately-available ocean-going vessels then this suggestion should be explored. After all, if British, Norwegian, or Dutch freighters sailed along the coasts, they would be "available" in an emergency and so the United States military position would be improved, freight rates lowered, and men and materials made available for other pressing needs.

To those who object to having foreign sailors sail for the United States two observations are pertinent. First, the United States has been quite willing to use foreigners as soldiers in its defense. Hundreds of thousands of foreigners trained by Americans serve in foreign armies. In time of war, why not rely on well-trained foreign sailors? If more United States sailors are needed, they can be trained by both foreign and American seamen. Second, in *mutual* defense we already go on the principle that citizens of allied nations can all play a part with resulting greater use of all the skills and strength available to the alliance. The same principle can be applied to shipping.

These examples of suggested changes in United States maritime policies follow from the simple guide for the formulation of shipping policy presented earlier in this chapter. A national shipping policy based solely on military considerations and conditioned by an awareness of the collective character of United States military policy would do much to insure that the maritime needs of defense were being obtained at the lowest cost and the least friction among allies. Other aspects of policy would undergo fewer changes. *Conferences* would be condoned as at present on the grounds that some excess capacity should be maintained at all times and the conference system provides a practical means of regulating rates in these circumstances. The *MSTS nucleus fleet* would be retained at whatever level would guarantee the government the necessary tonnage (government plus private) to fulfill certain military requirements.

The argument for this case has been made at various points throughout this book. The strengths, weaknesses, and practical characteristics of these and other elements of policy have been explored. Among the specific recommendations for changes in policy that result from this book, four stand out as most important.

First, cargo-preference legislation should be repealed. It offers a short-run solution to a pressing problem. Ultimately it may cause damage. It adversely affects relations among allies. As a corollary policy the government should strive to influence other governments to eliminate discrimination against United States shipping. This could be coupled with offers to abandon cargo preference in exchange for foreign agreement to rescind regulations and practices inimical to the interests of United States shipping companies.

Second, attempts should be made to open the coasting trades to foreign-flag vessels. The military objections do not appear important while the advantages to national defense are many. More and cheaper transportation should be welcomed by all. Only the labor unions and a few shipping companies would suffer until talents and properties could be used elsewhere. Shippers, taxpayers, and national defense would gain. We have suggested only that "attempts" should be made. Perhaps the threat of foreign competition would be enough to encourage the introduction of more efficient, lower-cost shipping operations in the coasting trades.

Third, the United States-flag merchant fleet should be internationalized to the fullest extent consonant with mutual military necessity. This would not only minimize defense costs but would improve the international economic position of other countries vital to the defense of the United States.

Fourth, shipbuilding activity should be maintained at the lowest level consistent with adequate national defense. Under no circumstances should it be permitted to fall below this level. The government should stand ready to bolster shipbuilding immediately should output threaten to drop below defense-minimum levels. Preferably, the Department of Defense should be charged with the responsibility of maintaining a "pilot-type" of shipbuilding operation just as it is for other war industries.

Broadly speaking, except for the cargo-preference and cabotage restriction laws and the statements of policy in various maritime acts passed by Congress, the major policy suggestions made here require no legislative action. However, these three probably cannot be revised for some time. Yet, world political, economic, and military conditions may soon force policy makers to consider the possibility of their revision. We all know that times have changed. In the light of these changes there is good reason to suggest that the maritime policies of the United States be changed, too.

STATISTICAL APPENDIX

Table 1

WATER-BORNE FOREIGN TRADE OF THE UNITED STATES, 1921, 1925, 1930-55 [a]

[In millions of tons of 2,240 lbs.]

	Imports			Exports			Imports and Exports		
Year	Total	U.S. flag	Per cent U.S. flag	Total	U.S. flag	Per cent U.S. flag	Total	U.S. flag	Per cent U.S. flag
1921	33.2	23.5	70.8	48.6	18.6	38.3	81.8	42.1	51.5
1925	43.1	21.2	49.2	49.7	15.7	31.6	92.8	36.9	39.8
1930	47.6	24.8	52.1	49.7	14.9	30.0	97.3	39.7	40.8
1931	35.9	17.1	47.6	40.0	11.1	27.8	75.9	28.2	37.2
1932	28.7	13.3	46.3	31.8	8.1	25.5	60.5	21.4	35.4
1933	26.6	11.0	41.4	32.4	8.4	26.0	59.0	19.4	32.9
1934	29.8	12.8	43.0	37.8	9.4	24.9	67.6	22.2	32.8
1935	34.0	14.1	41.5	38.1	8.7	22.8	72.1	22.8	31.6
1936	38.4	13.2	34.4	39.7	8.6	21.7	78.1	21.8	27.9
1937	42.1	13.4	31.8	54.6	10.9	20.0	96.7	24.3	25.1
1938	32.8	12.1	37.0	55.6	10.4	18.7	88.4	22.5	25.5
1939	37.5	11.1	29.6	55.1	9.4	17.1	92.6	20.5	22.1
1940	39.9	15.5	38.8	54.4	11.6	21.3	94.3	27.1	28.7
1941 [b]									
1942 [c]	24.5	15.5	63.3	37.2	14.5	39.0	61.7	30.0	48.6
1943 [c]	27.7	22.1	79.8	42.6	22.6	53.1	70.3	44.7	63.6
1944 [c]	29.8	23.4	78.5	49.3	30.4	61.7	79.1	53.8	68.0
1945 [c]	35.2	28.0	79.5	55.0	33.7	61.3	90.2	61.7	68.4
1946 [c]	43.9	28.9	65.8	77.7	44.5	57.3	121.6	73.4	60.4
1947 [c]	52.9	33.6	63.5	111.0	54.5	49.1	163.9	88.1	53.8
1948 [c]	60.2	36.2	60.1	78.8	30.8	39.1	139.0	67.5	48.6
1949 [c]	69.1	36.9	53.4	64.2	23.3	36.3	133.3	60.2	45.2
1950 [c]	86.3	37.7	43.7	56.0	18.2	32.5	142.3	55.9	39.3
1951 [c]	90.2	38.2	42.4	103.0	38.7	37.6	193.2	76.9	39.8
1952 [c]	95.9	37.2	38.8	92.0	27.2	29.6	187.9	64.4	34.3
1953 [c]	106.3	34.4	32.4	71.9	17.4	24.1	177.9	51.7	29.1
1954	107.5	32.3	30.0	69.3	16.3	23.5	176.8	48.6	27.5
1955	126.0	33.4	26.5	100	19.7	19.7	22.6	53.1	23.5

[a] Excludes, prior to 1946, cargoes (small in aggregate) carried by ships of less than 100 gross tons.

[b] Not available.

[c] Excludes U.S. Army and Navy cargo. Includes Alaska, Hawaii, and Puerto Rico. Beginning in July 1950, also excludes commodities classified for security reasons as "special category" and foreign aid shipments on Department of Defense controlled vessels. Excludes merchandise in transit. 1947-53 subject to revision. Figures for 1952 and 1953 are for statistical years consisting of 12 reporting periods during a calendar year. They will exclude small amounts transported during a given calendar year but reported during a period falling within another statistical year.

Source: For 1921-35, Department of Commerce, Shipping Board Bureau; for 1936-40 United States Maritime Commission; for 1942-45, War Shipping Admin-

Table 2

WATER-BORNE DRY-CARGO AND TANKER FOREIGN TRADE OF THE UNITED STATES, 1939, 1946-55 [a]

[In millions of long tons]

| | Dry cargo | | | | | | Tanker cargo | | | | | |
| | Imports | | | Exports | | | Imports | | | Exports | | |
Year	Total	U.S. flag	Per cent U.S. flag	Total	U.S. flag	Per cent U.S. flag	Total	U.S. flag	Per cent U.S. flag	Total	U.S. flag	Per cent U.S. flag
1939	27.4	7.3	26.6	34.1	7.6	22.3	10.1	3.8	37.6	21.0	1.9	9.0
1946	22.6	12.7	56.2	64.2	39.1	60.9	21.3	16.1	75.6	13.6	5.4	39.7
1947	28.6	15.5	54.2	97.6	49.8	51.0	24.2	18.2	75.2	13.4	4.7	35.1
1948	32.7	15.4	47.1	67.7	27.3	40.3	27.5	20.8	75.6	11.1	3.5	31.5
1949	35.0	12.7	36.3	55.0	19.9	37.2	34.1	24.3	71.3	9.1	3.4	37.4
1950	41.6	13.2	31.7	47.8	14.7	30.8	44.7	24.5	54.8	8.1	3.5	43.2
1951	44.7	15.9	35.6	90.4	34.3	37.9	45.1	22.7	50.3	12.9	4.3	33.3
1952	45.0	16.5	36.7	79.2	23.5	29.7	50.9	20.7	40.7	12.8	3.7	28.9
1953	51.2	15.4	30.1	59.9	14.3	23.9	55.1	19.0	34.5	12.0	3.1	25.8
1954	51.2	14.7	28.7	59.7	14.0	23.5	56.3	17.6	31.3	9.6	2.3	24.0
1955	61.1	17.7	29.0	89.7	17.6	19.6	64.9	15.7	24.2	10.6	2.1	19.8

[a] Excludes U.S. Army and Navy cargo. Includes Alaska, Hawaii, and Puerto Rico. Beginning July 1950, excludes commodities classified for security reasons as "special category." 1947-53 data subject to revision.

Source: For 1939, U.S. Maritime Commission, Division of Research, "Water-Borne Foreign and Noncontiguous Commerce and Passenger Traffic of the United States," *Report No. 2610* (Washington: GPO, 1940).

For 1946-55, same as preceding table. The 1955 figures are subject to revision.

(*Source for Table 1 continued*)
istration; for 1946-50, Department of Commerce, Bureau of the Census, *Foreign Commerce and Navigation of the United States*, annual report, and records as cited in Department of Commerce, Bureau of the Census, *Statistical Abstract of the United States, 1952* (Washington: GPO, 1952), Table 649, p. 535; for 1951, Department of Commerce, Bureau of the Census, Foreign Trade Division, *Summary Report FT 973* (Washington: May 19, 1953); for 1952, U.S. Department of Commerce, Bureau of the Census, "Water-Borne Foreign Trade Statistics," *Summary Report FT 985* (Washington: June 15, 1954), p. 9. For 1953-54, Same, "United States Water-Borne Foreign Trade," *Summary Report FT 985* (Washington: July 24, 1955), p. 10. For 1955, Same, "Water-Borne Foreign Trade Statistics," . . . (monthly issues). The 1955 figures are subject to revision.

Table 3

NUMBER AND GROSS TONNAGE OF ACTIVE AND INACTIVE
UNITED STATES-FLAG MERCHANT VESSELS, 1939 [a]

[Tonnage in thousands]

Services	Combination		Freighters		Tankers		Total	
	No.	Gross tons	No.	Gross tons	No.	Gross tons	No.	Gross tons
Privately owned								
Nearby foreign[b]	27	172.2	36	141.5	27	188.0	90[c]	501.7
Overseas foreign	44	430.3	122	701.1	21	165.4	187	1,296.8
Coastwise	53	299.5	415	1,871.2	304	2,127.3	772[d]	4,298.0
Laid-up vessels	26	195.6	129	546.2	32	223.6	187[e]	965.4
Total privately owned	150	1,097.6	702	3,260.1	384	2,704.2	1,236	7,061.9
Government owned								
Nearby foreign[b]	4[f]	39.3	—	—	—	—	4	39.3
Overseas foreign	3	61.4	35	195.0	—	—	38	256.4
Coastwise	—	—	—	—	—	—	—	—
Special service	—	—	1	7.1	—	—	1	7.1
Laid-up vessels	6	110.4	113[g]	659.8	—	—	119	770.2
Total government vessels	13	211.1	149	861.9	—	—	162	1,073.0
Total American Fleet	163	1,308.7	851	4,122.0	384	2,704.2	1,398	8,134.9

[a] Seagoing vessels of 1,000 gross tons and over. Excludes vessels on inland waterways and the Great Lakes, those under control of the U.S. Army and Navy, and special types such as cable ships, tugs, etc.

[b] "Nearby" includes Canada, Mexico, Central America, West Indies and North Coast South America to and including the Guianas.

[c] Includes 5 vessels (6,422 g t), under 2,000 gross tons.

[d] Includes 43 vessels (63,269 g t), under 2,000 gross tons.

[e] Includes 21 vessels (31,134 g t), under 2,000 gross tons.

[f] Panama RR vessels.

[g] Includes 2 Panama RR vessels.

Source: U.S. Maritime Commission, Division of Research, "Quarterly Report on the Employment of American Steam and Motor Merchant Vessels of 1,000 Gross tons and over as of June 30, 1939," *Report 300* (Washington: June 30, 1939), Table 1.

Table 3A

NUMBER AND TONNAGE OF ACTIVE AND INACTIVE UNITED STATES-FLAG MERCHANT VESSELS, 1948-55 [a]

[Tonnage in thousands]

As of June 30, 1948

Trade	Combination			Freighters			Tankers			Total		
	No.	Gross tons	DWT	No.	Gross tons	DWT	No.	Gross tons	DWT	No.	Gross tons	DWT
Active vessels												
U.S. foreign trade	41	440	357	996	7,002	10,009	100	978	1,570	1,107	8,420	11,936
U.S. domestic trade	7	46	28	198	1,263	1,832	272	2,440	3,925	477	3,749	5,785
Foreign to foreign	—	—	—	57	399	583	82	782	1,248	139	1,181	1,831
Inactive vessels												
Temporarily inactive	8	103	67	118	770	1,078	49	407	636	175	1,280	1,781
U.S.M.C. reserve fleet	21	187	149	1,548	10,917	15,172	23	81	120	1,592	11,185	15,441
Total active & inactive	77	776	601	2,887	20,351	28,674	526	4,688	7,499	3,490	25,815	36,774

As of June 30, 1949 [b]

Trade	Combination			Freighters			Tankers			Total		
	No.	Gross tons	DWT	No.	Gross tons	DWT	No.	Gross tons	DWT	No.	Gross tons	DWT
Active vessels												
U.S. foreign trade	43	466	375	807	5,870	8,566	98	988	1,594	948	7,323	10,536
U.S. domestic trade	4	20	13	156	983	1,438	222	1,997	3,180	382	3,001	4,631
Foreign to foreign	—	—	—	6	41	60	50	508	821	56	550	881
Inactive vessels												
Temporarily inactive	9	92	62	63	414	597	106	891	1,417	178	1,397	2,077
U.S.M.C. reserve fleet	23	224	158	1,767	12,548	17,781	25	113	166	1,815	12,886	18,107
Total active & inactive	79	803	610	2,799	19,858	28,444	501	4,499	7,179	3,379	25,160	36,234

(See page 209 for footnotes)

Table 3A (Continued)

Trade	Combination			Freighters			Tankers			Total		
	No.	Gross tons	DWT	No.	Gross tons	DWT	No.	Gross tons	DWT	No.	Gross tons	DWT
As of June 30, 1950[b]												
Active vessels												
U.S. foreign trade	45	483	389	494	3,621	5,255	93	920	1,477	632	5,025	7,121
U.S. domestic trade	6	45	28	177	1,158	1,708	251	2,338	3,737	434	3,542	5,474
Foreign to foreign	—	—	—	11	75	112	68	695	1,120	79	770	1,232
Inactive vessels												
Temporarily inactive	4	47	27	42	255	383	40	274	434	86	577	845
U.S.M.A. reserve fleet	28	288	195	2,122	15,142	21,468	27	128	190	2,177	15,559	21,853
Total active & inactive	83	864	639	2,846	20,253	28,927	479	4,357	6,959	3,408	25,475	36,526
As of June 30, 1951[b]												
Active vessels												
U.S. foreign trade	46	510	404	719	5,224	7,641	120	1,166	1,885	885	6,901	9,931
U.S. domestic trade	5	41	24	176	1,159	1,721	245	2,232	3,587	426	3,433	5,333
Foreign to foreign	—	—	—	24	170	251	79	786	1,244	103	956	1,496
Inactive vessels												
Temporarily inactive	7	81	46	52	347	509	10	64	102	69	493	658
U.S.M.A. reserve fleet	196	1,594	1,484	1,454	9,979	14,851	13	39	60	1,663	11,612	16,395
Total active & inactive	254[c]	2,227	1,959	2,425[d]	16,880	24,975	467[c]	4,289	6,880	3,146	23,398	33,815

(See *page 209 for footnotes*)

Table 3A (Continued)

As of June 30, 1952[b]

Trade	Combination			Freighters			Tankers			Total		
	No.	Gross tons	DWT	No.	Gross tons	DWT	No.	Gross tons	DWT	No.	Gross tons	DWT
Active vessels												
U.S. foreign trade	61	743	548	823	5,979	8,648	107	1,048	1,686	991	7,769	10,882
U.S. domestic trade	1	7	4	135	863	1,302	259	2,414	3,884	395	3,284	5,190
Foreign to foreign	—	—	—	9	65	96	52	501	808	61	567	904
Inactive vessels												
Temporarily inactive	10	91	52	106	756	1,100	31	246	392	147	1,093	1,544
U.S.M.A. reserve fleet	188	1,512	1,439	1,556	10,820	16,064	12	38	59	1,756	12,370	17,562
Total active & inactive	260	2,353	2,044	2,629	18,482	27,210	461	4,247	6,827	3,350	25,082	36,081

As of June 30, 1953[b]

Trade	Combination			Freighters			Tankers			Total		
	No.	Gross tons	DWT	No.	Gross tons	DWT	No.	Gross tons	DWT	No.	Gross tons	DWT
Active vessels												
U.S. foreign trade	50	636	456	786	5,754	8,297	97	992	1,589	933	7,380	10,342
U.S. domestic trade	5	39	23	167	1,090	1,638	265	2,531	4,064	437	3,659	5,725
Foreign to foreign	—	—	—	11	79	125	34	340	546	45	418	671
Inactive vessels												
Temporarily inactive	5	41	22	39	261	369	54	463	731	98	765	1,122
U.S.M.A. reserve fleet	197	1,618	1,538	1,627	11,325	16,799	12	38	59	1,836	12,981	18,395
Total active & inactive	257[f]	2,333	2,039	2,630[g]	18,508	27,227	462[h]	4,363	6,988	3,349	25,204	36,255

(See page 209 for footnotes)

Table 3A (Continued)

As of June 30, 1954[b]

Trade	Combination			Freighters			Tankers			Total		
	No.	Gross tons	DWT	No.	Gross tons	DWT	No.	Gross tons	DWT	No.	Gross tons	DWT
Active vessels												
U.S. foreign trade	49	617	443	576	4,268	6,095	84	952	1,516	709	5,837	8,053
U.S. domestic trade	5	39	23	154	1,044	1,581	239	2,345	3,719	393	3,428	5,324
Foreign to foreign	—	—	—	—	—	—	16	166	268	16	166	268
Inactive vessels												
Temporarily inactive	1	6	3	141	980	1,467	94	862	1,373	236	1,849	2,843
U.S.M.A. reserve fleet	197	1,652	1,227	1,765	12,462	18,092	12	38	54	1,974	14,152	19,373
Total active & inactive	252[f]	2,315	1,695	2,636[a]	18,754	27,235	445[h]	4,363	6,930	3,333	25,432	35,860

As of June 30, 1955[b]

Trade	Combination			Freighters			Tankers			Total		
	No.	Gross tons	DWT	No.	Gross tons	DWT	No.	Gross tons	DWT	No.	Gross tons	DWT
Active vessels												
U.S. foreign trade	49	617	443	612	4,508	6,532	66	750	1,193	727	5,876	8,168
U.S. domestic trade	1	19	10	160	1,096	1,650	264	2,665	4,220	425	3,779	5,880
Foreign to foreign	—	—	—	—	—	—	11	113	184	11	113	184
Inactive vessels												
Temporarily inactive	14	114	68	28	189	288	47	465	742	89	768	1,099
U.S.M.A. reserve fleet	185	1,547	1,166	1,760	12,447	18,070	38	290	451	1,983	14,284	19,687
Total active & inactive	249[f]	2,298	1,687	2,560[a]	18,239	26,539	426[h]	4,282	6,790	3,235	24,820	35,017

(See opposite page for footnotes)

Notes to Table 3A

ᵃ Seagoing vessels of 1,000 gross tons and over. Excludes vessels on inland waterways, the Great Lakes, those under control of the U.S. Army and Navy, and special types such as cable ships, tugs, etc. Tonnage figures do not add because of rounding to the nearest thousand.

ᵇ The figures for each year from 1949 to 1955 omit certain government-owned ships transferred to foreign flags under lend-lease or other agreements. These are: 8 vessels of 27,000 gross tons (38,000 dwt) transferred to the Philippine flag under the Philippine Rehabilitation Act, and 83 vessels of 518,000 gross tons (786,000 dwt) transferred to the U.S.S.R. under lend-lease.

The figures for 1949 and 1950 exclude certain vessels on loan in bare-boat charter to U.S. military agencies. These came to 43 vessels of 271,000 gross tons (359,000 dwt) in 1949 and 17 vessels of 94,000 gross tons (128,000 dwt) in 1950. The figures for 1951 exclude the following vessels comprising both the above categories of transfers, and perhaps others as well: 13 combination ships of 146,000 gross tons (114,000 dwt); 314 freighters of 2,209,000 gross tons (3,208,000 dwt); 4 tankers of 17,000 gross tons (25,000 dwt).

The totals excluded for these years are (tons in thousands):

	1949	1950	1951	1952-55 (each year)
Number	135	108	331	91
Gross tons	817	639	2,372	545
DWT	1,183	952	3,347	823

ᶜ Comprises 57 combination passenger and cargo ships of 619,000 gross tons and 467,000 deadweight tons, 23 transports, hospital ships, etc., of 203,000 gross tons and 149,000 deadweight tons, carried in this classification in previous reports; and 174 freighters of 1,405,000 gross tons and 1,343,000 deadweight tons originally constructed as cargo vessels, but converted to transports, hospital ships, etc., and included in the freighter classification of previous reports.

ᵈ Includes 75 ships of 472,000 gross tons and 696,000 deadweight tons converted for use as store ships, tenders, etc.

ᵉ Includes 2 tank ships of 14,000 gross tons and 21,000 deadweight tons converted for use as distilling ships.

ᶠ Includes ships originally constructed as combination passenger and cargo ships and freighters, later converted to troop transports, hospital ships, etc., and not reconverted to their original types.

ᵍ Includes ships converted to store ships, repair ships, cargo attack, etc.

ʰ Includes tankers converted to distilling ships.

Source: For 1938 and 1948, United States Maritime Commission, *Report to Congress, For the Fiscal Year Ended June 30, 1948* (Washington: GPO, 1949), Appendix C, p. 68. For 1949, Same, . . . *1949* (Washington: GPO, 1950), Appendix A, p. 62. For 1950, U.S. Department of Commerce, *Annual Report of the Federal Maritime Board [and] Maritime Administration* (Washington: GPO, 1950), Appendix A, p. 56. For 1951, Same, . . . *1951* (Washington: GPO, 1952), Appendix A, p. 98. For 1952, Same, . . . *1952* (Washington: GPO, 1953), Appendix J, p. 64. For 1953, Same, . . . *1953* (Washington: GPO, 1954), Appendix F, p. 64. For 1954, Same . . ., *1954* Washington: GPO, 1955), p. 54. For 1955, Same, . . . *1955* (Washington: GPO, 1956), p. 62.

Table 4

UNITED STATES INTERCOASTAL TRADE VIA THE PANAMA CANAL,
FISCAL YEARS, 1929-30 TO 1953-54

[In thousands of tons of 2,240 lbs.]

Fiscal Year	Atlantic to Pacific	Pacific to Atlantic	Total
1929-30	3,162	7,329	10,491
1930-31	2,380	6,426	8,806
1931-32	1,917	4,706	6,623
1932-33	1,595	4,832	6,427
1933-34	2,075	6,850	8,925
1934-35	2,163	5,801	7,964
1935-36	2,579	5,141	7,720
1936-37	2,575	3,965	6,530
1937-38	2,342	4,053	6,395
1938-39	2,392	4,493	6,885
1939-40	2,796	4,919	7,715
1940-41	2,948	3,934	6,882
1941-42	950	1,002	1,952
1942-43[a]	—	17	17
1943-44[bc]	1	67	68
1944-45[bc]	78	108	186
1945-46	866	787	1,653
1946-47	1,466	1,463	2,929
1947-48	1,719	2,119	3,838
1948-49	1,450	1,641	3,091
1949-50	1,846	5,530	6,376
1950-51	2,061	3,670	5,731
1951-52	2,140	2,139	4,279
1952-53	2,214	2,657	4,871
1953-54	2,316	2,701	5,017

[a] Beginning with the 1943 *Annual Report of the Governor of the Panama Canal*, the classification of coastal areas was changed from "Atlantic Coast" and "Pacific Coast" to "East Coast U.S." and "West Coast U.S.," respectively. There was no change in coverage, however.

[b] "West Coast U.S." included Canada.

[c] Use of standard cargo declaration form discontinued June 30, 1943, and resumed November, 1945. Figures for fiscal years 1943-44, 1944-45, and 1945-46, therefore, are not comparable with those for other years in this series.

Source: For 1929-30 to 1947-48, *Annual Report of the Governor of the Panama Canal* (Washington: GPO, 1932-48) as cited in Wytze Gorter and George Hildebrand, *The Pacific Coast Maritime Shipping Industry, 1930-1948*, Vol. 1, "An Economic Profile" (Berkeley and Los Angeles: University of California Press, 1952), p. 95. For 1948-50 to 1950-51, *Annual Report of the Governor of the Panama Canal*, cited, appropriate issues. For 1951-52 and 1952-53, *Second Annual Reports, Panama Canal Company* [*and*] *Canal Zone Government* (Washington: GPO, 1954), p. 71-72. For 1954, Same, *Third Annual Reports* . . . (Washington: GPO, 1955), p. 71, 73.

Table 5

NUMBER AND GROSS TONNAGE OF STEEL SELF-PROPELLED MERCHANT VESSELS—BY TYPES OF SHIPS—BUILT IN THE PRIVATE SHIPYARDS OF THE UNITED STATES AND DELIVERED, 1914-55 [a]

Year	Cargo		Tanker		Passenger and Passenger-Cargo		Total		
	No.	Gross tons	No.	Gross tons	No.	Gross tons	No.	Gross tons	
1914	16	85,542	8	44,917	—	—	24	130,459	Pre World War I
1915	19	92,675	2	11,709	2	16,510	23	120,894	
1916	43	187,529	23	155,896	1	6,063	67	349,488	
Total	78	365,746	33	212,522	3	22,573	114	600,841	
1917	81	382,292	39	247,003	—	—	120	629,295	World War I
1918	355	1,465,520	27	182,852	4	23,590	386	1,671,962	
Total	436	1,847,812	66	429,855	4	23,590	506	2,301,257	
1919	634	2,894,641	43	279,098	3	16,549	680	3,190,288	Post World War I
1920	382	1,829,782	57	390,960	11	91,916	450	2,312,658	
1921	49	269,030	70	554,595	19	214,072	138	1,037,697	
Total	1,065	4,993,453	170	1,224,653	33	322,537	1,268	6,540,643	
1922	10	78,442	5	44,073	3	41,293	18	163,808	
1923	10	75,524	2	15,513	7	33,947	19	124,984	
1924	5	41,232	1	6,546	6	35,824	12	83,602	
1925	8	62,162	—	—	3	18,850	11	81,012	
1926	2	16,302	1	8,952	5	28,789	8	54,043	
1927	9	73,179	3	30,470	7	51,294	19	154,943	

Table 5 (Continued)

Year	Cargo		Tanker		Passenger and Passenger-Cargo		Total	
	No.	Gross tons	No.	Gross tons	No.	Gross tons	No.	Gross tons
1928	—	—	2	20,630	3	44,190	5	64,820
1929	4	24,685	1	9,096	2	23,614	7	57,395
1930	1	7,964	10	92,933	5	50,311	16	151,208
1931	—	—	5	41,981	9	108,968	14	150,949
1932	2	16,122	—	—	13	129,348	15	145,470
1933	—	—	—	—	4	49,527	4	49,527
1934	2	9,544	—	—	—	—	2	9,544
1935	—	—	2	19,022	—	—	2	19,022
1936	—	—	8	63,428	—	—	8	63,428
1937	—	—	15	121,852	—	—	15	121,852
Total	53	405,156	55	474,496	67	615,955	175	1,495,607
1938	8	43,476	16	137,930	2	4,252	26	185,658
1939	14	91,560	11	119,429	3	30,063	28	241,052
1940	31	227,275	16	148,509	6	68,943	53	444,727
1941	61	423,019	28	267,979	6	58,107	95	749,105
Total	114	785,330	71	673,847	17	161,365	202	1,620,542
1942	652	4,678,988	61	612,121	11	101,844	724	5,392,953
1943	1,410	10,116,973	231	2,163,147	20	219,753	1,661	12,499,873
1944	1,175	8,457,190	240	2,485,923	48	461,291	1,463	11,404,404
1945	833	5,384,610	188	1,769,583	46	509,169	1,067	7,663,362
Total	4,070	28,637,761	720	7,030,774	125	1,292,057	4,915	36,960,592

Pre World War II

World War II

Table 5 (Continued)

Year	Cargo		Tanker		Passenger and Passenger-Cargo		Total	
	No.	Gross tons	No.	Gross tons	No.	Gross tons	No.	Gross tons
1946	71	515,833	8	80,055	9	76,666	88[b]	672,554
1947	38	194,253	5	22,662	7	69,558	50[c]	286,473
1948	22	97,643	6	51,480	1	15,359	29[d]	164,482
1949	1	3,100[e]	33	535,773	—	—	34[e]	538,873
1950	3	37,726[f]	23	377,773	—	—	26[f]	415,499
1951	4	28,993	4	71,138	2	47,438	10	147,569
1952	19	176,529	8	127,341	4	93,286	31	397,156
1953	22	214,103	23	356,223[g]	—	—	45[g]	570,326
1954	12	107,670[h]	26	456,091	—	—	38[h]	563,761
1955	4	49,930	4	55,312	—	—	8	105,242
Total	196	1,425,780	140	2,133,848	23	302,307	359	3,861,935
41 Yrs.	6,012	38,461,038	1,255	12,179,995	272	2,740,384	7,539	53,381,417

Notes:

[a] Includes vessels of 2,000 gross tons and over.

[b] Includes 1 carfloat, 2 dredges, 1 small cargo and 1 small passenger vessel—7,360 tons.

[c] Includes 8 dredges, 1 small cargo and 2 small tankers—39,053 tons.

[d] Includes 4 small cargo vessels—4,596 tons.

[e] Includes 1 dredge of 3,100 displacement tons.

[f] Includes 1 dredge of 21,572 displacement tons.

[g] Includes 1 tanker of 1,784 tons.

[h] Includes 1 passenger-auto ferry of 1,495 tons.

Source: Shipbuilders Council of America, *Annual Report* (New York, April 2, 1956), Appendix, Table 24, slightly altered.

Table 6

NUMBER AND DISPLACEMENT TONNAGE OF STEEL COMBATANT AND AUXILIARY NAVAL VESSELS BUILT IN THE SHIPYARDS OF THE UNITED STATES AND DELIVERED, 1914-55

| Year delivered | Private yards | | | | Navy yards | | | | Grand Total | | | | | |
| | Auxiliary | | Combatant | | Auxiliary | | Combatant | | Auxiliary | | Combatant | | Total | |
	No.	Tons	No.	Tons	No.	Tons	No.	Tons	No.	Tons	No.	Tons	No.	Tons
1914	1	1,408	15	36,871	—	—	3	27,408	1	1,408	18	64,279	19	65,687
1915	2	10,730	—	—	1	14,500	7	8,135	3	25,230	7	8,135	10	33,365
1916	—	—	19	100,405	2	29,000	1	31,400	2	29,000	20	131,805	22	160,805
1917	2	7,600	8	37,104	3	29,500	3	3,087	5	37,100	11	40,191	16	77,291
1918	3	23,320	74	71,673	—	—	15	42,609	3	23,320	89	114,282	92	137,602
1919	—	—	128	179,112	1	14,800	5	5,493	1	14,800	133	184,605	134	199,405
1920	—	—	81	102,619	2	25,858	9	41,488	2	25,858	90	144,107	92	169,965
1921	2	27,850	29	67,452	3	39,325	6	38,347	5	67,175	35	105,799	40	172,974
1922	—	—	7	6,680	—	—	4	4,800	—	—	11	11,480	11	11,480
1923	—	—	23	118,600	—	—	4	3,640	—	—	27	122,240	27	122,240
1924	—	—	10	26,750	3	31,200	1	2,000	3	31,200	11	28,750	14	59,950
1925	—	—	5	10,250	—	—	1	2,000	—	—	6	12,250	6	12,250
1926	—	—	—	—	1	10,600	1	2,000	1	10,600	1	2,000	2	12,600
1927	—	—	2	66,000	—	—	—	—	—	—	2	66,000	2	66,000
1928	—	—	—	—	—	—	1	2,710	—	—	1	2,710	1	2,710
1929	—	—	1	10,000	—	—	—	—	—	—	1	10,000	1	10,000
1930	—	—	3	30,000	—	—	3	15,460	—	—	6	45,460	6	45,460
1931	—	—	1	10,000	—	—	2	20,000	—	—	3	30,000	3	30,000
1932	—	—	1	10,000	—	—	1	1,540	—	—	2	11,540	2	11,540
1933	—	—	1	10,000	—	—	1	1,110	—	—	2	11,110	2	11,110

Table 6 (Continued)

Year delivered	Private yards Auxiliary No.	Tons	Combatant No.	Tons	Navy yards Auxiliary No.	Tons	Combatant No.	Tons	Grand Total Auxiliary No.	Tons	Combatant No.	Tons	Total No.	Tons
1934	—	—	5	27,900	—	—	4	40,000	—	—	9	67,900	9	67,900
1935	—	—	—	—	—	—	8	11,360	—	—	8	11,360	8	11,360
1936	—	—	17	35,920	—	—	5	8,430	—	—	22	44,350	22	44,350
1937	—	—	10	42,360	—	—	17	33,940	—	—	27	76,300	27	76,300
1938	—	—	13	72,900	—	—	7	27,250	—	—	20	100,150	20	100,150
1939	—	—	16	32,600	—	—	11	33,010	—	—	27	65,610	27	65,610
1940	4	36,500	12	31,705	—	—	15	22,690	4	36,500	27	54,395	31	90,895
1941	1	9,180	15	45,915	3	12,640	16	91,915	4	21,820	31	137,830	35	159,650
1942	10	93,765	94	342,760	6	21,690	35	89,835	16	115,455	129	432,595	145	548,050
1943	62	391,765	387	883,470	1	9,000	158	301,840	63	400,765	545	1,185,310	608	1,586,075
1944	69	393,127	387	809,305	2	17,300	82	284,555	71	410,427	469	1,093,860	540	1,504,287
1945	24	174,122	144	456,615	1	8,680	34	194,830	25	182,802	178	651,445	203	834,247
1946	18	108,044	60	268,100	1	8,000	6	60,480	19	116,044	66	328,580	85	444,624
1947	3	14,898	5	66,100	—	—	—	—	3	14,898	5	66,100	8	80,998
1948	—	—	2	31,700	—	—	—	—	—	—	2	31,700	2	31,700
1949	—	—	7	58,400	—	—	3	4,620	—	—	10	63,020	10	63,020
1950	—	—	—	—	1	7,968	1	30,800	1	7,968	1	30,800	2	38,768
1951	—	—	1	765	—	—	2	1,675	—	—	3	2,440	3	2,440
1952	1	680	5	12,916	—	—	5	6,210	1	680	10	19,126	11	19,806
1953	—	—	16	50,900	—	—	1	1,218	—	—	17	52,118	17	52,118
1954	1	11,600	12	35,960	—	—	—	—	1	11,600	12	35,960	13	47,560
1955	7	67,400	7	78,360	—	—	—	—	7	67,400	7	78,360	14	145,760
Totals	210	1,371,989	1,623	4,278,167	31	280,061	478	1,497,885	241	1,652,050	2,101	5,776,052	2,342	7,428,102

Source: Shipbuilders Council of America, *Annual Report* (New York: April 2, 1956), Tables 25, 25-1, 25-2, Appendix.

Table 7

MONTHLY AVERAGE NUMBER OF EMPLOYEES IN THE SHIPBUILDING AND REPAIRING INDUSTRY OF THE UNITED STATES, 1923-55

[In thousands]

Year	Total	Private yards	Navy yards
1923	87.9	68.1	19.7
1924	75.6	55.6	20.0
1925	76.6	55.0	21.6
1926	79.9	58.0	21.9
1927	81.1	60.3	21.0
1928	68.8	47.3	21.4
1929	84.1	60.3	23.8
1930	85.2	63.9	21.4
1931	70.7	49.4	21.2
1932	60.8	39.7	21.1
1933	56.5	33.8	22.7
1934	65.3	44.4	20.9
1935	68.5	48.7	19.8
1936	92.4	62.4	30.1
1937	101.8	67.7	34.1
1938	94.6	59.2	35.4
1939	119.1	72.5	47.4
1940	180.3	102.7	77.5
1941	377.0	236.0	141.0
1942	1,004.0	761.7	242.3
1943	1,655.5	1,336.9	318.6
1944	1,568.6	1,242.5	326.1
1945	1,033.9	741.9	292.0
1946	354.1	210.0	144.1
1947	224.0	137.3	86.6
1948	213.9	124.2	89.7
1949	171.8	88.1	83.7
1950	145.7	72.0	73.6
1951	223.2	102.2	121.2
1952	267.6	134.2	133.4
1953	255.0	131.2	123.8
1954	218.3	108.4	109.8
1955	206.5	99.5	107.0

Note: The industry includes establishments primarily engaged in building and repairing all types of ships, barges, canal boats and lighters of 5 gross tons and over.

Source: For 1923-53, U.S. Department of Labor, Bureau of Labor Statistics, *Employees in the Ship Building and Repairing Industry, By Region* (August 1954), processed. For 1954-55, Same, *Employment and Earnings* (appropriate monthly issues).

Table 8

DELIVERIES OF NEW MERCHANT VESSELS, BY TYPE AND COUNTRY WHERE BUILT, FISCAL YEARS, 1949-55

Country in which built and type of vessel	1948		1949		1950		1951		1952		1953		1954		1955	
	No.	DWT	No.	DWT	No.	DWT	No.	DWT	No.	DWT	No.	DWT	No.	DWT	No.	DWT
United States																
Combination	2	20,878	—	—	—	—	2	24,200	1	12,810	—	—	—	—	—	—
Freighters	27	204,008	4	44,472	—	—	2	15,236	3	35,500	11	135,100	20	269,000	3	42,000
Tankers	4	44,300	14	345,485	40	1,065,308	10	264,113	2	46,174	18	478,833	22	553,000	16	441,000
Total	33	269,186	18	389,957	40	1,065,308	14	303,549	6	94,484	29	613,933	42	822,000	19	483,000
United Kingdom																
Combination	24	202,258	23	191,983	24	214,640	14	101,469	7	52,800	7	46,095	7	49,000	8	48,000
Freighters	131	818,734	126	900,841	121	826,118	82	633,363	78	561,557	91	723,195	76	613,000	103	818,000
Tankers	15	179,185	35	435,720	47	656,812	64	937,650	66	1,223,358	57	920,196	66	1,080,000	52	1,013,000
Total	170	1,200,177	184	1,528,544	192	1,697,570	160	1,672,482	151	1,837,715	155	1,689,486	149	1,742,000	163	1,879,000
Sweden																
Combination	2	12,590	3	8,800	3	7,350	2	10,650	—	—	2	2,000	—	—	—	—
Freighters	30	167,130	35	244,085	28	158,898	26	157,758	20	114,210	17	114,495	31	207,000	26	218,000
Tankers	8	135,600	17	245,065	21	290,610	24	362,195	30	497,485	31	528,925	31	547,000	29	577,000
Total	40	315,320	55	497,950	52	456,858	52	530,603	50	611,695	50	645,420	62	754,000	55	795,000
Netherlands																
Combination	7	28,740	14	81,040	2	16,975	4	30,050	3	21,685	3	7,957	3	14,000	—	—
Freighters	22	122,486	14	75,105	17	89,400	19	100,349	11	50,760	23	111,255	32	211,000	30	155,000
Tankers	—	—	—	—	5	51,002	8	127,020	7	117,070	13	191,720	14	221,000	18	328,000
Total	29	151,226	28	156,145	24	157,377	31	257,419	21	189,515	39	310,932	49	446,000	48	483,000

Table 8 (Continued)

Country in which built and type of vessel	1948 No.	1948 DWT	1949 No.	1949 DWT	1950 No.	1950 DWT	1951 No.	1951 DWT	1952 No.	1952 DWT	1953 No.	1953 DWT	1954 No.	1954 DWT	1955 No.	1955 DWT
Norway																
Combination	—	—	—	—	1	2,850	—	—	—	—	—	—	—	—	—	—
Freighters	18	60,926	10	35,225	19	74,930	15	59,663	12	51,685	13	70,350	13	67,000	18	92,000
Tankers	—	—	—	—	3	7,255	3	7,430	6	69,450	7	76,038	13	110,000	8	113,000
Total	18	60,926	10	35,225	23	85,035	18	67,093	18	121,135	20	146,388	26	177,000	26	205,000
Denmark																
Combination	—	—	2	3,350	3	13,100	1	570	2	9,274	2	1,820	—	—	1	2,000
Freighters	15	91,740	12	64,267	11	70,430	12	70,925	12	73,232	8	56,302	17	94,000	12	87,000
Tankers	1	15,500	4	64,150	2	33,400	6	95,680	4	64,000	5	77,650	6	100,000	7	131,000
Total	16	107,240	18	131,767	16	116,930	19	167,175	18	146,506	15	135,772	23	194,000	20	220,000
France																
Combination	7	30,407	1	7,500	3	17,400	4	26,300	6	41,693	16	122,098	6	39,000	1	2,000
Freighters	—	—	12	66,100	15	101,970	23	140,047	17	84,555	20	114,972	8	48,000	16	101,000
Tankers	4	35,702	4	54,150	1	2,550	5	75,200	4	96,100	1	17,200	8	157,000	15	376,000
Total	11	66,109	17	127,750	19	121,920	32	241,547	27	222,348	37	254,270	22	244,000	32	479,000
Japan																
Combination	—	—	—	—	—	—	—	—	—	—	1	10,700	—	—	3	26,000
Freighters	—	—	—	—	20	100,325	41	344,614	64	590,440	45	447,103	28	377,000	23	331,000
Tankers	—	—	—	—	1	18,500	17	159,902	8	141,453	21	493,164	16	378,000	15	259,000
Total	—	—	—	—	21	118,825	58	504,516	72	731,893	67	950,967	44	715,000	41	616,000
Germany																
Combination	—	—	—	—	—	—	5	25,931	2	19,420	1	11,500	5	40,000	3	28,000
Freighters	—	—	—	—	—	—	60	198,322	66	365,019	99	543,434	106	615,000	98	596,000
Tankers	—	—	—	—	—	—	—	—	10	140,850	13	191,690	31	591,000	28	550,000
Total	—	—	—	—	—	—	65	224,253	78	525,289	113	746,624	142	1,246,000	129	1,174,000

Table 8 (Continued)

Country in which built and type of vessel	1948 No.	1948 DWT	1949 No.	1949 DWT	1950 No.	1950 DWT	1951 No.	1951 DWT	1952 No.	1952 DWT	1953 No.	1953 DWT	1954 No.	1954 DWT	1955 No.	1955 DWT
Italy																
Combination	—	—	—	—	—	—	6	40,100	9	48,712	10	34,150	1	1,000	1	10,000
Freighters	—	—	—	—	—	—	6	21,940	4	25,100	2	7,400	2	7,000	5	26,000
Tankers	—	—	—	—	—	—	1	26,000	1	18,000	6	127,400	15	329,000	13	203,000
Total	—	—	—	—	—	—	13	88,040	14	91,812	18	168,950	18	337,000	19	239,000
All others																
Combination	5	45,160	8	66,776	7	36,900	6	33,735	3	17,800	2	10,496	5	29,000	2	10,000
Freighters	42	227,522	35	216,911	32	146,575	13	46,634	7	23,755	19	89,035	33	140,000	22	116,000
Tankers	4	43,400	4	35,400	5	77,250	5	63,656	6	74,850	4	37,741	18	206,000	18	162,000
Total	51	316,082	47	319,087	44	260,725	24	144,025	16	116,405	25	137,272	56	375,000	42	288,000
Total																
Combination	40	309,626	51	359,449	43	309,215	44	293,005	33	224,194	44	246,816	27	172,000	19	126,000
Freighters	292	1,722,953	248	1,647,006	263	1,568,646	299	1,788,851	294	1,975,813	348	2,412,641	366	2,608,000	356	2,582,000
Tankers	36	453,687	78	1,179,970	125	2,202,687	143	2,118,846	144	2,488,790	176	3,140,557	240	4,272,000	219	4,153,000
All types	368	2,486,266	377	3,186,425	431	4,080,548	486	4,200,702	471	4,688,797	568	5,800,014	633	7,052,000	594	6,861,000

Note: Includes only seagoing steam and motor vessels of 1,000 gross tons and over. Excludes vessels built for operation on the Great Lakes and inland waterways and special types such as cable ships, tugs, etc.

Source: For 1948, United States Maritime Commission, *Report to Congress, For the Fiscal Year Ended June 30, 1948* (Washington: GPO, 1949), Appendix B, p. 66. For 1949, Same, . . . *1949* (Washington: GPO, 1950), Appendix C, p. 66. For 1950, U.S. Department of Commerce, *Annual Report of the Federal Maritime Board [and] Maritime Administration, 1950* (Washington: GPO, 1950), Appendix C, p. 60. For 1951, Same, . . . *1951* (Washington: GPO, 1952), Appendix C, p. 102. For 1952, Same, . . . *1952* (Washington: GPO, 1952), Appendix C, p. 56. For 1953, Same, . . . *1953* (Washington: GPO, 1953), Appendix A, p. 58. For 1954, Same, . . . *1954* (Washington: GPO, 1955), p. 50. For 1955, Same, . . . *1955* (Washington: GPO, 1956), p. 56.

Table 9

SHIPS LAUNCHED IN THE WORLD AND THE UNITED STATES,
1937-55

[Vessels of 100 gross tons and over]

United States

	Sea		Great Lakes		World	
Year	Number	Gross tons (thousands)	Number	Gross tons (thousands)	Number	Gross tons (thousands)
1937	103	195.8	20	43.7	1,101	2,690.6
1938	62	163.1	43	38.1	1,119	3,033.6
1939	94	376.4	76	45.6	941	2,539.4ª
1940	93	528.7	74	50.7	495	1,754.2ª
1941	177	1,032.0	10	3.3	510	2,491.2ª
1942	803	5,479.8	58	191.1	1,300	7,815.4ª
1943	1,584	11,448.4	41	131.2	2,078	13,884.8ª
1944	1,242	9,288.2	19	50.9	1,738	11,169.5ª
1945	842	5,839.9	38	127.7	1,326	7,192.7ª
1946	95	500.9	1	0.4	690	2,114.7ª
1947	65	162.1	5	2.8	787	2,102.6ª
1948	42	123.5	7	2.9	872	2,309.7ª
1949	60	619.4	6	13.9	926	3,131.8ª
1950	47	435.5	5	1.6	1,013	3,492.9ª
1951	50	134.6	14	31.2	1,022	3,642.6
1952	51	373.5	13	94.0	1,074	4,395.6
1953	63	481.7	5	46.6	1,143	5,096.1
1954	44	450.9	2	26.0	1,233	5,252.6
1955	24	70.6	2	2.5	1,447	5,316.7

ª Returns not complete.

Source: Lloyd's Register of Shipping, *Register Book Appendix* (London: 1953), Section 6, Table 12, p. 28-29. For 1952, Same, . . . (London: 1954). For 1953, Same, *Statistical Tables 1954* (London: December 1954), Table 12, p. 28-29. For 1954, Same, *Annual Summary of Merchant Ships Launched in the World During 1954* (London: February 1955), p. 8. For 1955, Same, . . . (London: February 1956), p. 8.

COMPOSITION OF MSTS NUCLEUS FLEET BY TYPE OF ADMINISTRATIVE ARRANGEMENT, OCT. 1, 1949 TO JAN. 1, 1955

[Thousands of tons]

Date	Commissioned			Contract operated			Civil Service			Total			Service Craft		
	No.	Gross	DWT	No.	Gross	DWT	No.	Gross	DWT	No.	Gross	DWT	No.	Gross	DWT
10-1-49	37	408.0	448.5	57	583.0	913.1				94	991.0	1,361.6			
1-1-50	36	398.1	432.7	55	561.8	880.2				91	959.5	1,312.9			
4-1-50	31	347.4	357.1	51	519.4	814.4	72	680.2	467.0	154	1,547.0	1,638.5	1		
7-1-50	28	315.9	307.2	41	414.4	649.9	104	731.3	519.1	173	1,461.6	1,476.2	1		
10-1-50	28	313.6	297.5	57	583.0	913.1	120	930.5	698.2	205	1,827.1	1,908.8	12		
1-1-51	29	320.9	299.5	57	583.0	913.1	129	924.5	693.0	215	1,828.4	1,905.6	12		
4-1-51	36	395.6	429.2	57	583.0	913.1	133	942.9	722.0	226	1,921.5	2,064.3	12		
7-1-51	33	339.6	365.6	57	583.0	913.1	136	953.3	734.2	226	1,875.9	2,012.9	12		
10-1-51	30	300.0	296.0	58	586.2	917.1	135	953.3	735.6	223	1,839.5	1,948.7	12		
1-1-52	27	298.8	295.2	58	586.2	917.1	139	972.2	745.7	224	1,857.2	1,958.0	13		
4-1-52	28	306.0	298.8	100	681.0	1,020.7	140	958.4	755.2	268	1,972.4	2,074.7	11		
7-1-52	29	314.4	306.4	100	681.0	1,020.7	144	1,016.2	777.0	273	2,011.6	2,104.1	10		
10-1-52	29	314.4	306.4	100	681.0	1,020.7	140	1,012.5	763.8	269	2,007.9	2,090.9	10		
1-1-53	28	306.0	298.8	100	681.0	1,020.7	136	1,001.9	744.3	264	1,988.9	2,063.8	10		
4-1-53	27	294.3	280.5	100	681.0	1,020.7	135	1,003.4	745.6	262	1,978.7	2,046.8	6		
7-1-53	26	287.0	271.9	100	681.0	1,020.7	132	1,001.9	744.3	258	1,969.9	2,036.9	6		
10-1-53	26	287.0	271.9	100	681.0	1,020.7	131	1,001.4	743.9	257	1,969.4	2,036.5	6		
1-1-54	26	287.0	271.9	100	681.0	1,020.7	129	1,000.2	743.1	255	1,968.2	2,035.7	6		
4-1-54	26	287.0	271.9	97	649.6	971.5	123	984.4	724.0	246	1,921.0	1,967.4	5		
7-1-54	25	278.6	264.1	89	607.0	923.7	118	938.4	701.9	232	1,824.0	1,889.7	3		
10-1-54	23	261.5	244.7	87	586.3	890.8	112	919.3	686.5	222	1,767.1	1,822.0	(a)		
1-1-55	19	221.9	181.3	81	523.3	792.4	110	905.7	678.9	210	1,650.9	1,652.6	(a)		

a Certain small ships were moved from other categories to a special miscellaneous category for vessels used in inter-island and special operations. This accounts for the absence of figure here.

Source: Worksheet records. John McCarron, MSTS, July 13, 1954 and letter to author from B. E. Lewellen, Assistant Chief of Staff, Operations, MSTS, October 10, 1955.

SELECTED BIBLIOGRAPHY

The purpose of this bibliography is to give the lay reader or the man in a hurry a short list of items useful to an understanding of the principal aspects of the current maritime policies of the United States. It does not contain statistical sources, references to laws and regulations, or a listing of such well-known reports as *The Bulletin* of the American Bureau of Shipping, or the annual reports of the American Merchant Marine Institute, the Shipbuilders Council of America, and the Federal Maritime Board. Only a few books about shipping in general have been listed. Most of the books and articles written before 1940 have not been included. What remains represents merely one man's judgment regarding the works appropriate to such a restricted bibliography, keeping in mind the advisability of including references to the views of the industry, the government, and the interested outsider.

Scholars, research workers, and those interested in studying particular aspects of shipping policy can compile more extensive bibliographies from the footnotes in the text and the source references appended to the statistical tables.

Books

Dearing, Charles L. and Wilfrid Owen. *National Transportation Policy*. Washington: The Brookings Institution, 1949. 459 p.

Hutchins, John G. B. *The American Maritime Industries and Public Policy. 1789-1914*. Cambridge: Harvard University Press, 1941. 627 p.

Marx, Daniel Jr. *International Shipping Cartels: A Study of Self-Regulation by Shipping Conferences*. Princeton: Princeton University Press, 1953. 323 p.

Mance, Osborne [assisted by] J. E. Wheeler. *International Sea Transport*. London: Oxford University Press, 1945. 198 p.

McDowell, Carl E., and Helen M. Gibbs. *Ocean Transportation*. New York: McGraw-Hill, 1954. 475 p.

Mears, E. G. *Maritime Trade of the Western United States*. Stanford: Stanford University Press, 1935. 538 p.

Radius, Walter A. *United States Shipping in Transpacific Trade, 1922-1938*. Stanford: Stanford University Press, 1944. 204 p.

Viner, Jacob, and others. *The United States in a Multi-National Economy*. New York: Council on Foreign Relations, 1945. 174 p.

Zeis, P. M. *American Shipping Policy*. Princeton: Princeton University Press, 1938. 254 p.

Articles

Adler, J. H. "British and American Shipping Policies: A Problem and a Proposal," *Political Science Quarterly*, (June 1944), pp. 193-219.

de Wilde, John C. "Ship Subsidies and the Future of World Shipping," *Foreign Policy Reports* (March 14, 1934), pp. 1-12.

Hutchins, John G. B. "One Hundred Fifty Years of American Navigation Policy," *Quarterly Journal of Economics* (February 1939), pp. 238-260.

Kalijarvi, Thorsten V. "The Cargo Preference Principle in Merchant Shipping," *The Department of State Bulletin* (July 12, 1954), pp. 63-69.

Koushnareff, Serge G. "Postwar Merchant Marine Developments," *Foreign Commerce Weekly* (March 17, 1952), pp. 3-4, 28.

McDonald, Eula. "Toward a World Maritime Organization", *The Department of State Bulletin* (Jan. 25, 1948; Feb. 1, 1948), pp. 99-107, 115; and 131-137 resp.

Marx, Daniel Jr. "Current American Ship-Operating Subsidies," *Journal of Business of the University of Chicago* (Oct. 1948), pp. 239-259.

——————————— "The Merchant Ship Sales Act of 1946," *The Journal of Business of the University of Chicago* (Jan. 1948), pp. 12-28.

Oyevaar, J. J. "The New Maritime Organization," *The United Nations Bulletin* (March 15, 1948), pp. 237-240.

Smith, Judah E. "Transportation in the Balance of Payments," *Survey of Current Business* (Sept. 1953), pp. 20-24.

GOVERNMENT PUBLICATIONS

Studies, monographs, special reports.

Graduate School of Business Administration, Harvard University. *The Use and Disposition of Ships and Shipyards at the End of World War II.* Washington: GPO, 1945. 325 p.

Postwar Planning Committee. *The Postwar Outlook for American Shipping.* Washington: GPO, 1946. 128 p.

President's Advisory Committee. *Report of the President's Advisory Committee on the Merchant Marine.* Washington: GPO, 1947. 69 p.

U. S. Bureau of Foreign and Domestic Commerce. *Shipping and Shipbuilding Subsidies,* by Jesse E. Saugstad. Trade Promotion Series No. 29. Washington: GPO, 1932. 611 p.

U. S. Department of Commerce. *Maritime Subsidy Policy.* Washington: Author, April 1954. 125 p. plus Appendices.

U. S. Department of Commerce. *A Review of Direct and Indirect Types of Maritime Subsidies with Special Reference to Cargo Preference Aid.* Washington: Author, April 1956. 65 p.

U. S. House. *Report on Audit of United States Maritime Commision.* 81st Cong., 2d sess., House Doc. 465. Washington: GPO, 1950. 160 p.

——————— *Scope and Effect of Tax Benefits Provided in the Maritime Industry.* 82d Cong., 1st sess., House Doc. 213. Washington: GPO, 1951. 29 p.

U. S. House. Committee on Merchant Marine and Fisheries. *A Review of Maritime Subsidy Policy in the Light of Present National Requirements for a Merchant Marine and a Shipbuilding Industry.* 83rd Cong., 2d sess. Committee Print. Washington: GPO, 1954. 132 p.

U. S. Maritime Commission: *Economic Survey of the American Merchant Marine.* Washington: GPO, 1937. 85 p.

——————— *Long-Range Shipbuilding Program for the United States Ocean-Going Merchant Fleet.* Washington: Author, 1947. (Mimeographed.) 32 p.

——————————— *A Study of Tramp Shipping Under the American Flag.* Washington: Author, 1949. (Mimeographed.) 42 p.

Congressional hearings.

U. S. House. Committee on Merchant Marine and Fisheries. *Long Range Shipping Bill.* Hearings, 82d Cong. 2d sess. on S. 241. Washington: GPO, 1952. 517 p.

——————————— *Proposed Amendments to the 1936 Merchant Marine Act.* Hearings, 83rd Cong., 1st sess. Washington: GPO, 1953. Part 1, 573 p.

——————————— *Study of the Operations of the Maritime Administration and the Federal Maritime Board.* Hearings, 84th Cong., 1st sess. Washington: GPO, 1955. 347 p.

——————————— *Study of Operations of Military Sea Transportation Service.* Hearings, 83rd Cong., 2d sess. Washington: GPO, 1954. 548 p.

——————————— *To Facilitate and Encourage New Ship Construction, Including National Defense Reserve of Tankers.* Hearings, 83rd Cong., 1st sess., on H.R. 6353 and H.R. 6441. Washington: GPO, 1954. 85 p.

——————————— *Vessel Replacement Program.* Hearings, 84th Cong., 1st sess., on H.R. 4118 and H.R. 5959. Washington: GPO, 1955. 384 p.

U. S. Senate. Committee on Armed Services. *Long-Term Charter of Tankers By Navy.* Hearings, 83rd Cong., 2d sess., on S 2788. Washington: GPO, 1954. 64 p.

U. S. Senate. Committee on Interstate and Foreign Commerce. *Cargo Preference Bill.* Hearings, 83rd Cong., 2d sess., on S 3233. Washington: GPO, 1954. 143 p.

——————————— *Merchant Marine Studies.* Hearings, 83rd Congress., 1st sess. Washington: GPO, 1953. Part 1, 678 p.

——————————— *Military Sea Transport Service.* Hearings, 83rd Cong., 1st sess., on S. 1439 and S. 1881. Washington: GPO, 1953. 185 p.

——————————— *Merchant Marine Study and Investigation.* Final Report, 81st Cong., 2d sess., Report 2494. Washington: GPO, 1950. 387 p.

_____ *Merchant Marine Study and Investigation.* Hearings, 81st Cong., 1st and 2d sess., pursuant to S. Res. 50. Washington: GPO, 1949 and 1950. Parts 1-7. 1,898 p.

INDUSTRY PUBLICATIONS

American Tramp Shipowners Association. *Tramp Shipping and the American Merchant Marine.* New York: Author, 1954. 39 p.

Committee on American Shipping Lines Serving Essential Foreign Trade Routes. *What's the Score on American Shipping?* New York: Author, 1953. 15 p.

Fourteen Shipping Companies Holding Operating-Differential Subsidy Contracts Under the Merchant Marine Act of 1936. *Attainable Objectives for the Privately Owned American Dry Cargo and Passenger Fleet Based on the Merchant Marine Act of 1936.* New York (?): Author, 1953. 96 p.

The Transportation Council. *Analysis of Construction and Operating Subsidies Under Merchant Marine 1936, as Amended. Submitted by the Ocean Shipping Panel to the Transportation Council for the Department of Commerce.* New York (?): Author, 1953. 32 p.

_____ *Minority Report of John Gammie of the Ocean Shipping Panel to the Transportation Council for the Department of Commerce.* New York: Author, 1953. (Mimeographed.) 12 p.

_____ *Comments of W. A. Kiggins, Jr. and James Sinclair (Panel Members) on Reports Submitted by the Ocean Shipping Panel to the Transportation Council.* New York: Author, n.d. (Mimeographed.) 2 p.

INDEX

The index does not cover material in tables, the appendix, the bibliography, or publications cited in footnotes.